RESPONSIBILITY

RESPONSIBILITY

J. R. LUCAS

Fellow of Merton College, Oxford

CLARENDON PRESS · OXFORD

1993

Oxford University Press, Walton Street, Oxford OX2 6DP

Oxford New York Toronto
Delhi Bombay Calcutta Madras Karachi
Kuala Lumpur Singapore Hong Kong Tokyo
Nairobi Dar es Salaam Cape Town
Melbourne Auckland Madrid
and associated companies in
Berlin Ibadan

Oxford is a trade mark of Oxford University Press

Published in the United States
by Oxford University Press Inc., New York

British Library Cataloguing in Publication Data
Data available

Library of Congress Cataloging in Publication Data
Lucas, J. R. (John Randolph), 1929–
Responsibility / by J. R. Lucas.
p. cm.
Includes index.
1. Responsibility. I. Title.
BJ1451.L83 1993 170–dc20 92–30980
ISBN 0–19–824008–2

Set by Hope Services (Abingdon) Ltd.
Printed in Great Britain by
Biddles Ltd., Guildford and King's Lynn

I dedicate this book to my pupils, who have been the chief authors of my philosophical understanding. Many of them have come to positions of responsibility in public life, in business and finance, as lawyers, teachers, pastors, and priests. If they read what I have written, they will find that their experience has taught them lessons I never learnt, and they will want to amplify some of my arguments, correct some of my conclusions, and probe the problems they have wrestled with but I have overlooked. And if some are led to put me right in public and make good the deficiencies of this book, I shall be well content.

Oxford
December 1991

CONTENTS

Introduction

Really it ought to be longer, much longer. At every stage I have ignored possible objections to my line of argument, and passed over in silence what other thinkers have put forward. To do them justice, I ought to give them a fair run for their money, and only after I had made the best case for their point of view that I could, go on to explain why none the less I felt bound to disagree. But then it would have been a very long book indeed, and although big books are popular with publishers and widely purchased, they are more often displayed than read. I want to be read. What I have to offer is not a definitive treatment of responsibility, covering the subject completely and giving the last word on it, but a single organizing idea which makes sense of a large range of moral, legal, and political discourse. It is possible to hold different views from those I put forward here, about punishment, reward and desert, the Atonement, free will, rationality, consequentialism, political accountability, and business ethics, but the account I give brings these topics together, and offers a unified view of them all.[1] I have therefore concentrated on the common thread of argument, and left out much that could usefully have been said on individual issues, in the hope that the reader, seeing how the whole hangs together and persuaded of the value of a synoptic view, will think through the detailed difficulties and objections for himself. In the end, philosophy cannot be read, or taken on board second-hand, but must be thought through afresh oneself, and all I can do is to provide hints for the reader to undertake a first-hand philosophical enquiry. In order that he may grasp my main theme, and see which chapters he may safely skip, I give here a brief overview of my whole argument.

In the first chapter I bring out the point that responsibility is, as its etymology shows, concerned with having to answer a

---

[1] For a similar defence, see Jonathan Glover, *I: The Philosophy and Psychology of Personal Identity*, Harmondsworth, 1988, p. 11.

certain question, namely why one acted as one did. The question
can fail in a number of ways: because the wrong person is being
asked, because what one did was not really an action, or because
it was wrongly characterized. I am largely indebted to Aristotle's
discussion in book III of the *Nicomachean Ethics*, but, since they
are not central to the argument, I leave a discussion of Aristotle's
views to Appendix I. In the second chapter I summarily dismiss
the arguments of the determinists who make out that none of our
actions are really actions of ours, but are only reactions to stimuli, entirely determined by our genetic make-up and previous
experience.

In the third chapter I consider consequences, which often bear
on the correct description of an action, and consequentialism,
which claims that consequences are all-important. I argue against
consequentialism. Actions are important not simply as causes in
the course of events but as communications; and what they signify is therefore as relevant as what they bring about. There is a
difference between what we do, which manifests what we have in
mind to do, and what we do not do, which for the most part
does not. We are responsible for what we do, but not for what
we do not do, unless we are under some special obligation to do
it. When we are under a special obligation—so that we cannot
brush off the question 'Why did you not . . . ?' with a 'Why
should I?'—we have a negative responsibility. Negative responsibility is an important extension of the concept, which underlies
much of our social and political thinking; it is further developed
in Chapter 9, where the responsibility of officials, judges, and
members of the professions is discussed.

In Chapter 4 I delineate the general structure of the reasoning
in the answers that may be given to the question of why one did
something. It is dialectical, often leaving room for further argument, though cogent if no further objection is raised. Reasons are
shareable and interpenetrable, and there is a continuous spectrum
between those that are primarily first-personal, simply explaining
why the agent acted as he did, and those that are omni-personal,
claiming the allegiance of every rational agent.

The shareability of reasons makes it possible to share responsibility, and in Chapter 5 I consider the ways we can be responsible for actions taken by another, either on our instructions or on
our advice, or because we were in some sense accomplices before

or after the act. Collective responsibility can extend a long way, far further than is comfortable. We often find ourselves feeling responsible for what our ancestors, compatriots, or co-religionists have done, and seek some means of dissociating ourselves and disavowing actions taken by members of our group. This, I maintain, is the underlying rationale of punishment, and in Chapter 6 I develop a 'vindicative' theory of punishment, which construes it primarily as a message to the person being punished, but overheard also and importantly by others, to the effect that what he did was unacceptable. This view is at odds with most of the current orthodoxies; I try to accommodate them in the course of my argument, but leave to Appendix 2 a more straightforward exposition of their strengths and weaknesses.

Many thinkers have held that punishments are negative rewards. I agree, but make the argument go the other way, and having construed punishments as tangible tokens of disapprobation, in Chapter 7 I elucidate rewards as tangible tokens of esteem. I distinguish desert, which is concerned with what an agent has done, from merit, which is concerned with what he is; and I argue against John Rawls' contention that desert ought not to be a basis for distributing good things. Desert is not the only basis, but it is the pre-eminent one, which, in default of good reason to the contrary, we ought to adopt. It is particularly appropriate for distributing the fruits of co-operative endeavour, and where these accrue unevenly, a monetary transfer enables the score to be made even. Money raises many questions about its responsible use, and these are laid out in Chapter 8.

In Chapter 10 two lines of argument converge. Responsible government is an exercise of negative responsibility, as distinguished in Chapter 3 and developed in Chapter 9; governments are responsible for their exercise of power, and various institutions have been tried in the course of history in the hope of making rulers to some extent responsible to some supervisory body. Governments also share responsibility with those they govern, and institutions have been developed to share knowledge not only of what is being done, but of why it is being done. The dialectical nature of reason outlined in Chapter 3 requires that the governed not only be told what the reasoning is, but be allowed to enter into the reasoning itself. Some sort of parliamentary discussion and debate is necessary, though inevitably conducted for the most part through representatives. Votes and elections are seen as artifices for eliciting definite decisions from indefinite opinions. They have their merits, but the dangers of majoritarian democracy, in particular where national minorities are concerned, are real and not yet resolved.

The concept of responsibility has less application to the intimate world of personal relationships, in which first-personal rather than omni-personal reasoning is paramount, but irresponsibility can be deeply corrosive, particularly in matters of sexual morality and family obligation. I discuss these, together with issues of loyalty to the group, and reach unfashionable conclusions, being much harder on permissiveness than advanced thinkers of the present age, and softer on homosexuality than would be approved by popular sentiment. Questions of responsibility are, however, at the periphery rather than the centre of our understanding of personal relationships, and in Chapter 12 I move beyond responsibility to a discussion of identification with and acceptance by other human beings and God, and offer a rethinking of the Atonement.

Chapter I
Why Did You Do It?

I.I WHY DID YOU DO IT?

The concept of responsibility is one that has developed and grown over the ages. We take it for granted, but the Homeric heroes had little use for that concept, centring their moral vocabulary on merit and kudos instead.[1] Since Aristotle first tried to give a systematic account of it, the concept has ramified, and now we have complicated notions of ministerial responsibility and responsible government which are fairly far removed from the original root.

Etymology can help. Although words often change their meaning, they are likely to retain some impetus from their original use. In the case of the word 'responsible' this is certainly so. If we survey its contemporary uses in ethics, politics, psychiatry, and ordinary discourse, we find a bewildering array of different senses which have no obvious pattern or rationale. But if we consider first the original meaning of the word, we can see a common thread running through all its subsequent developments.

Etymologically, to be responsible is to be answerable—it comes from the Latin *respondeo*, I answer, or the French *répondre*, as in RSVP. I can equally well say I am answerable for an action or accountable for it. And if I am to answer, I must answer a question; the question is 'Why did you do it?' and in answering that question, I give an account—in Greek λόγον (*logon*)—of my action. So the central core of the concept of responsibility is that I can be asked the question 'Why did you do it?' and be obliged to give an answer. And often this is quite unproblematic. But sometimes I cannot answer, cannot be expected to answer, the question 'Why did you do it?', and then I say 'I am not

---

[1] A. W. H. Adkins, *Merit and Responsibility*, Oxford, 1960, repr. Chicago, 1975, esp. ch. 3. But see also H. Lloyd-Jones, *The Justice of Zeus*, Berkeley, Calif., 1971; and Mary Margaret Mackenzie, *Plato on Punishment*, Berkeley, Calif., 1981, ch. 6.

responsible'. I cannot stop you asking, of course, but in disclaiming responsibility I am saying that I am not obliged to answer because the question has been improperly addressed to me. And by considering the conditions under which we are not responsible, we can obtain a clearer idea of what it is actually to *be* responsible.[2]

1.2. 'YOU', 'DO', 'IT'

The question 'Why did you do it?' can be impugned in three ways: on the score of the 'You', the 'Do', or the 'It'. It may be that the question is perfectly appropriate in its context, but is wrongly addressed to me. It may be that the question is correctly addressed, but what happened was not properly an *action* of mine. It may be that the question is correctly addressed and I had indeed acted, but what I actually did was not what you say I did.

'You': Mistaken Identity

It may be that the question is perfectly appropriate in its context, but is addressed to the wrong person. 'Don't ask me.' I say, 'I didn't do it: ask him'. Such disclaimers are very important in the criminal law, and in a very different way in politics.[3] For the most part they are thought to raise few philosophical problems. Philosophers are much more concerned with failures of the 'do' and the 'it'.

'Do': Active and Passive; Could Not Help It

It may be that the question is correctly addressed, but what happened was not properly an action of mine. It was I who was blown out to sea, but being blown out to sea was not something

---

[2] H. L. A. Hart, "The Ascription of Responsibility and Rights", *Proceedings of the Aristotelian Society*, 49, 1948, pp. 171–94; repr. in A. G. N. Flew, *Logic and Language*, i, Oxford, 1951, pp. 145–65. That a concept is best elucidated by considering its opposite was suggested by Aristotle, *Nicomachean Ethics*, v. 1. 5–12, $1129^a17–1129^b12$. It was first suggested to me by D. F. Pears in a lecture. F. A. Hayek (*Law, Legislation and Morality*, ii, London, 1976, p. 36) says it is a "feature that has again and again, as though it were a new discovery, been pointed out . . .".

[3] See further §3.8 and §9.1.

that I did. It happened to me, rather than was my doing. I could not help it; I did not really do it: therefore I cannot properly be asked why I did it. Similarly, if my body moves but is made to move by some outside stimulus. If bandits wire me up so that my muscles contract willy-nilly on the trigger, then clearly the deed was not mine but theirs. Or if they inject me, or hypnotize me. Or if I have an epileptic fit. There is a fuzzy boundary here, which causes much trouble to lawyers and psychologists, but the clear cases are clear.

'It': Description of Action

It may be that the question is correctly addressed and I had indeed acted, but what I actually did was not what you say I did. The 'It' in the question 'Why did you do it?' fails. If I am a linesman for the Central Electricity Generating Board and turn on the current on a high-voltage line, and it so happens that a youth has climbed a pylon and is touching the line, he will die. But I have not killed him. All I did was to switch on the current, and provided I did that properly and with due precautions, I am guiltless of the youth's death. If you ask 'Why did you kill him?', I disown responsibility not because it was someone else, not because I was not acting at all, but because what I did was not killing him. If you ask me 'Why did you switch on the electricity?' I can tell you, but to the question 'Why did you kill the youth?' I can give no answer, because the question is improperly put.

Of course, disclaimers are more often made than accepted. We do not—we cannot—always take a man's word for it that he is not answerable for his actions under any description he cares to disown. There is much dispute over what is the right description of an action. Feinberg notes the "accordion effect", whereby a description can be puffed up to include various consequences or slimmed down to exclude them, and be a bare minimal account of bodily movement,[4] but the choice of description is not, *pace* Salmond, a merely verbal one.[5] It has important moral, social,

---

[4] Joel Feinberg, "Action and Responsibility", in Max Black (ed.), *Philosophy in America*, London, 1965, p. 145.

[5] J. Salmond, *Jurisprudence*, London, 1957, p. 402, quoted by Feinberg, "Action and Responsibility", in Max Black (ed.), *Philosophy in America*, London, 1965:

and legal implications, and has for this reason been greatly refined by the lawyers, and developed into the law of tort. Our present concern, however, is not how arguments about the right description of an action may be developed, but where they have their point of entry. And it is clear that an ascription of responsibility can be defeated on the score of the 'It' being wrongly characterized.

1.3. THE SIGNIFICANCE OF ACTIONS

Any piece of bodily behaviour can be described in a number of different ways, depending in part on its effects but more particularly on the context in which it takes place and the intention or presumed intention of the agent. The difference between my bumping into you and my barging you out of my way lies not in what happens but in what I meant to happen, and my lifting my finger might be an admonition to a small child or a bid at an auction.[6] But effects are important. If I intend to bring something about—if I moved my body in order to bring that something about—then certainly I can be said to have done it, and to be responsible for it. It implements my intention and shows what I was minded to do.

The significance of intention is made clear in our locutions for disclaiming responsibility for unintended consequences. We do not deny that the thing happened, but say 'I did not mean to'. The outcome was not one I intended, not one I was minded to bring about, and does not manifest my mind or express my intentions. But if there are some things I did not mean to bring about, there must be others that I did mean to bring about, and which do manifest my mind and express my intentions. They signify. They are not only causes of effects in the course of events, but carriers of meaning between communicating agents. Usually the intention behind an action matters much more than the consequences that flow from it in the impersonal course of events. Insults rankle more than injuries. It is the example I set to others, if I walk across the grass in the Quad, or fail to enter a

"The distinction between an act and its consequences, between doing a thing and causing a thing, is a merely verbal one."

[6] See §2.6, p. 21.

library book in the register, that is at issue, not the physical damage to the grass or actual unrecorded absence of the book. It is my flouting the law or some other rule of conduct that shows I had *mens rea* and am guilty of an offence, not the causal consequences.[7] Actions are very largely communications, and carry a meaning which they acquire not by linguistic convention, as with ordinary language, but by virtue of their causal effects, though construed in some conventional social setting.

1.4. CONJUGATION

Action, like language, is a bearer of meaning, and like language alters its significance as we alter our temporal, personal, or modal standpoint. It is helpful to conjugate. I need to think not only of the reasons I give after the event, but of those I bear in mind when deciding what to do, and those I turn over in my mind as I deliberate about what I shall do. And I need to think not only of my reasons before, at, and after the moment of decision, but of the reasons you might have urged on me, had you been advising me, and similarly in the past tense of the judgement you, or anyone else, might pass on the deed I actually did. Justification conjugates with deliberation, with advice, and with judgement. I deliberate about what I shall do, and give advice about what you should do; I acknowledge what I have done, and you ask me why I did it. If my reasons were good, I boast about it, and you praise me: if my reasons were bad, I apologize, and you blame me.

The concept of responsibility operates within a web of other concepts, all concerned with reasons I may urge upon you before the event, adopt for myself, give in justification after the event, or adopt as a basis for judging someone else worthy of praise or blame. In particular, there is a double temporal standpoint, analogous to that of the perfect tense.[8] In justifying my actions now, I am saying what my reasons were then: for it is what I had in

---

[7] See §3.7.
[8] See Hans Reichenbach, *Elements of Symbolic Logic*, New York, 1947, §51, pp. 287–96; J. R. Lucas, *The Future*, Oxford, 1989, ch. 2; J. R. Lucas, *On Justice*, Oxford, 1980, pp. 42–3.

mind at the time that determines the meaning of what I did and so very largely its significance now.

But sometimes I cannot justify now what I did then. I make mistakes; I do wrong. And then, after the event, I shall need to admit that it was wrong, and that I acted for the wrong reasons. I shall need both to own up to it and to disown it: I own up in admitting that I did indeed do it, and disown it in acknowledging that the reasons I acted on then are reasons I can no longer endorse now. I accept responsibility and apologize, perhaps also making reparation for what I have done wrong. I do not deny my agency and my involvement, nor the bad complexion that must be put upon my deeds, but express μεταμέλεια (*metameleia*), or μετάνοια (*metanoia*), regret, repentance, or a change of heart, so that what I did then is no longer a manifestation of what I mean now, and those who rightly condemn what I did need no longer be estranged from me now, but can once again be at one with me, if only they will accept my apologies and forgive me for what I now no longer meant to do.

I am not, however, always willing to say sorry, at least not if I am really meaning it. And in any case my view of my past actions and their justification may differ from yours. You may think that what I did was wrong and inexcusable: I may disagree for a number of different reasons, and may reckon that I have nothing to apologize or ask your forgiveness for. We may dispute about what I did, my reasons for, and the rights and wrongs of, my doing it. This is why we need to consider not only how we deliberate about the future and decide in the present, but how we account for deeds done in the past, and need to see this not only from the first-personal standpoint but from second- and third-personal standpoints too. Fallibility requires us to conjugate. My reasons may have seemed good at the time, but afterwards it is not only my judgement that counts. If my reasons are indeed accepted, it can be the occasion for praise, but if they are not, I may be blamed; and sometimes in admitting responsibility I am owning up to actions I need to apologize for. And then if I apologize sufficiently, expressing adequate contrition, in word but perhaps also in deed, you may forgive me and restore me to the fellowship of the moral community.

Since none of us is infallible, there are many possibilities of disagreement in these conjugations. You may accuse me unjustly of having done something I never did. More subtly, you may tax me with having done wrong where, though I am undoubtedly the man involved, I do not think I am to blame. The concepts of responsibility, justification, and excuse operate in this area, and since we are naturally, though sometimes wrongly, anxious to avoid blame, they are distorted, and often badly misunderstood.

1.5. 'RESPONSIBLE'

If I accept that I may be legitimately questioned, I shall have that possibility in mind, and consider what answers I should give to questions that may be asked of me. I shall think about what I am doing, rather than act thoughtlessly or on impulse, and act for reasons that are faceable rather than ones I should be ashamed to avow. Equally, I shall give thought to the situation generally, keep an eye out for anything that needs to be done, and take care that nothing in my sphere of responsibility that needs to be done is left undone, and that if anything goes amiss I shall be ready to put things right again. That is what it is to be a responsible person.

A responsible person is one who can be left in charge, who can be relied on to cope, who will not slope off, leaving the job undone, or switch off, leaving the business unattended to. So long as a responsible person is responsible, you can sleep easy, knowing that no extra vigilance on your part is called for, and that he will see to it that all goes well.

'Responsible' in this sense is an adjective, denoting a quality of character and mind, not a position within a web of dialectical obligation. Often it seems the best English translation available for Aristotle's term φρόνιμος (*phronimos*), which plays a key part in his moral philosophy. There is the same sense of all-round reasonableness and reliability, not confined to any particular topic, and entering into most other desirable qualities of character. It is a term of high commendation, though from an external point of view. We want to have responsible people about in positions of authority, performing their duties reliably and well. We are not, however, committed to liking them, loving them, wanting to be in their company, or enjoying their conversation. I could reasonably speak well of my friends' girlfriends, or of potential sisters- and daughters-in-law, by describing them as responsible, but it would be curious if I chose that as the chief commendation of my own girlfriend or wife. It is always good to be responsible, but in entering into a personal, I–thou relationship we look for something that goes beyond responsibility.[9]

1.6 AGENCY

Responsibility, though central in our moral and political thinking, can none the less be impugned. It presupposes that there are agents, that agents act for reasons, and that it is up to an agent whether he acts or not. All these assumptions have been contested. The concept of agency and personal identity is difficult to elucidate, and some philosophers have sought to dissolve it into a number of disparate strands. Many philosophers have doubted the rationality of human agents, and indeed the possibility of there being any cogent moral reasons at all. Arguments can be adduced against both these contentions, but they are not conclusive. It could be that we should one day be persuaded that human beings were not agents in the sense we had hitherto assumed, or that no good reasons for action were possible. In that case we should abandon our concept of responsibility. Up to a point, we can argue from the unwelcomeness of such a conclusion to the untenability of the premiss, but only up to a point. From a metaphysical point of view we cannot rule out by any quick argument the possibility that all our present concepts are founded on some pervasive human error, and to address such questions properly would take us far beyond the confines of the present work. Our present purpose is to elucidate the concept of responsibility as it is actually used, assuming that it is not altogether an erroneous one. We therefore leave these fundamental contentions rejected though not conclusively refuted. Equally, we shall reject the third contention, that agents are not free to do anything other than what they actually do. But since this is a much more widely felt difficulty, we cannot give it quite such short shrift, and shall devote the next chapter to a cursory consideration of the arguments.

---

[9] See further chs. 11 and 12.

Chapter 2
Free Will

Most of the questions that arise over the suitability of asking someone 'Why did you do it?' are practical: Am I addressing the right person? Have I asked him the right question? Is he obliged to answer me? But the questions about the 'You' and the 'Do' are more strictly philosophical. It often seems that although on the surface I am clearly responsible for some actions, at a deeper level I am forced to admit that no actions are really mine, because it is never up to me—ἐπί μοι (*epi moi*)—whether I do them or not; they are not actions at all, but mere reactions of the human organism to the environment. On some theories of strict determinism what I do is the inevitable causal consequence of things that happened long ago, and which are now unalterable, certainly unalterable by me. So in some sense which is important, but difficult, to elucidate, they are not really my actions and I cannot be held responsible for what my hormones, my genes, my childhood traumas, or the state of the universe at the Big Bang have made me do.[1]

---

[1] It is worth quoting Sir Isaiah Berlin's eloquent account of the implications of determinism: "And it may, indeed, be a true doctrine. But if it is true, and if we begin to take it seriously, then, indeed, the changes in the whole of our language, our moral terminology, our attitudes towards one another, our views of history, of society, and of everything else will be too profound to be even adumbrated. The concepts of praise and blame, innocence and guilt and individual responsibility from which we started are but a small element in the structure, which would collapse or disappear. Our words—our modes of speech and thought—would be transformed in literally unimaginable ways; the notions of choice, of responsibility, of freedom, are so deeply embedded in our outlook that our new life, as creatures in a world genuinely lacking in these concepts, can, I should maintain, be conceived by us only with the greatest difficulty." From "Historical Inevitability", repr. in I. Berlin, *Four Concepts of Liberty*, Oxford, 1969, p. 113, quoted by Jonathan Glover, *Responsibility*, London, 1970, p. 78.

2.2. IGNORING IT

Some philosophers discount problems of free will: they claim not to understand what determinism amounts to, or not to be able to decide even in principle whether it is true, or not to see its relevance to issues of responsibility. Admittedly, much thinking about determinism is confused, and there are many different versions of it, and different arguments for and against. But the claim that there is no problem about free will is difficult to sustain in the face of its being a topic of recurring concern to thinking people through the ages. A problem that bothered Aristotle, Augustine, the Schoolmen, the Reformers, and Kant, as well as innumerable lesser thinkers down to the present day, is not likely to be due to some simple confusion. Those who cannot see what all the fuss is about are more likely to be reporting their own lack of intellectual acuity than the real non-existence of a problem.

2.3. COMPATIBILISM

Many philosophers of the empiricist tradition have allowed that determinism is a real issue, and believe that it is true, but hold that it is compatible with responsibility.[2] They hold that for an agent to be responsible he must be free, not from causal necessity but from compulsion and constraint. The paradigm example of not being free is being in prison. A prisoner cannot be taxed with not going to visit his ailing aunt, because he is constrained to stay in prison. Only if I am compelled to do, or not to do, something am I exempt from having to say why I did, or did not, do it. Since, whatever the psychologists may say, it is manifestly the

---

[2] In addition to Hobbes and Hume, the following modern authors may be consulted: Moritz Schlick, *Problems of Ethics*, tr. David Rynin, New York, 1939; A. J. Ayer, "Freedom and Necessity", *Polemic*, 5, 1946, repr. in his *Philosophical Essays*, London, 1954, in his *The Concept of a Person*, London, 1963, and in G. Watson (ed.), *Free Will*, Oxford, 1982; C. L. Stevenson, *Ethics and Language*, Newhaven, 1944, ch. 14; Philippa Foot, "Free Will as Involving Determinism", *Philosophical Review*, 1957, pp. 439–50; Paul Edwards, "Hard and Soft Determinism", and John Hospers, "What Means This Freedom", in Sidney Hook (ed.), *Determinism and Freedom*, New York, 1958; D. C. Dennett, *Elbow Room*, Oxford, 1984.

case that we are not compelled to do most of the things we do, it follows that we are responsible. Indeed, quite apart from the particular exegesis offered, it must be the case that we are, by and large, responsible for our actions, since we use the word 'responsible', and its use determines its meaning. Whatever criteria we apply for deciding whether someone is responsible or not, those criteria determine the meaning of the word, and hence allow that in some cases at least it is properly applied.

The argument as stated is unconvincing. Although it is certainly true that a man is unfree *if* he is constrained or compelled, it does not at all follow that he is unfree *only if* he is constrained or compelled. To make that plausible, we need to take the words 'constrained' and 'compelled' in a very wide sense. In the ordinary sense of the words, the kleptomaniac is not constrained or compelled to steal: nobody is moving his limbs against his will, nobody is sticking a knife or the barrel of a gun into him, threatening him with instant death if he does not do as he is told. If we say, none the less, that he is constrained to steal by his neuroses or childhood traumas, we are stretching the concept, and can no longer argue that in its stretched sense it may not turn out, in the light of new discoveries, to cover all cases of human decision-making. If the compatibilist keeps to the strict sense of 'constrained' and 'compelled', there are counter-examples to his proposed elucidation of what freedom really means: if he accommodates these by saying that in these cases the agents are, really, acting under some compulsion or constraint, then he has no grounds for denying that it may turn out that all our actions are in like case. Nor can he base any general argument on the fact that we have the word 'responsible' and know how to use it. There is no valid argument from language to reality. We have the concept 'flying saucer': it does not follow that flying saucers exist.[3]

2.4. 'OUGHT' IMPLIES 'CAN'

The central issue in the dispute between compatibilists and their opponents is the conditions under which a person may properly

---

[3] For a brief discussion of compatibilism, see Ted Honderich, *Punishment: The Supposed Justifications*, London, 1969, pp. 102–8, paperback edn., 1984, pp. 113–18.

claim not to have to answer the question 'Why did you do it?' It
is generally agreed that ability to have done or not to have done
the deed in question is required: 'ought' implies 'can'—if I could
not have done it, there is no question that I ought to have done
it, and if I could not have not done it, there is no question that I
ought not to have done it. The dispute is over the nature of the
'can', or, more confusingly, as Austin pointed out, the 'could'.[4]
G. E. Moore suggested that the 'could' in 'I could have done
otherwise' means 'I would have done otherwise, if I had chosen'.
Once again the suggested exegesis is not convincing. Many people reckon that it is not what they mean when they say 'I could
have done otherwise': indeed, it precisely misses the point at issue
in their worries over free will. Arguments from meaning are
always suspect, and if a suggested analysis fails to commend itself
to those who use the term, it is unlikely to merit much attention:
users of language may not be very good at articulating the rules
governing the use of the words they use, but they have a fair
sense of what they meant to mean, and their emphatic repudiation of an analysis is decisive.

Even if Moore's analysis does not commend itself, it may still
be argued that the 'can' in ' "ought" implies "can" ', is different
from the 'can' excluded by determinist necessity. Thus Glover
argues that the former concerns 'what is possible for me in terms
of my capacities and opportunities', while the latter is about
'what is possible (logically) given the truth of certain statements'.
'It is', he maintains,

a consequence of determinism that all courses of action except one are
ruled out as being incompatible with a set of true statements. But this is
not peculiar to the predictions of the determinist. True statements about
the past have the same consequences. It is true that yesterday I stayed
indoors instead of going out. So I cannot (logically) have spent yesterday out of doors, for if I had done so this would falsify the statement
which we know to be true: that I stayed indoors. But this does not mean
that I lacked either the capacity or the opportunity to go out. Similarly,
on the basis of causal laws, it may in principle be predictable that I will

---

[4] J. L. Austin, 'Ifs and Cans', *Proceedings of the British Academy*, 1956,
pp. 109–32; repr. in his *Philosophical Papers*, Oxford, 1961, pp. 153–80. Austin
points out that in English the word 'could' is ambiguous between a simple past
tense of 'can' and a conditional, which is constitutionally "iffy".

go out tomorrow. But this in no way shows that tomorrow I will lack either the capacity or the opportunity to stay indoors.[5]

But the argument is fallacious. It depends on assimilating the unalterability of future events which the determinist claims, to the temporal unalterability of past ones, which is a logical corollary of tense logic. Granted the truth of the statement that yesterday I stayed indoors instead of going out, it is logically impossible that I went out: but granted the truth of statements about some antecedent state of the universe, it is not logically impossible that I should act not in accordance with the prediction made about me by the determinist. It is, on the contrary *logically* possible that I should, and if I did, it would constitute evidence that the laws of nature on which the determinist based his prediction were not without exception true. On the hypothesis of physical determinism it is physically impossible for me to act in any other way than as predicted, but that physical impossibility is not the same as a logical impossibility, and no valid argument can be based on assimilating the two.

The claim that the 'can' in "'ought' implies 'can'" concerns 'what is possible for me in terms of my capacities and opportunities' is false. Although we exculpate the person who lacks the capacities and opportunities to do what he otherwise ought to do, we do not stop there. In any ordinary sense the kleptomaniac has the capacity and the opportunity not to steal, but once we are persuaded that in view of his psychological make-up he is bound to steal rather than not steal, we cease to regard him as responsible for what he does. In the ordinary sense of the words, capacities and opportunities are defined in terms of *general* conditions, the sort of thing a person can do if he so wishes. But when it comes to holding a person responsible, we consider not just the general features, but the particular circumstances of the case. Any restriction of choice—that I was tired, that I had just received bad news, that I was acting under hypnotic suggestion—can be successfully pleaded, provided only that it is true, to exculpate myself from the charge of not having done what I ought to have done. Witness the fact that in our ordinary, non-determinist way of thinking, we do not tell people that they ought to alter the past, because we know that they cannot, as a

[5] Jonathan Glover, *Responsibility*, London, 1970, pp. 74–5.

matter of temporal logic, do that: in judging past deeds, we back-
date the 'ought' to the time when the decision was still, according
to our ordinary, non-determinist way of thinking, open, and
speak of what they ought then to have done. If the 'can' in
"'ought' implies 'can'" concerned only 'what is possible for me
in terms of my capacities and opportunities', there would be no
fear of determinism. There would be a clear distinction between
externally assessable capacities and opportunities and the internal
restrictions on choice that psychologists and neurophysiologists
seek to uncover; and the success of their endeavours would pose
no threat to our day-to-day ascriptions of responsibility. It is
only because our sense of the exculpatory 'can' is not so limited
that we feel obliged to revise our standards of responsibility in
the light of new discoveries, and fear that we may end by having
to exculpate everybody, because nobody can act other than he
does. Our willingness to revise our ascriptions of responsibility
and our fear that we might have to revise them away altogether
indicate that the 'can' in "'ought' implies 'can'" is a much more
particularised 'can' than 'what is possible for me in terms of my
capacities and opportunities'.

2.5. THE DOUBLE STANDPOINT

Kant, and more recently Strawson, have adopted the heroic
course of acknowledging the incompatibility between determinism
and responsibility, and attempting simply to live with it.[6] There
are two standpoints, that of the agent and that of the spectator,
and correspondingly two attitudes to people, the reactive and the
objective. If we adopt the spectator's standpoint and the objective attitude, questions of responsibility no longer arise, and it
would be inappropriate to blame someone or feel resentment
towards him on account of what he had done. Although we are
sometimes tempted to get angry with a car that will not start or

---

[6] I. Kant, *Groundwork of the Metaphysic of Morals*, tr. H. J. Paton, London,
1948, pp. 118–21 [105–10/450–53]. P. F. Strawson, "Freedom and Resentment",
Proceedings of the British Academy, 1962, repr. in P. F. Strawson (ed.), *Studies in
the Philosophy of Thought and Action*, Oxford, 1968, pp. 80–4; in P. F. Strawson,
Freedom and Resentment, London, 1974, pp. 11–13; and in Gary Watson (ed.),
Free Will, Oxford, 1982, pp. 59–80. See further Galen Strawson, *Freedom and
Belief*, Oxford, 1986.

curse a computer that loses our files, we know that these responses are irrational, and that we should not react in that way towards them, but only dispassionately understand their workings, predict their behaviour, and manipulate them to our own advantage. We can, on occasion, adopt this attitude to our fellow human beings too, and regularly do so once we come to believe that they are abnormal, and merely the plaything of their circumstances.

Thus far the argument merely articulates, though with considerable subtlety and skill, the standard position, in which determinism, if we accepted it as true, would undercut our taking up the agent's standpoint and adopting a reactive attitude to ourselves and our fellow human beings. But, on the view set out, actually to abandon that standpoint and attitude would be an impossibility. It is simply not on: the reactive attitude is too deeply rooted in our conceptual structure. Nor, indeed, were it possible, would it be rational to eschew the reactive attitude generally. For the only reasons that could be relevant to such a choice, were it open to us, would be those concerned with the richness and texture of human life, and these would all point in the direction of keeping our traditional attitudes towards ourselves and one another.

Neither of these arguments carries weight. It is possible to take the objective attitude not only to some people but to all. Kafka has a brief account of what it felt like once in Prague when other people ceased to be people, and were just like snowflakes blown about in the wind. Scepticism about other minds is like scepticism about material objects—not a natural state of mind, but an intelligible one, and one that sometimes forces itself on us. Most of us can, like Hume, force ourselves back into a reactive frame of mind by playing, if necessary, a game of backgammon with a friend, but even that can fail, and those suffering from autism never succeed in acquiring reactive attitudes to others.

It is difficult to assess the considerations bearing on the rational choice of standpoints since, if determinism is true, there is no choice to be made, and we take up whatever attitude our heredity and environment determine. If such a choice were open, it would be proper at one level to look for reasons of a general pragmatic type, for at that level they would be the only reasons available.[7] But once truth is admitted to our conceptual scheme, it cannot be ignored. If determinism is true, it is worthy to be believed. Once a man is allowed to adopt the objective attitude of a spectator, he will seek to see things as they are, and will assess the tenability of the agent's standpoint not only in terms of its potential for human happiness and fulfilment, but on the score of its compatibility with the truth. Unless truth is altogether extruded from the conceptual scheme of the metaphysician (as, indeed, it may be from that of the determinist[8]), he will reckon that if something is true he ought to believe it, and if that requires him to give up the reactive attitude, he ought to give it up, no matter what the cost in terms of the impoverishment of the texture of human life.

2.6. PHYSICAL DETERMINISM

There are several different versions of determinism. In time past it was often argued that God foreknew the future, or, less theologically, that propositions about future events were already true, and written, so to speak, in the Book of Destiny. In our more scientific age it is often supposed that the basic science, physics, to which all other sciences can be reduced, is itself deterministic, and that all our thoughts and actions are to be explained in terms of the electrons, neutrons, and protons of which our bodies are composed, and that these go round in fixed, definite orbits, so that, given their initial positions and velocities, their positions and velocities at any subsequent time are unalterably fixed, and could, in principle at least, be precisely calculated. Determinism need not, however, rest on that or any other particular scientific view of the world. It is possible to argue simply from the success of science generally, and to maintain that as we have succeeded in explaining one phenomenon after another, so in the fullness of time we shall be able to explain all our doings in terms of our environment and heredity. Freud's claim to be able to explain even the most mentalistic phenomena, such as dreams, in terms of early childhood experience, has seemed to lend credence to

---

[7] Compare the pragmatic justification of induction, given in, for example, J. R. Lucas, *Space, Time and Causality*, Oxford, 1985, pp. 24–6.
[8] See §2.10 below.

such a suggestion. In the absence of convincing argument to the contrary, it seems reasonable to suppose that one day there will be no decision or act of choice we cannot account for satisfactorily in terms of antecedent circumstance. Indeed, it is often argued that the very hypothesis that there were such inexplicable events would constitute a surrender to irrationalism, and the denial of the very rationality that advocates of responsibility are anxious to uphold.

Although physical determinism is not the only form of determinism, it is in our present age the most plausible and widely believed. Classical physics is deterministic. Given a full description of a system with the initial positions and velocities of each particle of matter we can, in Newtonian mechanics, calculate the positions and velocities of each particle at every subsequent time. Although a one–one correlation between brain states and our mental experience has not been proved, it is widely regarded as plausible. In that case, granted a full Newtonian description of a person's brain together with incoming stimuli, it should be possible for a Laplacian intelligence to calculate its state at any later time, and hence also to predict all the accompanying experience, including decisions and acts of choice. Even if exception were made for mental phenomena, it would still be possible to calculate all future positions of those material particles which constitute the body, and hence all bodily movements. Although some philosophers have argued that since bodily movements are not the same as actions,[9] predicting bodily movements is not the same as predicting actions,[10] the fact is that actions can only be expressed in bodily movements, so that, at the very least, most actions would be ruled out by a predicted bodily movement; indeed a sufficiently long sequence of bodily movements, including those of the tongue and lips, would constitute specific actions. So, granted that our bodies are made of material particles and that these particles obey Newtonian, or other similarly deterministic, laws, our actions could in principle be predicted and accounted for in terms of some antecedent state of the universe, over which we ourselves could have exercised no control.

[9] See §1.3.
[10] A. I. Melden, *Free Action*, London, 1961, p. 72, quoted in Ted Honderich, *Punishment: The Supposed Justifications*, London, 1969, pp. 113–14, paperback edn. 1984, pp. 123–4. R. S. Peters, *The Concept of Motivation*, London, 1958.

But the fundamental theories of physics are not deterministic. Although Newtonian mechanics and the Special and General Theories of Relativity are, quantum mechanics is not. Its state descriptions are in terms of "ψ-functions", and when a measurement is made, the square of the modulus of the eigen-function gives the *probability* that the corresponding eigen-value will be the one measured. It is very difficult to make sense of this. Einstein could not bring himself to believe that God plays dice. Many physicists have laboured to devise "hidden variable" theories which would provide a determinist substrate for quantum mechanics in the way that the kinetic theory of gases does for thermodynamics. They have failed. Not only that, but in the course of the last sixty years there have emerged a number of theoretical results (due to von Neumann, Bell, and Kochen and Specker) and experimental observations (due to Aspect) which together constitute a powerful argument against there being any fundamental deterministic theory compatible with quantum mechanics.[11] It is never possible to rule out with absolute certainty what theories scientists may come up with in time to come. All we can say is that quantum mechanics is itself established to a very high degree of accuracy, and seems to leave no room for a fundamentally deterministic physics.

Quantum mechanics is probabilistic. But the Law of Large Numbers means that probabilities approximate to certainties where large numbers of cases are involved, and the numbers of material particles in human organisms are huge. Their movements might be supposed to be predictable in the same way as those of the planets are. The probability of my doing a quantum leap into the heavens is vanishingly small, and can for all practical purposes be discounted. But to generalise this into an argument for determinism is to ignore the nature of organisms.

[11] John von Neumann, *Mathematical Foundations of Quantum Mechanics*, tr. Robert T. Beyer, Princeton, NJ, 1955, ch. 4, §2. J. S. Bell, "On the Problem of Hidden Variables in Quantum Mechanics", *Review of Modern Physics*, 38, 1966, pp. 447–75; repr. in J. A. Wheeler and W. H. Zurek (eds.), *Quantum Theory and Measurement*, Princeton, NJ, 1983, pp. 397–402. S. Kochen and E. Specker, "The Problem of Hidden Variables in Quantum Mechanics", *Journal of Mathematics and Mechanics*, 17, 1967, pp. 59–87; repr. in C. A. Hooker (ed.), *The Logico-Algebraic Approach to Quantum Mechanics*, i, Dordrecht, 1975, pp. 293–328. A. Aspect, J. Dalibard, and G. Roger, "Experimental Tests of Bell's Inequalities Using Time-Varying Analyzers", *Physical Review Letters*, 49, 1982, pp. 1804–7.

Organisms are "homeostatic" processes: they respond to changes in environmental conditions by altering so as to maintain the *same* condition. Thus mammals maintain the same blood temperature in cold weather as in hot. In that respect they are much more stable items in the world than mere inert collocations of material substance. But stability in some respects is purchased at the cost of sensitivity in others. My blood stays the same temperature whatever the weather, but I shiver in cold weather and sweat and pant in hot. In order to stay the same in one respect, an organism has to alter in others, and thus becomes sensitive to small, sometimes very small, changes in the environment. Birds are shape-conscious, and react immediately to anything having the shape of a predator. Human beings are highly developed organisms, capable of great persistence, achieving their purposes in spite of innumerable obstacles and setbacks, but responding to very slight differences in stimuli by radical alterations of behaviour. A dot on the horizon will alter a steersman's behaviour, and it makes all the difference to our responses if we hear or see in a message the word 'not'. It cannot be argued that because we are large lumps of flesh, the Law of Large Numbers must apply, and smooth out the random fluctuations of quantum uncertainty into statistical certainty on the macroscopic level. We are large, and all too often lumpish, but we are also neural networks, capable on occasion of greatly amplifying small variations, and sensitive in some areas at least to only a few quanta of energy.[12]

It is not possible to reinstate determinism in the face of quantum mechanics by appeal to the Law of Large Numbers, but some thinkers have sought to set the indeterminist implications of modern physics on one side by arguing that indeterminism could not give the advocate of responsibility what he wanted. For indeterminism asserts that some physical events are uncaused, that is

---

[12] The original paper was S. Hecht, S. Schlaer, and M. H. Pirenne, "Energy Quanta and Vision", *Journal of General Physiology*, 25, 1942, pp. 819–30; see further M. H. Pirenne, *Vision and the Eye*, London, 1967, pp. 89–91. H. B. Barlow and J. D. Mollon, *The Senses*, Cambridge, 1982, pp. 127–30, report that a stimulus entering the pupil and containing an average of 73 quanta was definitely seen on 50 per cent of the trials, and that the ear is more sensitive and can detect an even smaller amount of energy. Many of the quanta entering the pupil do not reach the retina, or fail to excite a rod; the number of effective absorptions is probably ten to fifteen. Further calculations, borne out by experiments with toads, lead the authors to conclude "that a rod does not require the absorption of more than a single quantum in order to initiate a signal".

to say, random. But random events are not the sort we ask people to account for: if I am acting at random, it is a sign that I am out of my mind, or at least absent-minded, and I shall not be able to say, if asked, why I acted as I did.[13]

The argument is fallacious. It depends on an equivocation. The word 'random' in its first occurrence is being used to deny that there is a physical cause, and in subsequent occurrences to deny that there is any explanation whatsoever. But the two are not the same. I can perfectly well explain an action without giving a physical cause for it. 'I went to see him because he was ill' is a perfectly good explanation of my action, and would show that it was not a random, pointless one, but it does not give a physical cause in terms of antecedent conditions and laws of nature. Few of us can give a physical explanation in terms of physical causes of any event—we do not know enough physics. But we can, and could long before any physics was known, give adequate explanations of many of our actions. So the absence of a physical cause cannot be a bar to actions being explicable, or to our being responsible for them.

2.7. EVERY EVENT HAS A CAUSE

The argument from randomness turns on an ambiguity in the word 'cause'. As our use of the word 'because' shows, it can be used of any explanation. But since the seventeenth century it has been increasingly used in a narrower sense, and this narrower sense is even more strongly carried by the adjective 'causal'. Causal causes are, or approximate to, physical causes. The use of the essentially negative concept 'random' makes it easier not to notice the equivocation, but it often occurs also if we adopt the

[13] The most forceful contemporary exponent of this argument is A. J. Ayer, in "Freedom and Necessity", *Polemic*, 5, 1946, pp. 38–9; repr. in A. J. Ayer, *Philosophical Essays*, London, 1954, p. 275 and in A. J. Ayer, *The Concept of a Person*, London, 1963, p. 254. See also, P. H. Nowell-Smith, "Freewill and Moral Responsibility", *Mind*, 70, 1961, p. 296; R. E. Hobart, "Free Will as Involving Determinism", *Mind*, 43, 1934, p. 5; Philippa Foot, "Free Will as Involving Determinism", *Philosophical Review*, 1957, pp. 439–50. For a general criticism, see C. A. Campbell, *On Selfhood and Godhood*, London, 1957, pp. 175–6; Ted Honderich, *Punishment: The Supposed Justifications*, London, 1969, p. 110, paperback edn. 1984, p. 120; J. R. Lucas, *The Freedom of the Will*, Oxford, 1970, pp. 55–9, 109–10.

so-called Law of Universal Causation, that every event has a cause.

We may hold that every event has a cause as a methodological principle or as a general cosmological truth, or simply as a result of introspection into our own experience. It is certainly a good rule always to look for explanations, always to ask the question 'Why?' And to ask is to suppose that there is an answer. But it is not to suppose that the answer is of a particular type. It is not a good methodological principle to lay down in advance the types of answers that our 'Why?' questions may elicit. We may hope that everything is ultimately explicable, and act on the assumption that it is so; but then we must be open to the possibility that explanations may be of different types, indeed, sometimes of types we had never anticipated. The explanations of actions, in particular, are unlikely to be always or illuminatingly causal: far more likely that they should be rational explanations, citing reasons why a rational agent might, or should, have performed them. Alternatively, if we insist on looking only for explanations of a particular, say causal, type, then we must hold ourselves open to the possibility that no such explanations exist. What we may not do is to take explanation in its widest sense, so that the principle that every event has a cause is a reasonable one to adopt, and then interpret it in a narrow sense, so as to justify an assumption that there must be a causal explanation even though we cannot find one.

The claim that every event has a cause may be regarded as a cosmological thesis about the nature of the universe. Many different arguments have been adduced for some such cosmological principle, and they are not all bad arguments. But again we need to be on our guard against adopting such a principle on the basis of arguments which take it in a wide sense, and then applying it in a narrow one. This is not to say that we could not conceive of the universe as being totally explicable according to just one single canon of explanation. Spinoza seems to have viewed the universe in that way. But there are deep arguments against a totally integrated, monistic universe. Not everything seems to be completely dependent on everything else. There seems to be a plurality of substances and explanations, and hence a certain measure of contingency at each level of explanation. If that is so, then in particular complete causal explanations will not always be forthcoming.

2.8. THE LOGIC OF DECISION-MAKING

Many people are led to determinism by reflecting on their own
experience of decision-making. As they look back they are able
to discern in each case some cause why they decided as they did.
They conclude that all their decisions were caused, and that
therefore they were not free to decide other than they did. Once,
however, we distinguish causes from causes, the force of this
argument is destroyed. All my actions were indeed done for reasons, because of which I did them. But it does not follow that I
had to do them, or was unfree to do anything else. The reasons
were *my* reasons, ones which I freely adopted, not some external
condition outside my control, perhaps even existing and unalterably operative long before I was born. I could have not acted on
them. Although I sent a subscription to Save the Whale because
whales were an endangered species, I did not *have to* send a subscription—I could have decided to buy a bottle of gin instead.
The case is quite different from that of a determined action. If I
wrote the cheque because the laws of physics, together with the
state of the universe at some past time, entailed that I should,
then, had I not written the cheque, the laws of physics would
have been falsified. Hence, conversely, the necessity of the laws of
physics, together with the unalterability of the past, yields an
unalterable physical necessity of my having sent the subscription.
Whereas if I had merely chosen to spend the money on gin
instead of whales, no laws of physics would have been falsified—
it would have been just one more instance of the frailty of
human nature and my tendency to choose immediate pleasures
rather than ultimate goods.

Often determinism is formulated in terms of the predictability
of human actions, but we need to distinguish between predicting
what I shall actually do, and what I must necessarily do. Actual
predictions do not compromise freedom, but are often exercises
of it. I know I shall have lunch at home tomorrow, because I,
unlike a prisoner, am free to decide where to have lunch, and I
have already decided to have lunch at home. If I tell you, you
know too where I shall have lunch tomorrow, but my freedom is
not thereby circumscribed. I could always change my mind, and
at the last moment decide to have bread and water at the office,
or go and have a solitary blow-out at a restaurant instead. Of

course, if I do, knowing that you were planning to meet me at lunch, I shall thereby show myself unreliable. Although I am free to go back on my word in the sense that I am not subject to any deterministic necessity to keep it, I am not morally free to break it, and if I do, I shall forfeit my reputation as a reliable character. Often we ascribe epithets such as 'reliable', 'trustworthy', etc., on the strength of previous behaviour, and then seem to be committed to determinist conclusions, since if we have said a man is a man of his word, then he cannot break it without our ascription having been wrong. That indeed is the case. But it does not follow that once we have described someone as a man of his word he deterministically must keep it, but only that if, contrary to our expectation, he were to break it we should then have to withdraw retrospectively our description of him: "I thought he was reliable, but he was not," we should have to say. Retrospective withdrawal, rather than any circumscription of freedom, is how we accommodate the many fallible predictions of human behaviour we constantly make, and need to make, in our day-to-day affairs.

Two linked misunderstandings of decision-making lend determinist overtones to our ordinary predictions of human actions. When we decide, we often, in difficult cases at least, deliberate. We weigh considerations *pro* against considerations *con*, and assess the balance of argument. Once we have reached a decision, we explain and justify it by citing the reasons which were, in our judgement, weightier, and which therefore won the day. If the balance of argument was in favour of a certain course of action, we justify it by reference to the pros: if against, to the cons. We do *not*, normally, refer, after the decision has been taken, to the considerations on the other side, which did not prevail. They fade from our consciousness, and we remember and cite only those that support the decision we eventually arrived at. Our decision then seems much more inevitable than it really was. Everything was going for it, and nothing that we remember could have led us the other way. But in reality what we are witnessing is a lapse of memory not a lack of freedom.

Because we deliberate, the logic of decision-making is open-textured and adversative, not tight and deductive.[14] We establish

---

[14] See H. L. A. Hart, "The Ascription of Responsibility and Rights", *Proceedings of the Aristotelian Society*, 49, 1948, pp. 171–94; repr. in A. G. N.

prima-facie and presumptive cases which in the absence of counter considerations carry the day. But they do not entail the conclusions, only establish them *other things being equal*. It is always possible that other things are not equal: it would not be inconsistent to concede the facts cited in the arguments and to deny the conclusion—if someone were to do that, he would not be ruled out of court on account of having misused language, but expected to substantiate his objections and give reasons why the conclusion did not stand. Predictions made on this basis do not necessitate. They do not follow as a matter of deductive logical necessity from the facts cited and the arguments adduced, but only as a reasonable conclusion to be drawn in the absence of further considerations. We report such predictions, and understand them when reported to us, subject to a tacit *ceteris paribus* clause: he will have lunch at home *unless he unexpectedly changes his mind*. Provided such *ceteris paribus* clauses are made explicit, our everyday predictions do not appear to foreclose freedom, but if they are left implicit, it is easy to fall into determinist fallacies. In particular it is easy to oscillate between keeping the open texture as part of the argument, which then is inherently non-necessitating, and making it an explicit extra premiss, which then yields a necessary deduction. You may predict, on the basis of my own statements or from observation of my Thursday lunching habits, that I shall lunch at home tomorrow; and ordinarily you would be well aware that you were only saying that I would, not that I was bound to, and that I was free to change my mind, and that if I did, I would not lunch at home. But you may also inadvertently include the *ceteris paribus* clause as a premiss, most commonly by describing me as a reliable, or trustworthy, man. In that case I cannot but come home for lunch. Once it is granted both that I undertook to be home and that other things are equal, there is no let-out: the three propositions—that I reliably promised, that other things were equal, and that I did not keep my promise—form an inconsistent triad. Under a sufficiently full description I must come home to lunch on pain of inconsistency, and since the description seems to describe conditions holding at the time of the prediction rather than at the time of the action

Flew, *Logic and Language*, i, Oxford, 1951, pp. 145–65. For further references and fuller discussion, see §4.3, pp. 58–60.

predicted, it seems that I am not after all free to do otherwise than as predicted.

Once the argument is fully formulated, it is easy to fault it. The *ceteris paribus* clause includes among other things a *homine volente* condition: he will come home to lunch unless he changes his mind. If he does change his mind, we are not faced with an inconsistency, some breach of logical necessity, but with a deductive argument in which one of the premisses has proved false. But we blind ourselves to the possibility of its proving false by incorporating it in the description of the antecedent situation, which forms the basis of the prediction and is already past and so, it seems, unalterable. When you ascribe virtues such as reliability to me, or any other frail human being, your description is not of an unalterable past fact, but is vulnerable to future failures on my part. "Call no man reliable until he is dead"—every characterization of a free agent is tinged with future non-necessity, and subject to the possibility of its having to be retrospectively withdrawn were he to let us down.

2.9. FREEDOM AND RATIONALITY

The arguments so far show that determinism bears on responsibility, that modern physics is not determinist, and that other arguments often urged in favour of determinism are invalid. They do not show that determinism is false. We have no good reason for thinking it true, and every reason for hoping that it is false, but hopes are not arguments, and if we were simply to take it that determinism must be false because it would upset us if it were true, we should be open to the charge of wishful thinking. There are, however, further arguments, not absolutely conclusive but sufficient to warrant a judgement in favour of the freedom of the will, which arise from an extension of the incompatibility of determinism and rational decision-making. It would disturb the balance of this book to go into these arguments fully, but it is worth giving a brief indication of their nature and scope.

Once the incompatibilist position is rejected, determinism is seen to be incompatible not only with rational decision-making with regard to actions in the external world, but with regard to internal judgements too. Rational judgement, like rational action, presupposes freedom. If there is no free will, we are not independent rational beings reaching reasoned conclusions on the basis of the evidence and arguments, but mere automata, whose output depends solely on antecedent conditions, and need not at all correspond with the truth. In that case the conclusion reached by the determinist that determinism is true is itself just a conditioned reflex, not a rational response, and the fact that the determinist expresses such a view is to be taken by us merely as a fact about him, not an argument to be entertained rationally by us. If determinism is true, all arguments in favour of determinism are to be discounted, for there is in the end no rationality, and hence no rational arguments. Equally, if we are to consider whether or not determinism is true, we cannot view ourselves as determined: we must think of ourselves as rational beings who can debate rationally whether or not determinism is true, and are therefore committed to its being false. It is a presupposition of thought, something like Descartes' *Cogito, ergo sum.* I cannot think, except on the supposition that I exist: we cannot argue, except on the supposition that we are rational, and not just automata.[15]

2.10. GÖDEL

The arguments of the last section are difficult to articulate clearly. They are typical of a common type of argument in metaphysics, where the proponent of a rival scheme is convicted of sawing off the branch he is sitting on, or, to change the metaphor, of being hoist with his own petard. One difficulty is that such arguments are self-referential, and self-referential arguments have been under suspicion on account of the paradoxes discovered by Russell and others in the foundations of mathematics at the beginning of this century. In an effort to circumvent these difficulties and to articulate the argument exactly and cogently, I put forward a version formulated in terms of Gödel's theorem.

---

[15] This argument has been put forward by many thinkers, and controverted by many others. For the former, see J. E. McTaggart, *Philosophical Studies*, London, 1934, p. 193; Warner Wick, "Truth's Debt to Freedom", *Mind*, 82, 1964, pp. 527 ff.; Ted Honderich, *Punishment: The Supposed Justifications*, London, 1969, pp. 123–30, paperback edn. 1984, pp. 132–9. For the latter, see Jonathan Bennett, *Rationality*, London, 1964, pp. 16–17; David Wiggins, "Freedom, Knowledge and Necessity", in G. Vesey (ed.), *Knowledge and Necessity*, London, 1970, pp. 132–54.

The argument turns on the difference between truth and provability-in-a-formal-system. Gödel's theorem shows that, granted the consistency of ordinary mathematics, the former cannot be reduced to the latter. The concept of truth comes from the same logical stable as that of rationality. Both are open-ended, capable of extension in all sorts of unanticipated ways. Both are mentalistic concepts, characteristically sought and exercised by rational agents with minds of their own, who are swayed by reasons and seek to know the truth. The concept of provability-in-a-formal-system, by contrast, can be defined in purely formal, mechanical terms. It corresponds to calculability by a Turing machine, and to the schematic account which, according to the determinist, can be given of all human actions and decisions. If the determinist's account is correct and all-embracing, therefore, we cannot really have a full concept of truth, but only some partial surrogate; and if, *per contra*, we have enough of a concept of truth to be able to follow and apply Gödel's theorem, it follows that the account given by the determinist is incorrect, or at best incomplete.[16]

The structure of the argument is complicated, and the details technical. It has caused much controversy. Many of the criticisms have been based on simple misapprehensions of the argument, and have set out to refute contentions I never put forward. It would be out of place to attempt to review criticisms and answer them in detail here,[17] but one general reason for thinking that the Gödelian argument is not entirely wrong is the very wide disagreement among critics about where exactly the arguments fail. Each picks on a different point, allowing that the points objected to by other critics are in fact all right, but hoping that his one point will prove fatal. None has thus far. There may, of course, still be some decisive argument yet to be formulated. But at present it is reasonable to reckon that if we really have concepts

---

[16] This argument was originally put forward by J. R. Lucas in "Minds, Machines and Gödel", *Philosophy*, 36, 1961, pp. 112–27, repr. in Kenneth M. Sayre and Frederick J. Crosson (eds.), *The Modeling of Mind*, Notre Dame, Ind., 1963, pp. 255–71; and in Alan Ross Anderson (ed.), *Minds and Machines*, Englewood Cliffs, NJ, 1964, pp. 43–59. A fuller statement of the argument is given in J. R. Lucas, *The Freedom of the Will*, Oxford, 1970.

[17] For a survey and discussion of the leading criticisms, see J. R. Lucas, "Minds, Machines and Gödel: A Retrospect", in P. Millican and A. Clarke (eds.), *Proceedings of the 1990 Turing Colloquium*, Oxford, 1992. For a full rebuttal of those criticisms, see Roger Penrose, *Shadows of the Mind*, Oxford, 1994, pt. 1.

of rationality and truth, then the restrictive accounts of our ratiocinations that determinists want us to accept are necessarily inadequate.

It is not a conclusive disproof of determinism. Determinism could still be true, and our idea of ourselves as rational, truth-seeking creatures an illusion. What we can say, however, is that if determinism is true, it is rationally inaccessible: we cannot be led to it by rational argument, for if it is true, we are not leadable by rational arguments at all. And although it remains logically possible that it is true—it does not involve us in any straight inconsistency—it is incompatible with the presuppositions of our thought, and it is rational to hold that rational thought is possible, and hence that determinism is false.[18]

---

[18] There are many other works I have not discussed in this chapter. Every generation needs to articulate the arguments afresh, finding the conclusions of previous generations to be missing the point. Among recent works the reader may find helpful are: Austin Farrer, *The Freedom of the Will*, London, 1958; C. A. Campbell, *In Defence of Free Will*, London, 1967; R. L. Franklin, *Freewill and Determinism*, London, 1968; M. R. Ayers, *The Refutation of Determinism*, London, 1968; G. Watson (ed.), *Free Will*, Oxford, 1982; P. van Inwagen, *An Essay on Free Will*, Oxford, 1983; Ted Honderich, *Determinism*, London, 1988; R. Double, *The Non-Reality of Free Will*, Oxford, 1991.

Chapter 3

Consequences and Negative Responsibility

3.1. ACTIONS AND THEIR CONSEQUENCES

Actions are two-faced. They are done by agents, intentionally and therefore expressing what the agent has in mind. But they are also causes of effects in the public external world of events, and have consequences irrespective of whether they were intended or not. Actions typically both manifest reasons and bring about results. Both aspects of action are essential, but it is common for thinkers to concentrate on one to the exclusion of the other. Where blame is at issue, or apology called for, the agent thinks only of his intentions, and says "I didn't mean to": the impersonal spectator, on the other hand, tends to discount the agent's perspective, and to consider actions solely in the light of their consequences, and to hold people responsible for all the consequences of their action or inaction.

Either exclusion eviscerates the concept. If we think of actions solely as communications conveying the agent's intentions, we ignore the conditions which alone make communication possible. It is not just that the way to hell is paved with good intentions, but that there is a conceptual link between what is intended and what actually happens, and it is only in virtue of our sharing a common world of cause and effect that we can construe the bodily behaviour of another as expressing his intentions towards us. We can understand the plea "I did not mean to" only against a background of people generally intending to bring about the results that flow from the movements of their bodies.

Equally, however, we fail to give an adequate account of actions if we try to see them simply as causes, and do not see them also from the agent's point of view, and ask ourselves what his reasons were for doing as he did. This is what is right about Collingwood's contention that all history is contemporary history.[1] The historian, in order to make sense of what people in time past were doing, must put himself imaginatively in their place and ask himself what they were up to: it is not that they really become contemporary with him, but that he must imaginatively become contemporary with them. He must ask, without benefit of hindsight, 'Why did he do it?' 'What was his situation?' 'What alternatives were open to him?' This it is difficult to do, because the historian has also to occupy another standpoint which is not primarily first-personal. Our interest is in the course of events, what actually happened, not what was aimed at. History is the record of achievements, not aspirations. Ulysses S. Grant may have been a less good general than Robert E. Lee, but he had a greater impact on the course of events. We are interested in the Battle of Waterloo, which, as it happened, Wellington won, not in Wellington, who could well have been defeated at Waterloo if Blücher had not arrived in time. The historian has to see things from both standpoints: he has to use the language of action—and to use the language of action at all he must enter into the first-personal point of view of those who acted, and consider what they meant to do as well as what actually resulted from their efforts. But, in choosing what to relate, his concern is with consequences not intentions, to tell us what actually happened, not what was meant to happen.

3.2. CONSEQUENTIALISM

Once we acknowledge that the consequences of actions count, it is tempting to adopt an entirely consequentialist position, in which the distinction between an action and its consequences ceases to signify, and each course of action is evaluated entirely and exclusively in the light of its consequences.[2] Even if we admit that actions are not merely causes, it is very largely as causes that

---

[1] R. G. Collingwood, *The Idea of History*, Oxford, 1946, esp. pp. 213–16.

[2] It is important to stress the 'exclusively': many other moral theories evaluate actions in the light of their consequences—it would be difficult not to, since most actions are focused on some state of affairs one means to bring about (see below, §3.3 and §3.7, pp. 38, 47–8). It is a mistake to contrast consequentialism with some doctrine that takes no account of consequences. The question is only whether anything else is relevant.

they are significant for us. The terminology of the Theory of Games[3] strongly suggests that the pay-offs, in terms of which outcomes are to be evaluated, are consequences, and most games-theorists unwittingly assume a consequentialist outlook.

There are many varieties of consequentialism. The best known is utilitarianism. Utilitarians evaluate consequences by their total utility, usually thought of as the happiness or pleasure enjoyed by each person as a result of those consequences. According to the utilitarian we should evaluate an action by working out what consequences flow from it, and then considering the ensuing state of affairs from the point of view of each sentient being, and seeing how much happiness it would cause him. Having done this, we then add up each individual's happiness to form a grand total of happiness resulting from that action. If we do the same for every alternative course of action, we can then see which will produce the best outcome, and reckon that to be the best. In the terminology of the Theory of Games, each outcome is evaluated by simply taking the sum of all its pay-offs.

Utilitarianism is widely accepted as the obviously right moral theory, but it has also been much criticized. Some of the criticisms are criticisms of utilitarianism as a particular type of consequentialism, others of consequentialism generally. Some can be countered. Although there are problems in measuring utility, or happiness, or pleasure, there are other ways of evaluating consequences, and these might not be open to those objections. We can imagine a celestial consequentialist operating the felicific calculus to work out how to maximise bliss; or a demonic educator trying to bring about the greatest knowledge by the greatest number; or a Platonic utopia in which the frontiers of knowledge were to be advanced as far as possible; or even a public health authority in the years after the Second World War seeking to maximise the body weight of the populace. These may not all be laudable ideals, and perhaps only the more laughable ones have goals that are easily measured, compared, and aggregated. But these failings are not failings of consequentialism *per se*, and since we do, in fact, evaluate consequences in a rough and ready way, it is hard to maintain that they are in principle impossible to evaluate.

---

[3] See further §3.5 below.

Consequentialism has difficulties of time perspective. It is not clear when the consequences are to be evaluated: is it on the morrow of the action, or the following year, or in the long run, when we are all dead, and everything will be much the same whatever we have done? This criticism, too, can be met. If we could evaluate states of affairs generally, we could integrate our evaluations over time, to yield a diachronic assessment of their total value over all time. It may seem rebarbative to introduce integral signs and the differential dt into moral discourse, but it is no worse than what economists already do in their cost–benefit analyses.

Consequentialism has many merits. It offers a unitary scheme of evaluation, which takes full account of the fact that consequences are important. Consequences are much more definite than motives or intentions: consequences are states of affairs, and it is moderately easy to distinguish between one state of affairs and another, and to decide which, if either, obtains. Reasons, by contrast, are much more indeterminate: they interpenetrate one another,[4] and often there is no way of telling what were the reasons behind a particular action. Although the scheme for evaluating states of affairs put forward by utilitarianism runs into difficulties, states of affairs are the sort of thing that could be evaluated objectively, and often are. We often do take consequences into account in deciding what to do, and are able to assess their value, and it is not clear that there is anything else that could enter into our reckoning with equal validity and weight.

A different line of argument goes back to Protagoras.[5] In deciding what to do, we are deciding what we shall do, how we shall affect the course of events in the future; we should therefore be forward-looking, and orient ourselves towards the future, taking account of what will be the effect of our actions, but not harping on the past. What is done cannot be undone. It is no use crying over spilt milk. The rational man turns his face resolutely away from the past, and husbands his energies for issues on which he can have some influence, unworried by water already under the bridge.

These are powerful arguments, more powerful still when not

---

[4] See §4.5.   [5] Plato, *Protagoras*, 324b.

stated baldly but implicitly appealed to in the give-and-take of actual argument. Any considerations adduced by a non-consequentialist are easily rubbished: if he adduces some deontological consideration—that some particular action is contrary to the moral law, for example—he can be accused of superstitious rule-worship;[6] if he adduces some past fact as relevant, he can be told to let bygones be bygones, and to concentrate his energies on making the best of the situation as it is; in general, if ever the non-consequentialist recommends a different course of action, it will be sub-optimal, as far as consequences are concerned, and it seems irrational to want to produce a sub-optimal outcome.

The arguments seem overwhelming, and often, within a certain context, are. They are overwhelming when we are considering a single operator operating in an impersonal world he is manipulating to serve such purposes as he happens to have. Under those conditions his actions should be viewed as mere interventions in the course of events intended to achieve his particular ends. But most actions are not like that. They involve more than one person. They are communications as well as causes. And they involve more than one temporal standpoint: characteristically they form part of projects extending over long periods of time. Contrary to proverbial wisdom, it is worth crying over spilt milk if it conveys, to oneself as well as to others, that the spilling was not intentional, was not typical of one's behaviour, was not part of one's autobiographical record one would be proud to recite. The crying does not get the milk back into the churn, but does alter the significance of the event.

3.3. ACTS AND OMISSIONS

An exclusive emphasis on consequences obliterates the distinction, important in our ordinary moral thinking, between action and inaction. According to the consequentialist we are as much responsible for the consequences of what we do not do as for the consequences of what we do do: sins of omission are on exactly the same footing as sins of commission, and if at any time I fail

---

[6] See J. J. C. Smart and B. A. O. Williams, *Utilitarianism: For and Against*, Cambridge, 1973, pp. 6–7.

to alleviate the sufferings in the remotest part of the Third World, I am as responsible as if I had deliberately chosen to bring them about.

From a conceptual point of view such a doctrine of unlimited negative responsibility is flawed. It misconstrues the nature of action. Actions are "homeostatic": to act is to take compensating moves to offset the unexpected variation of circumstance; actions are focused on some end-result, and therefore away from others. I must keep my eye on the ball, and therefore turn a blind eye to other needs. If I am doing medical research, I ought not to sell my equipment to relieve immediate hunger. Projects are long-term, and though it is always possible that my project is unworthy, and meet to be abandoned, in general I should be slow to do this, and, having once put my hand to the plough, continue to the end of the furrow. Once I recognise myself as an agent, I must accept the concomitants of agency, one of which is that in acting I necessarily narrow my focus of concern, and concentrate on doing some things at the expense of ignoring others.

The doctrine of unlimited negative responsibility is a hard doctrine. It loads everyone with unbearable burdens and induces unassuageable feelings of guilt. For that very reason, we sense, it must be wrong. I cannot be responsible for alleviating all the ills in the world. I am not God, not omnipotent, cannot take on myself unlimited responsibility with only finite resources. Moreover, an all-pervasive feeling of guilt is, in practice, counterproductive: while it screws some people up to incessant, though often dissipated, effort, it dulls in others the sense of real responsibility that leads to effective action. What is the general responsibility of all becomes the responsibility of nobody in particular. And since, however much one does, there will still be an unending catalogue of tasks undone for which one will be blamed, it is tempting to call it a day early on, and wallow with everybody else in a ritual beating of the collective breast, generally feeling bad about things without actually doing anything to make anything any better.

In criticizing the consequentialists' doctrine of unlimited negative responsibility, I do not maintain that nobody should have a wide-ranging concern for the general welfare of mankind, but merely reject the Procrustean tenet that this is the only concern that any moral agent should have. Although that may be a vocation for some, for many it is a good vocation to make just a few people happy, as in family life. The man who gives his children only sardine sandwiches for Christmas, so as to give more to Oxfam, is not self-evidently doing right. One may even spend something on oneself.[7] This is not to say that money should be spent on one's family or oneself regardless of the needs of others, as it too often is. Many people are selfish, and many devote their lives to the trivial and valueless, and it would be far better if they gave money and time to help their less fortunate fellow human beings. But that is a call for generosity, not an obligation arising from their being always responsible for every ill they could conceivably have prevented.

3.4. DIFFICULTIES OF CONSEQUENTIALISM

Although we may criticize consequentialism for viewing actions in the wrong light, these criticisms do not carry much weight in particular cases. Specific criticisms need to be made and pressed home, if the consequentialist is not to win each argument as it arises.

Although the difficulties faced by the utilitarian in evaluating states of affairs are not by themselves decisive, they are indicative of one weak point in the consequentialist case. The consequentialist rubbishes the deliberations of others by not allowing that they can rationally attach weight to tenuous entities such as moral principles or reasons. But this is an exercise of selective scepticism. If he is sceptical of the value of the deliberations of others, they are entitled to be sceptical of the process whereby he reaches his judgements. Neither is beyond question. If the consequentialist defends his assessments of consequences on the grounds that we do, as a matter of fact, often judge policies in the light of their consequences, and often agree on how those consequences are to be assessed, the non-consequentialist can equally protest that we often judge actions by reference to their motives, and often agree on how those motives are to be assessed. Although motives, reasons, and intentions may be more difficult to determine, they are not obviously more difficult to evaluate. Only if the consequentialist had a copper-bottomed way

[7] See further §8.5.

of assigning value to states of affairs which was not applicable to motives, reasons, and intentions, would he be entitled to be sceptical about the way we take the latter and not the former into account when we deliberate or judge actions. And this condition is not adequately met by any serious version of consequentialism.

Consequentialists take it for granted that the concepts of cause and effect are not problematic. But even an empiricist account presupposes some principle of classification whereby we can say that events of type C are the causes of events of type E; and once we are dealing with human affairs, it is a matter of dispute which principle of classification should be used. What rule it should fall under may well depend on what reason informed it. Was it an instance of law-conformity or law-breaking, or merely a walking across the grass? The most potent causes of human behaviour are messages, and the meaning of messages depends on the reasoning they embody, which can be understood and entered into by a rational agent, but cannot in general be reduced to externally specifiable universal rules.

Once we leave the level of in-principle calculability and descend to that of practical decision-making, the advantage lies with the non-consequentialist. Consequences are difficult to foresee. Even after the event, it is often difficult to say what exactly were the consequences of a particular action, and what would have happened if it had not been done. The precepts of the deontologist are much more accessible. If I know that I should not lie, should not steal, should not cause pain gratuitously, I am already prepared for many of the situations I shall encounter in ordinary life. Sophisticated versions of consequentialism, such as rule utilitarianism, seek to accommodate these precepts as "rules of thumb", which we adopt because they are easy to apply and usually give the right answer; but in that very concession they acknowledge an epistemological weakness in consequentialism which would need to be made up for by cogent arguments of principle, not thus far forthcoming.

Another difficulty is the ambiguity of time perspective between the date of deliberation and that of subsequent judgement. Is it foreseen or actual consequences that are to be taken into account? Having taken the best advice available, a mother has her child inoculated against whooping cough, and it suffers severe brain damage in consequence. The risk of that happening was much lower than the risk of dying from whooping cough caught in the normal course of events, and her decision at the time was sensible, but it actually turned out disastrously. Judgements with benefit of hindsight are very different from those at the time of decision, and often less favourable. Consequentialism, with its emphasis on the exclusive importance of consequences, without qualification, blurs the important distinction drawn by traditional reasoning between consequences that were foreseen or foreseeable and those that actually ensued. The distinction is, it is true, difficult to draw and sometimes difficult to apply in practice, but it provides a framework, as we seek to assign responsibility *ex post facto*, for asking the relevant questions, and taking proper account of the difference between the date of judgement and the date of actual decision.

3.5. OTHER PEOPLE, OTHER TIMES

Consequentialism is illuminated by the Theory of Games. In the Theory of Games each decision-maker, or "player", has a number of choices, yielding a large number of "outcomes" according to the choices made by each player. Thus if there are four players each with three possible courses of action, there will be 81 (that is, $3 \times 3 \times 3 \times 3$) possible outcomes. Each outcome is evaluated by each player according to his system of values, and the value he assigns to it is called his "pay-off". The pay-off is normally expressed in numerical terms, with the suggestion that we are dealing with the cardinal, interpersonal utilities that utilitarians believe in, but there is no need to assume that they are always cardinal and interpersonal: for most purposes it is enough that each player can decide his order of priorities as between the various outcomes that may result from his and others' choices. The outcome is usually thought of as being entirely separate from the decisions that lead up to it, and the Theory of Games is naturally construed as imposing a consequentialist gloss on our reasoning, but it need not be so: the pay-off might be assigned in view of the way in which the outcome was brought about, so that it could reflect the fact that the decisions that led up to it were in accordance with promises previously made, or alternatively were instances of base ingratitude. What is essential is that the outcomes are evaluated differently by the different players whose actions brought them about.

Consequentialism is a special case in which there is only one player, who has sole say on which decisions should be taken, and who acts so as to bring about that outcome with the highest pay-off, itself evaluated without regard to the decisions that lead up to it but solely in terms of the consequences in themselves. But in real life there are always many players, not just one. My decisions do not alone determine the outcome, but only in conjunction with yours and those of many other people too. I cannot therefore adopt a simple maximising strategy, but must take into account the decisions you and others have already taken or may yet take.

The Theory of Games enables us to characterize co-operative activities as opposed to purely competitive ones. In a competition there are necessarily losers as well as winners. They are "zero-sum games" since my gain is your loss. In co-operative activities, however, there need be no losers, since by collaborating we both do better than we would have done on our own. These are "non-zero sum games". Many are of a simple unproblematic sort: there is one outcome which is better from every player's point of view, and so each has a good reason for choosing to act so as to bring it about. But some pose problems. Two in particular bear upon consequentialism: the Rule of the Road and the Battle of the Sexes. The Rule of the Road shows the importance of other people and gives the rationale for rules and conventions, and thus reveals the weakness of a purely consequentialist approach to moral judgement. The Battle of the Sexes shows the importance of other times and the bad consequences of a purely consequentialist approach. It also will be important in Chapter 8 in showing the need for some transferable tokens of value in order to even up the difference in pay-offs that different outcomes give to different players.[8]

The Rule of the Road shows the importance of norms—"co-ordination norms"—in enabling players in a many-person game to concert their decisions so as to secure outcomes that they all prefer. In driving, in communicating, in dancing, and in many other social activities, we need to co-ordinate our actions with

---

[8] See further §8.10.

one another, so as to avoid collision and concert our efforts. If two motorists, Mr Knight and M. Chevalier, are approaching each other, they will need to move over in order not to run into each other. Provided both go right, or both go left, they will pass each other safely: what is essential is that they do not each

Mr Knight	goes right	goes left
M. Chevalier *à droite*	each passes other safely 5 5	collision 0 0
à gauche	collision 0 0	each passes other safely 5 5

decide what he, on his own, thinks best, but both abide by some convention, or rule, or law, or mutual agreement. That is to say, I should not attempt to do whatever seems to me to be productive of the best consequences but should reliably act in the way that other people expect me to act. I should drive on the left and not cut corners, give way when the other driver has the right of way, and press forward when I have, so that other drivers know where they are with me, and can plan their own movements accordingly. There is a necessary imperfection of information about the future actions of free agents in the absence of publicly avowed rules: norm observance—deontology—is the key to co-ordination. A simple maximising strategy is impossible, and each player must conjugate over persons and keep in step with others, usually by means of their all abiding by some relevant convention. Whatever the apparent attractions of consequentialism for the single operator, they are shown to be illusory, even by consequentialist standards, once the agent sees himself to be not a solipsistic loner, but one person among many, each needing to recognise others as initiators of action with minds of their own whose decisions can be anticipated only if they adhere to well-known rules.

In the Battle of the Sexes He and She want to spend their holiday together, but He would prefer to go mountaineering in the Alps, whereas She would rather they both spent it sunbathing by

He \ She	goes to Alps	goes to sea
goes to Alps	8 lovely for him; good for her 10	4 "wish you were here too" 4
goes to sea	0 beastly for him; beastly for her 0	10 good for him; lovely for her 8

the sea. Since for either of them the second best is so much better than the third or fourth alternatives, it would pay either to settle for that if the very best appeared unattainable. And therefore it would pay the other to make it seem so. If She can throw a fit of hysterics and say she cannot abide the Alps and will not go there at any price, then He, if he is reasonable, will abandon his hopes of an Alpine holiday and settle for the sea, which he would like twice as much—8—as solitary mountaineering. But equally He may see that the moment has come to take a firm masculine line, and let the little woman face up to the realities of the situation, and either come along with him or go her separate way. And if once it becomes clear that this is the choice, She will have no option but to cave in, and buy a knapsack instead of a new bikini. It is thus irrational to be guided only by the pay-offs of the outcomes that are available at any one time, because that enables the other to manipulate one's choices. If I am to retain my autonomy, I cannot be altogether a consequentialist. If once you knew that I was guided by consequences alone, you could induce me to do whatever you wanted by rigging the situation in such a way that by the time I came to make a decision the least bad outcome available to me then was to fall in with your plans.

The Battle of the Sexes shows the importance not of other persons but of other times. If we are to avoid being manipulated by unscrupulous fixers, we need long-term assessments, and a guarantee of not discounting the past as being merely water under the bridge. We cannot alter the past, but we can still assess it and take it into account, and thus free ourselves from being at the mercy of anyone who can rig the outcomes at one particular time. In the Theory of Games it is often an advantage to be able to bind oneself absolutely, or equivalently to rule out certain options absolutely. The strategy of Mutually Assured Destruction only worked provided both sides believed that the other was not governed solely by consequentialist considerations, and really would retaliate if attacked, even though there would be, then, no advantage in doing so. In order to reinforce this expectation, mechanical devices were constructed which in the event of a nuclear attack would operate automatically without the possibility of being switched off by any consequentialist survivors. In a less grisly way the whole logic of making and keeping promises is to ensure that some actions of an agent need not be altered simply by reason of factors which had been future becoming, by the effluxion of time, past. If we discount all past considerations we not only lay ourselves open to manipulation, but give only a partial account of the context in which our decisions are made and from which they obtain their significance. I cannot be coherently oriented towards the future once I recognise that all my futures will one day be past.

3.6. THE CONSEQUENCES OF CONSEQUENTIALISM

Many of the difficulties in consequentialism are conceptual, and may not cut much ice with the consequentialist himself. But those based on the ill consequences of consequentialism are ones he cannot brush aside. Bernard Williams gives a telling example of a traveller in South America who comes on a village where a hit squad is about to shoot twenty of the villagers, and their captain says that if the traveller will himself pull the trigger on one of them, the others will go free.[9] The traveller's dilemma would not arise if consequentialism were true: he should pull the trigger without compunction, abdicating an effective say in the course of events, and allowing his responses to be determined by others more bloody-minded and less moral than he is. In a world partly inhabited by consequentialists a Gresham's Law would operate, whereby bad people would be able to twist good people into being accomplices of their wicked plans. Only non-consequentialists would be able to stand up to them, because only they, when

---

[9] J. J. C. Smart and B. A. O. Williams, *Utilitarianism: For and Against*, Cambridge, 1973, pp. 98–9.

faced with a situation which had been engineered to produce a disastrous outcome unless they acted contrary to their principles, would nevertheless be able to say *ruat caelum* rather than themselves take part in doing wrong.

The traveller's dilemma arises from the difference between the act of killing someone and the omission that results in other people being killed. Consequentialists deny that there is a difference. But that involves a loss of integrity.[10] By ignoring the difference between actions and non-actions, it makes of no account the special relation subsisting between an agent and his actions, which makes him primarily responsible for them, because they are what he sought to do, and are the expression of his mind. It is only because of their being the expression of his mind that their rationale is something others can expect to elicit from him by questioning. If we adopt consequentialism, the connexion between the agent's reasons and what actually transpired in the course of events is broken, and he can no longer feel that his actions are his, or that it is incumbent on him to answer for them. He ceases to own his actions, and can no longer see himself as an agent, a being whose very nature is shown in what he does. And that involves a loss of self-esteem that even a consequentialist should take into account.

Consequentialism dilutes responsibility. If we hold ourselves negatively responsible for our omissions to just the same extent that we are positively responsible for the actions we actually commit, then, as we have seen,[11] we all feel guilty all the time, but never do anything effective about anything. In the absence of realistic goals, which we can blame ourselves more for not reaching than for reaching, and hence less for reaching than for not reaching, we do not see to it that we actually achieve any of them. Consequentialism has the bad consequence of blunting our effective sense of personal responsibility.

Some consequentialists reckon to be able to accommodate these criticisms by turning the argument backwards and saying that a consequentialist would, on consequentialist grounds, adopt a respect for others, a respect for rules, and a refusal to abandon

[10] The importance of integrity was emphasized by Williams. See his *Morality*, Harmondsworth, 1972, p. 101, and J. J. C. Smart and B. A. O. Williams, *Utilitarianism: For and Against*, Cambridge, 1973, pp. 93–100.

[11] In §3.3 above.

principles. In the same spirit some utilitarians adopt a modified rule utilitarianism, which claims to be utilitarian, but actually delivers the same conclusions as ordinary morality. It is difficult to resist this manœuvre, as the position maintained is so elastic that it has little positive content. Still, perhaps when there was a conflict of rules or a particularly difficult case the consequentialist might revert to a consequentialist stance, so that the position would not be completely vacuous. But again there are difficulties in determining when the consequentialist should stick to rules and respect for the decisions of others, and when he should revert to a purely consequentialist stance, and how he could know he could rely on others relying on him not to bend the rules. Mutually Assured Destruction would not have worked if either side had been thought to be *au fond* consequentialist. A consequentialism which seeks to modify consequentialism so as to accommodate the bad consequences that would follow from a strictly consequentialist position is an unreliable guide to action, and in any case fails to meet the conceptual objections to assimilating action and inaction, and treating both as merely causes of events, without reference to what the agent was intending to do.

Consequentialism has bad consequences. The foregoing arguments can each be used as a simple *reductio ad absurdum* of consequentialism in terms the consequentialist must allow as telling, and any attempt to accommodate them within a consequentialist schema results in the schema losing all its consequentialist edge. Much more generally, there are good reasons for rejecting consequentialism, and reckoning that the distinction between actions and their consequences may be morally relevant, and that there may be a difference between doing something and failing to avert a bad state of affairs. The connexion between an agent and his actions is of fundamental significance to his identity as an agent, and it makes the difference between his being a mere unit and being a real person with a mind of his own who has long-term projects, sees himself as one among many autonomous agents, and is concerned not only to intervene effectively in the course of events, but to communicate and make known to others what he has in mind. Although normally we act in order to bring about results, sometimes we act simply to make a statement. There are occasions when a man knows that his efforts will be unsuccessful, but still he goes on, in order to make public his protest and witness to the truth.[12]

3.7. MORAL EVALUATION OF ACTIONS AND CONSEQUENCES

Consequentialism is to be rejected. It does not follow that consequences are not morally relevant, nor that we are under no obligation to avert bad states of affairs. Consequences are always relevant, though sometimes not very relevant, and some bad states of affairs are ones we are always under great obligations to avert. Consequences are necessarily relevant, because actions are homeostatic:[13] they home in on their result; the agent needs to adapt his behaviour to adventitious circumstances in order to ensure that, in spite of alterations in the situation, the desired result occurs. Although it is right to see actions as manifestations of mind, the mind of the agent is focusing on the event he is trying to bring about, which typically enters into the description of the action; often, indeed, the action could not be adequately characterized in any other way.

The homeostatic nature of action not only makes the intended consequences constitutive of the action, but also makes the agent generally aware of other possible consequences too. He does not just loose off an intervention in the course of events, leaving it then in the lap of the gods whether things work out as desired; rather, he has to go on seeing to it that things shall work out as desired. In adapting to the changing situation in order to ensure that in spite of alterations of circumstances the desired result shall none the less come about, he has to be mindful of the changing circumstances, and the causal possibilities of his movements in the light of them. An absent-minded agent is unlikely to achieve his aims. If he is to be effective, he needs to foresee possible eventualities, and to take avoiding action to prevent side-effects or undesirable outcomes. Hence a general presumption

---

[12] This was the original sense of the Greek word μαρτύριον (*martyrion*) from which our word 'martyr' is derived. For a fuller consideration of consequentialism, see Samuel Scheffler (ed.), *Consequentialism and its Critics*, Oxford, 1988, ch. 2; also Amartya Sen and B. A. O. Williams, *Utilitarianism and Beyond*, Cambridge, 1982.

[13] See §3.3 above.

that the agent knew not only the intended consequences of his actions, but other consequences too, and can be asked to account not only for what he meant to do, but for the other effects of his intervention as well.

An agent, therefore, needs to be open to the consideration of consequences, even though he is not obliged to consider consequences alone, and does not have to consider all consequences equally. According to the doctrine of double effect agents are more answerable for the intended consequences of their actions than for those that are foreseen but not intended. The sadist revels in the pain he causes: the dentist knows that his drill will cause equal agony, but his purpose is to save the tooth from further decay: pain is not the intended result of his efforts, and is not a manifestation of his purposes towards his patients, even though he knows it will come about. If he were versed in the classical languages, he would use a consecutive, rather than a final, clause to express the situation. According to Roman Catholic moral theologians there is a difference between aborting a baby, even for a good purpose such as saving the mother's life, and performing an operation, for example, for appendicitis, which will bring about a miscarriage even though that is not its purpose: the former is forbidden, whereas the latter is permissible. Critics fail to see the relevance of the distinction, and distrust mere professions of intention. But the distinction can be drawn in terms of homeostasis: if my purpose is an abortion, and the foetus resists my first attempts to dislodge it, I try again with more drastic methods to terminate the pregnancy, whereas if the appendix is successfully removed without disturbing the foetus, I breathe a sigh of relief, and do all I can to prevent the uterus from expelling it. Similarly the dentist whose drilling does not cause pain is not disappointed, and does not seek another more sensitive tooth to attack instead; and once local anaesthetics were available, he would use them as a matter of course. Intended consequences are those we make sure happen, come what may: with unintended ones we do not offset changes of circumstance to ensure that they happen none the less, but, if they are unwelcome, seek to avoid them if at all possible. That is not to say that I can disclaim responsibility for the unintended, though foreseen, consequences of my actions: I knew they would happen if I acted, and can be asked why I acted in such a way that they came about. But I can disown them as my purpose in acting. They are not what I meant to do; they do not express what I had in mind when I acted as I did. There is a moral difference between what I deliberately set about achieving and what happens as an unwanted result of my action or inaction. Manslaughter is bad, but murder much worse.[14]

Although I can properly say "I did not mean to" when asked about the ill consequences of my actions, I still have to justify my having brought them about. In the Second World War a submarine picked up an unexploded mine while in enemy waters. It surfaced, and a seaman was detailed to go and free it from the submarine's superstructure, in the knowledge that if any enemy aeroplane was seen, the submarine would immediately submerge, drowning the seaman in the process. His life would be sacrificed to save those of his shipmates. In time of war it is right to consign some men to their deaths in order that others shall not be killed by the enemy. Although the bad consequences of an action constitute some argument against doing it, the worse consequences of not doing it may constitute a stronger argument for.

Moral philosophers are much concerned with cases where we are presented with harsh choices between courses of action or inaction, either of which will result in great evils. Often imaginary situations are envisaged where I can save one person only at the cost of another's life. But the choice is not a bare choice between two evils: action and inaction are not on a par, though we cannot take it for granted that the consequences of inaction are always less significant than those of action. Normally the difference between doing and not doing is decisive. If I can save Jane only by killing Peter, there is, of course, a reason for killing Peter—only so can I save Jane, which is something I ought to do; but equally, there is a reason against—it would result in Peter's death. Although, as far as outcomes go, these are equally balanced, there is a further argument for not intervening, in that then I am not involved in anyone's death. So, too, in Williams' South American example, if the traveller, Jim, agrees to the captain's demand, and executes one hostage, he has to answer for it, and justify his action.[15] Maybe he can: to have averted the death of a further nineteen men may be a good enough reason for hav-

---

[14] See further §6.10.
[15] See Williams' example cited above in §3.6, pp. 45–6.

ing actually killed one. But if he refuses, and the guerrillas carry out their threat, he is not automatically and necessarily answerable for what happens. He has not killed anyone. The deaths are due entirely to the guerrillas' actions, not to his inaction. The chain of causal responsibility is broken by their autonomous action. They do not have to kill the hostages. It is entirely up to them whether they do or do not. The responsibility is therefore theirs, and can be laid at Jim's door only if he has ordered them, advised them, or urged them to kill, or has at least acquiesced in their action.[16]

The intervention of other autonomous agents constitutes an important limitation on our responsibility for the foreseen consequences of our actions. Only if further conditions are fulfilled, do we share responsibility with them for what they do in the light of our actions. We cannot, and ought not to, take it upon ourselves to make their decisions for them. Some modern environmentalists attempt to shoulder too great a burden of responsibility towards future generations. It is right that we should hold ourselves responsible to posterity, and hand on to them the world in no worse shape than it was handed on to us. We ought not to pollute the earth and sea and atmosphere, or squander finite resources so that there is none left for them. Though we shall not be there to answer to them for our actions, we can consider now what answer we could make then if we were there, and seek so to act now that our children's children will have no just cause to upbraid us then. But the world they live in then will have been fashioned by our successors as well as ourselves, and we must leave to our successors not only our world but also the burden of maintaining it, a burden it will be for them to make up their minds how to discharge. We cannot do that for them, and ought not to try. In particular, with the advent of genetic engineering, we need to be wary of eugenic enthusiasm. It may be right to eliminate certain clearly deleterious genes from the human gene pool, but if we seek to breed out sin, and to people the world in time to come with only perfect specimens of *homo sapiens*, we shall be attempting to decide ourselves what decisions others shall take, and thus to make them not people but puppets.

At first sight it would seem that only known consequences will be relevant to our evaluation of someone's decision: if he did not

[16] See further ch. 5.

know that certain consequences would result from his action, we cannot, it would seem, tax him with not having taken them sufficiently into account in reaching his decision to act. But that is not so. We hold a man responsible not only for the actually foreseen, but for the reasonably foreseeable, consequences of his action, and will not automatically excuse him if he pleads that he did not know that his action would be likely to engender them. This is because of the homeostatic nature of action: in acting he was attending to what he was doing simply in order to carry it out successfully in the face of adventitious alterations of circumstance, and was aware of the causal nexus surrounding his activity, and so could and should have foreseen the foreseeable consequences of what he was doing. What a person could, and should, foresee depends very much on the social and legal context in which he acts. We have a rough idea of the likely consequences of our actions, and owe a general duty of care not to undertake actions which may result in damage to someone else. Some consequences are so bad that we fence them round with precautions, and lay on everyone the duty of not doing anything that could lead to such an unacceptable outcome. Death, in particular, is much to be avoided. It is not enough not to mean to kill someone. One must not do anything which might lead to someone's death. I must not point a gun at anyone; I must always keep a gun broken or uncocked except when actually firing. Knowing that it is lethal, and must never be pointed at anyone, never be loaded except when about to fire is part of knowing what a gun is. Thus, although we can sometimes disclaim responsibility by saying "I did not know" or "I did not realise", we often counter that disclaimer with the retort "Well, you should have known".

The distinction between an action and its consequences is often difficult to draw. Since actions are manifestations of mind, the reasons for which an action is undertaken are essentially part of the description of the action, whereas a consequence is characterized without reference to the agent's reasons. But almost always the agent's reasons for moving his body are to produce some effects, and so the description is focused on the intended consequences of the bodily movement, not the bodily movement itself. Moreover, actions are described in a public language, and the agent's reasons are not publicly accessible, and are usually imputed on the basis of bodily behaviour which is public. There is room for dispute as to what the agent's reasons really were, and whether his actions should really be described in terms of some ulterior motive we suspect him of having had. One advantage of the language of actions and consequences is that it enables us to bypass many such disputes, and accept a minimal description of the action, allowing that the agent may still be held responsible for the consequences of his action as well as the action itself, and leaving it open for further debate whether in fact he is.

3.8. NEGATIVE RESPONSIBILITY

Often we do not act, and cannot be asked 'Why did you do it?', but may sometimes be asked 'Why did you not do it?' or "Why didn't you do something about it?" In those cases where we are obliged to answer this negative question, we have a "negative responsibility".

Negative responsibility extends the concept of responsibility only to a limited extent. We can be asked to explain why we did not do what it was incumbent on us to do. But once we reject consequentialism, we must acknowledge that there are things it is not incumbent on us to do: we are not automatically answerable for all our omissions as we are for our actions. We do not always have to answer the question 'Why didn't you do something about it?', but can often retort 'Why should I have?' Only if there is some special reason why I should have done something about it, am I obliged to justify my inaction. Else I can say with perfect propriety that it was none of my business.

When there is some special reason why I should have done something about it, I am said to have some duty of care, or more generally some responsibility in the matter. We all ought to see to it that certain sorts of bad outcome do not occur, and these may require us to undertake actions we would not normally do. If I do not stop as first arrival at the scene of an accident, if I do not raise the alarm on discovering a fire, if I pass by on the other side when someone is wounded and evidently in desperate need, I shall be taxed for my inaction, and asked 'Why didn't you stop?', 'Why didn't you raise the alarm?', or 'Why didn't you give help?'

These are very general duties of care, incumbent on us all, but for that very reason limited in scope. Most special responsibilities are wider in scope, but apply only to certain people. I have wide responsibilities as son, husband, father, colleague, and friend, but they are mine alone, and different from, though often comparable with, those that others have. Some responsibilities arise simply from having a position of special power or influence—we ascribe greater responsibility to the well-educated and the rich. Most special responsibilities are, however, voluntarily assumed. If I choose to act, I thereby take on a special responsibility of care, to consider all the possible consequences of my action, and to make sure that nothing untoward comes of what I do. Hence our responsibility, noted in the previous section, not only for the actually foreseen but for the foreseeable consequences of our actions. Often the assumption of responsibility is more explicitly voluntary. We take on a particular office or role, and thereby hold ourselves willing to look after a certain sphere of activity, and take on the obligation of seeing to it that nothing goes wrong within a certain sphere of activity, and all untoward events are warded off. We lay ourselves open not just to the question 'Why did you?' but 'Why didn't you ensure that such-and-such did not happen?' Besides the positive requirement to answer for what we actually do, we acquire a negative responsibility for bad situations we fail to avert.

The division of responsibilities into a number of separate spheres can be seen as a concomitant of our being players in a more-than-one-person game. We need to co-ordinate our actions if we are not to get in one another's way, and may need to subordinate our individual decision-making to some common strategy if we are to avoid some Prisoners' Dilemma.[17] It becomes a precondition of joint activity that we divide decision-making into separate areas of concern, and each minds his own business, τὸ τὰ αὑτοῦ πράττειν (*to ta hautou prattein*), doing his part and not sticking his nose into other people's concerns. These spheres of responsibility are inherently limited: I am responsible for what is my business, but not for what is yours. Within my sphere of responsibility I am under a duty to see to it that my job is properly done, and can be blamed if I fail to do what is needed, or

---

[17] See §4.7.

more generally if things in my area of concern go awry: it was my responsibility to see to it that they did not, and I ought to have taken adequate steps to ensure not only that they did not but that they could not.

Although I can be commissioned to perform a specific task, most responsibilities are general, to look after some area of concern generally. Such negative responsibility is doubly negative. Instead of aiming to achieve a good, I seek to avert evils. And that alteration of aspiration entirely changes the task of those who have negative responsibilities, and the criteria for successful discharge of them. There is no one goal of endeavour but a heterogeneous collection of awkwardnesses to be avoided and problems to be defused, with little at the end of the term of office to show for it except that things are no worse then than they were at the outset. Hence the feeling of failure that afflicts many who occupy high office, and the temptation of governments to steer the ship of state to destinations beyond the horizon rather than bending their best efforts to keeping it afloat on an even keel.[18]

Negative responsibility extends the concept of responsibility in two important, but inherently limited, ways. It recognises that as an agent I must be aware of consequences, and that I have a duty of care not only to ensure that in acting I do not run the danger of causing untoward consequences, but to make sure that very damaging or disastrous events cannot happen. If I am in the immediate vicinity of potential disaster, and can myself take action to avoid it—pulling a drowning child from the water—then I should: I should be reprehended if I did not. I have a special responsibility too for my family, my friends, my colleagues, my neighbours. There are many other responsibilities that we undertake or are assigned by some moral, social, or legal principle. Not only are these of great importance in themselves, but they underly the application of the concept of responsibility in social institutions and politics. If I assume some office or take on some job, I undertake responsibilities to see to it that certain bad things do not happen. In particular, if I take on high public office, I have to live with the consequences of my inaction as much as with those of my actions, and cannot keep my hands clean by not getting involved in awkward situations. But it is not

[18] See further §10.1.

a universal contagion. Although in some circumstances I may be properly blamed if I pass by on the other side, it is not, and could not be, my business to see to it that everything is done which could be done to alleviate the world's innumerable ills.

Chapter 4
Reasons

4.1. RATIONALITY AND DEEDS

The question 'Why did you do it?' elicits from the agent the rationale of his action, and provides the key connexion between rationality and deeds. In spite of many exceptions, which have absorbed much attention from philosophers and lawyers, we are in most cases answerable for the actions people suppose us to have done. We can give our reasons, and justify what we did in terms of reasons which issued through our agency into action. It is because there are rational agents operating in the world that the power of reason is effective, and is capable of influencing the course of events. Responsible action is the means whereby reason is not condemned to be futile and ineffective, but can, through the agency of responsible men, be not only a reason but a cause.

4.2. ARTICULATION AND ALTERNATIVES

When we try to articulate our reasons, we often find it difficult to articulate in words the reason that guided us in deciding what to do: to have a reason—λόγον ἔχειν (*logon echein*)—does not mean that one can give it—λόγον διδόναι (*logon didonai*). We are good, but inarticulate, deciders. We can rapidly size up a situation and reach a snap decision whether to fly or flee, but we cannot easily find adequate words to convey our reasons to others, or to subject them to close and critical examination. Again and again we sense that the reason has its reasons it finds hard to express.

Our inarticulateness should not surprise us. The important thing is to do the right thing, not to talk about it. If we make the right decision we shall probably not be called upon to justify it, and if we make the wrong one, we shall have to live with the consequences, however good our reasons for it were. Typically, we are having to decide on the basis of imperfect information, and often between alternatives that are all of them unappealing. We choose the least bad of the available alternatives, not on account of its intrinsic merits but because to do anything else would be worse. Often, therefore, our real reason is negative, depending on the range of options we reckon to be open to us, often in fact taken to be just two. We argue by *modus tollendo ponens*, plumping for *this* in order to avoid the altogether intolerable *that*. The pattern of argument turns up in many fields: in politics we are told that There Is No Alternative to accepting the government's policies and often elect Mr A for the simple and sufficient reason that he is not Mr B; and many theologians argue for their favoured position *ping* on the grounds that it is not *pong*, the only other alternative they can think of.[1] Many philosophies have developed in opposition to some other one, assumed to be the only alternative, and in our own time moral subjectivism and mathematical intuitionism have both been argued for on the grounds that Platonism must be false. With the passage of time perspectives change, and it no longer seems certain that thesis and antithesis are mutually exclusive and jointly exhaustive; some third alternative emerges, synthesizing the merits and avoiding the weaknesses of its predecessors, though with other weaknesses which in their turn give rise to a new philosophy whose chief commendation is that it is not the one that was previously holding sway.

Often there really is no feasible alternative and the decision is clear-cut. But not always: sometimes we hesitate between two or more courses of action, and deliberate, weighing up the pros and cons of each course. And then we need to articulate the different considerations to assess how they bear on the possible courses of action, and to discuss with others and seek their criticism and advice, which we also need when we want to concert our actions or to win approval and support for what we do.

4.3. DIALOGUE AND ERROR

The structure of deliberative reason has not been well understood. We have been too much under the influence of the deduc-

---

[1] See B. G. Mitchell, *How to Play Theological Ping Pong*, London, 1990, pp. 166–82, adopting a thought of E. Gombrich, *Art and Illusion*, New York, 1960, p. 370.

tive paradigm, and have supposed that every decision ought to be reached by formal reasoning, *more geometrico*, and have not enquired further into the real rationale of other forms of reasoning. Reasoning about practical affairs is dialectical, that is two-sided. It is not a matter of drawing conclusions which must, on pain of inconsistency, be conceded once the premisses are admitted, but of argument and counter-argument, prima-facie case and rebuttal, presumptions which may be defeated, but if not defeated hold good, and conclusions drawn not conclusively but only subject to a *ceteris paribus* clause, other things being equal.[2] Sometimes an argument simply fails to get off the ground; sometimes it gets off the ground, but is brought down again, by some other argument, often one that shows that if it were valid, it would prove too much; sometimes it is a perfectly reasonable argument, but is effectively countered by some further consideration in the other direction: we might size up the situation on the basis of information available to us, but you draw our attention to some further factor that entirely alters the aspect of the case. The holistic nature of practical reason makes it always open to reconsideration, in contrast to the monotonic nature of monologous deductive logic where an additional premiss may yield additional conclusions but can never diminish the number of those established.[3]

Reasoning about practical affairs thus lacks a decision procedure. I cannot absolutely prove that you are wrong simply because you have failed to follow the relevant procedure, and

---

[2] See §2.8, pp. 27–9. I owe this point originally to the seminal paper by H. L. A. Hart, "The Ascription of Responsibility and Rights", *Proceedings of the Aristotelian Society*, 49, 1948, pp. 171–94, reprinted in A. G. N. Flew, *Logic and Language*, i, Oxford, 1951, pp. 145–65. Hart's argument is criticized and developed by George Pitcher, "Hart on Action and Responsibility", *Philosophical Review*, 69, 1960, pp. 226–35; by P. T. Geach, "Ascriptiveness", *Philosophical Review*, 69, 1960, p. 221; and by Joel Feinberg, "Action and Responsibility", in Max Black (ed.), *Philosophy in America*, London, 1965, esp. pp. 134–43, and pp. 157–60. I develop Hart's main point in J. R. Lucas, "The Philosophy of the Reasonable Man", *Philosophical Quarterly*, 1965, pp. 97–106; in "Not 'Therefore' but 'But'", *Philosophical Quarterly*, 1966, pp. 289–306; and in J. R. Lucas, *On Justice*, Oxford, 1980, p. 41.

[3] Plato may have been making this point in *Protagoras,* 329 de; it is interesting that many current attempts to model everyday reason in artificial intelligence use non-monotonic logics—indeed the widely used programming language PROLOG is considered by many to be non-monotonic in character. I am indebted to Dr D. A. Gillies, of King's College, London, for this point.

replace your reasoning by the correct reasoning, as I can if, for example, you have failed to follow the rules in symbolic logic. It is always possible for you, an autonomous agent, to persist in your wrong decisions, manifesting wrong value-judgements. And so it is possible for a value-judgement to be maintained by you, and still to be a wrong one.

The necessary non-infallibility of you is a doctrine I find it easy to accept. But if it is true of you, it must also be true of me, since I am your 'you' when you are addressing me. So when it comes to value-judgements it is necessarily possible that I can be wrong. First-person fallibility is philosophically important in showing the non-egocentricity of value-judgements. I say non-egocentricity rather than objectivity or realism, because both the latter terms are unduly thing-like. Objectivity suggests material objects: 'real' comes from *realis*, a word coined by the Schoolmen from *res*, a thing. Mackie argues that values cannot exist, cannot be part of the fabric of the universe, because they would be such queer kinds of things that we could not imagine them existing or see how we could come to know them.[4] But this is to assume a highly Platonist ontology and epistemology. When we talk about values existing we are not claiming to be super astronomers revealing that out there, far beyond the stars, there exists a set of quasi-quasars, queerer than quarks, which just are there, cognisable by the eye of the mind, conferring value on deeds and persons. Such a view is easily knocked down. But that is not what is really at issue when we talk of realism and anti-realism in morals, or raise the question of whether value-judgements are objective. What is at issue is whether value-judgements are merely a means of propaganding other people to do what we want, or whether they are open to rational assessment as right or wrong, true or false, independently of their being asserted or accepted by any particular person. If we acknowledge first-person fallibility, we are not only leaving room for such an assessment, but tacitly allowing its logical propriety, whereas if we deny it, we are implicitly regarding the assertion of value-judgements as a purely pragmatic means of manipulating other people.

Value-judgements are in some sense and in some circumstances action-guiding. If I say 'You ought to go and see Aunt Agatha',

[4] J. L. Mackie, *Ethics: Inventing Right and Wrong*, Harmondsworth, 1977, pp. 38–42.

my advice has been accepted and my utterance has been successful if in fact you do go and see her. Of course often my advice is
not taken, and to that extent my utterances are not successful,
but that can be construed simply as a failure, and not as showing
anything about the intention behind the utterance, and hence
about its meaning and purpose. But what we now see is not only
that I hold myself open to try and justify a value-judgement and
not simply maintain it on the strength of my mere say-so, but
that I allow that my justification may be inadequate and my reasoning wrong, in which case I shall need to change my mind.
Value-judgements are not simply the emanations of the great and
wonderful me, but are, rather, themselves subject to rational
assessment. Once I allow that what I say may be wrong, and that
the value-judgements I reach are in principle corrigible, their status is entirely altered. It is the same sort of difference as that
between reports of sense-experience—'It seems to me as if there
were a pink elephant dancing on my bed'—and claims about the
external world—'There really is a pink elephant dancing on my
bed'. In the former case, provided I am a competent language-
user and honest, I cannot be corrected; in the latter case, however competent and sincere I am, there is always the possibility of
appeal to further considerations, and of my being obliged to
retract my previous claim. Claims about reality are inherently
corrigible, though often, if well founded, not in need of actual
correction; and though the terms 'realism' and 'objective' are
infelicitous, if the question is posed in those terms we shall be
less wrong if we adopt the realist rather than the anti-realist con-
strual of value-judgements, and say that they are objective rather
than subjective. In acknowledging the possibility that I may be
wrong, I make it possible also to claim that I actually am right.

It is often felt that the claim that value-judgements are inherently fallible must be mistaken because it would mean that we
were condemned to a paralysing tentativeness in all our decision-
making. But it is a logical, not a psychological, fallibility I am
arguing for. It is the same as with knowledge. It is logically possible that I am wrong whenever I claim to know anything not
itself an analytic tautology; it does not follow that I should, as
Plato argued in book v of the *Republic*,[5] withdraw the claim

[5] *Republic*, v, 477e–478a.

merely on account of that possibility. Although it is logically possible that I may be in error when I judge that killing people is wrong, and although I lay myself under an obligation to justify my view, and to listen to counter-arguments, I need not entertain any serious doubt about the substantial truth of what I say. Maybe there are special circumstances—in time of war, in self-defence, in defence of others in imminent danger of being themselves killed—in which it is not wrong, and there is room for argument over disputed cases such as capital punishment; but in the mainline cases I should have no doubts about the views I find myself holding on the sanctity of life, and, should I doubt my own reliability of judgement, I should draw support from the near-universal verdict of mankind. In other cases I may find it difficult to be so sure, but often should not in consequence be weak. We are typically called upon to make decisions under conditions of imperfect information and with inadequate time for full reflection and deliberation, and can never be quite sure that further factors will not emerge which would lead us to change our mind; but decide we must, and, granted that necessity, we should adapt Luther's principle, and make our mistakes boldly. *Pecca fortiter*: better a bad decision honestly reached, and firmly carried out, than no decision at all, or a weak-kneed attempt to evade responsibility.

4.4. SHAREABLE

Although you and I may both be wrong in our reasoning, we do not have to be. One of us may be right, and the other agree that he is right. We can agree, and both act for the same reasons. Reasons are inherently shareable in a way that material objects are not. The ownership of material objects is privative: if I own something, others do not; and though you and I can be joint owners, our joint ownership excludes others from owning what we together own. With reasons, however, it is quite different: my having a reason—say, a reason for believing that the four-colour theorem is true—does not preclude you or anyone else from having it too. On the contrary, it invites it. I give my reasons in order that you may have them too, but in giving them to you, I do not thereby stop having them myself. Although, in the interchange of argument, I may, as a result of your counter-arguments, come to abandon some argument I had previously accepted, I do not give up an argument on its being accepted by you. Indeed, our hope is that we shall come to be of a common mind, each having given up his bad reasons, and both accepting the good ones.

But, of course, we do not have to. Arguments may be meant to end in agreement, but often leave us in total disagreement about the point at issue. Many people have in consequence despaired of reason. Aristotle quotes Theognis, that if arguments by themselves were enough to make men good they would rightly carry rich rewards:[6] but he himself thought it worth while to devote his life to argument. Indeed, arguments cannot be altogether as ineffective as cynics suppose, or we should not waste breath on them. Nevertheless, we cannot absolutely argue a person into, or out of, acting in a particular way. It is constitutive of our concept of personal identity that each person has a mind of his own, and can make it up differently from anybody else. I may be swayed by different reasons from those that weigh with you. My reasons may be bad, but they weigh with me, and if I assess them differently from you, I am able to put them into effect, and make them the basis of my own actions. In important cases, when these are reasons for action that matter a lot, we dignify them with the name of values. When you and I agree about what ought to be done, we show that we have some values in common: when we disagree, we show that, in some respect, our values differ.

Although I am always able to disagree with anybody, I cannot in practice disagree with everybody always. At least in some respects, if only in sharing a common dislike, I have some values in common with somebody. Social and political life depends on the fact that I nearly always have some community of purpose with someone, but never necessarily complete community of purpose with anyone. Communities exist: there are enough things enough people agree about to make them viable. But they are always under strain: we can never eliminate the possibility of disagreement, and seldom in practice achieve complete unanimity on any point.

[6] Aristotle, *Nicomachean Ethics*, x. ix. 3, 1179^b4–7.

4.5. INTERPENETRABILITY

Whereas material objects are fairly easy to individuate, reasons are not. A material object occupies a region of space to the exclusion of anything else: two things cannot be in the same place at the same time. But reasons do not occupy space, nor do they have each an exclusive hold on the mind. I can act for more than one reason, and may find it hard to distinguish them, or say which of them was uppermost in my mind when I made my decision. Reasons "interpenetrate" one another. Sometimes they reinforce one another cumulatively, so that together they constitute an overwhelming case for a course of action, though each individually is questionable, and could be easily overturned; but equally they may tell in different directions, and we may acknowledge the force of some consideration, even though reckoning that in the particular case under discussion it is overridden by further considerations on the other side.

For this reason, disagreements are often less fundamental than they seem. Often you acknowledge the force of what I am saying, and recognise that your proposed action will indeed, as I say, have untoward consequences, which it would be much better to avoid, while I for my part recognise the integrity which impels you to speak out and witness to the truth at whatever cost. In such cases we are not in radical disagreement about values, and can be said to have both in common, differing only in the weight we give to them in this particular case. Although radical disagreement is possible, in which one side calls into question or denies some value central to the other's thought, it is not typical, and most arguments take place in a context of considerable agreement about principles, but dispute about how they should be applied in a particular case. Admittedly, we need on occasion to consider how we may argue with the Nietzschean and the nihilist, but we distort our understanding of moral argument if we concentrate on extreme examples exclusively.

Much discussion is needed to elicit and elucidate the various reasons that move us to action. Subtly different hypothetical cases may be needed to determine just how far one line of reasoning extends, and in what circumstances other considerations come into play. But often, also, it is only when we have to decide an actual case that we discover what our real reasons are.

Although when we come to answer the question 'Why did you do it?' we tend to give short and simple answers, it is well to remember that behind them lies a much more complex web of reasoning, which occupies the forefront of our minds when we deliberate, but tends to be half forgotten once the decision has been made.[7]

4.6. FIRST-PERSONAL AND OMNI-PERSONAL REASONS

Reasons are of many different sorts, varying in range and cogency. Some are wide-ranging and peremptory: reasons for not murdering and not breaking promises are addressed to everyone and are not in the least tentative. Others, however, are more limited in scope and tone: if thou art wondering whether to marry Mary or become a monk, I may enter into thy thoughts and give thee counsel, but am certainly not adducing reasons why anyone else should marry Mary or become a monk.[8] First-personal reasons, as we may term them, are ones which I am guided by, and offer to others in case they find them persuasive too: omni-personal reasons, as we may term those at the other extreme, are ones which, we claim, should be accepted by everyone, and can never be disregarded or put on one side, and can only be overridden by other omni-personal reasons which, in the relevant situation, are even weightier. The distinction is not new. Gellner distinguished U-type judgements, based on universalisable reasoning, from F-type judgements, which are more existentialist in character,[9] and Strawson held that while the former are open to rational assessment, the latter occupy "a region where there are truths but no truth".[10] The characterization is apt, but needs to be refined further.

The difference turns on applicability. First-personal reasons do

---

[7] See §2.8, p. 27.

[8] It is greatly to be regretted that English, unlike French, German, and many other modern languages, has almost lost the use of the second-person singular. At the risk of appearing quaint, I shall use the singular to distinguish occasions when I am addressing thee individually as thyself being guided by first-personal reasons from those when I am addressing you generally as subject to omni-personal ones.

[9] E. A. Gellner, "Ethics and Logic", *Proceedings of the Aristotelian Society*, 55, 1955, pp. 157–78.

[10] P. F. Strawson, 'Social Morality and Individual Ideal', *Philosophy*, 36, 1961, pp. 1–17, esp. p. 4.

not claim to apply to other people, whereas omni-personal reasons do. If I justify my action on the score of performing a promise, then I am claiming that everyone else, similarly circumstanced, should do likewise. Of course, there is much dispute about which circumstances actually alter cases, and which cases really are alike, but in principle an omni-personal reason can be universalised to some maxim applying to everyone within its scope, whereas a first-personal reason is one that weighs with me but need not apply to thee.

It might seem that there was no real difference between first-personal and omni-personal reasons, and that as the latter were refined to take account of more and more circumstances they would come to be applicable to only one person, namely me; and that if my first-personal reasons were genuine reasons at all, and not mere expressions of my arbitrary will, they would, at least in principle, apply to some other person. And indeed there is a gradation, and many reasons are in between the two extremes, and may contain some purely first-personal considerations and others of universal application. But there is a difference none the less, a difference in orientation rather than actual application. First-personal reasons are necessarily unique, though they may be adopted by others, who make them, adapted to their case, their own: omni-personal reasons are necessarily applicable in principle to more than one person, though sometimes only one person actually falls within their scope. Omni-personally I can consider what ought to be done by anyone in your situation, by anyone in your shoes: but when I discuss thy first-personal reasons, I put myself not merely in thy shoes, but in thy skin, and try to project myself to a viewpoint which differs in innumerable relevant ways from my own. Thou, as a different person from me, with a mind of thine own, can decide what to do in all sorts of ways: when we take into account not only past actions actually done, but future ones that might be done, there is an infinite complexity in each individual, which makes him qualitatively different from every other one. My first-personal reasons set out to take this infinite complexity into account, and for that reason attach to the particular individual, me, and resist explication in terms of some finite set of features specifying a whole range of possible cases. And similarly, when I profess loyalty or love, I go beyond the finite set of features I am actually acquainted with, and claim, Godlike, to love thee for thyself alone, and not thy yellow hair.

The strategies of argument are different. With omni-personal reasons the argument is close-knit. I can properly claim that what is sauce for the goose should be sauce for the gander, and wonder what the world would be like if everyone were to act on them. Since, if they carry the day, they carry consequences, they are more vulnerable on the score of the consequences they seem to imply. If everyone must keep his promises, must I then give back the gun in accordance with my promise to the homicidal maniac? But whereas my omni-personal reasons are likely to be faulted on the score of being too cogent, of proving too much if they prove anything at all, my first-personal reasons are in danger of seeming too tenuous to carry any conviction whatsoever with thee. Still, reasons are shareable, and in giving a first-personal reason, I show that I care for some value enough to act on it, and if I care for a value, I shall want it to be valued by others; and so in giving my reasons why I acted in some particular way, there is always some suggestion that if thou wert I, thou wouldst, and shouldst, have acted similarly. But there is always also some recognition that thou couldst not have been I, without having been no longer thou: there is always some difference, and it may be a crucial one. I shall need to refer not just to my own vocation or the promptings of my own δαίμων (*daimon*), but to my own particular abilities, interests, or weaknesses.

Often the chief problem is to get thee to understand the complex web of considerations which, taken all together, lead me to a particular decision. It is a matter of formulation and exposition, to make intelligible a whole set of considerations which thou shouldst be able to appreciate, even if thou rejectest them as an adequate guide to action for thyself. But communication, difficult though it is, does not suffice. I may succeed in explaining what my first-personal reasons were that led me to be a drop-out and steal my mother's jewellery to finance our squat, and thou mayst understand just how it was with me, and still hold that my reasons did not justify what I did. It is not the case that first-personal reasons are immune to criticism, although it is often assumed that they are, and that there is no other alternative to the objective, omni-personal maxim than the purely subjective and arbitrary leap of faith. But that is not so. As I talk to thee about Mary or monkdom, or thou to me about my alternative lifestyle, I can come to the opinion, and may even tell thee, that thy reasons, though indubitably thine are bad, just as thou mayst probe the sogginess of my thought processes. It is one thing to know what our reasons are, another to judge whether they are good or bad. The reasons given in answer to the question 'Why did you do it?' may be first-personal or omni-personal, but are not on that account good. What my reasons actually were is a matter of autobiographical fact: whether they were good a matter of evaluative judgement.

First-personal reasons can, with difficulty, be assessed from outside. I can, if I am sufficiently sensitive, enter into thy point of view, and from that standpoint judge the cogency of thy first-personal reasons. But some difference remains. There is the ineliminable otherness of thee, in that thou always canst make up thy mind differently from me, adopting as ultimately decisive different first-personal reasons from the omni-personal ones I press on thee as mandatory. In the gap between what thou must, and what thou canst, do thou exercisest thy own actuality, beyond the reach of my determining. And for all the omni-personal reasoning I urge on thee, it is up to thee to decide what thou wilt do, and to say why.

The distinction between first-personal and omni-personal reasons is of the greatest consequence. The whole realm of personal relations depends on my being able to act individually but not arbitrarily. St Augustine and his successors found it difficult to reconcile grace with free will because they thought that if men's actions merited God's favour, they would require it, enabling men to manipulate God and secure salvation by works. Some of the Schoolmen, however, distinguished "condign" merit, which omni-personally demanded an appropriate response, from "congruous" merit, which made it intelligible why one might respond without making it mandatory that one must.[11] In politics we are led to value freedom and abridge the claims of justice, so that each individual may act out his first-personal reasons rather than be simply, as the Stoics would have it, the vehicle of an omni-personal reason; and conversely we recognise that in many cases

[11] William of Auvergne, *De Meritis*, in *Omnia Opera*, Venice, 1591, 298a, cited by Christopher Kirwan (*Augustine*, London, 1989, p. 116), to whom much of my understanding of Augustine is due.

there may be good reasons why someone should not decide against us, and yet these reasons are not omni-personal ones which should be given mandatory force, and that if the decision goes against us, we are entitled to be disappointed but not indignant, because no justiciable injustice has been done.

4.7. THE THEORY OF GAMES

In the previous chapter the Theory of Games was invoked to establish the need for conjugation: rationality required that reasons be conjugated over person and tense.[12] But it shows more. It establishes also that reason is essentially dynamic, by showing up the irrationality that can occur if we refuse ever to rethink our own priorities in the light of others'. The argument is a *reductio ad absurdum*. We assume, as is normal in the Theory of Games, that our priorities are indeed static, assigning to each person a fixed set of values, and then work out the consequences of their interaction in a particular case.

The Prisoners' Dilemma was first discerned by Protagoras, and greatly impressed Plato, and later Hobbes, who made it the cornerstone of his argument for Leviathan. In its modern form it is due to A. W. Tucker. He considers two prisoners, held incommunicado, who have jointly committed a serious crime. The prosecution does not, however, have sufficient evidence to convict either of them, and they know it. But it does have evidence to convict each of them of a less serious crime, say tax evasion, for

Prisoner B → Prisoner A ↓	keeps silent	confesses
keeps silent	-1 both jailed for tax evasion -1	0 B let off: maximum jail for A -10
confesses	-10 A let off: maximum jail for B 0	-6 both jailed with reduced sentences -6

----

[12] In §3.5.

which the penalty is one year's imprisonment. The prosecution then suggests some plea bargaining to each: if either will confess to the major crime, and give evidence so as to secure the conviction of the other, he will be pardoned for both the major and the minor crime. If he confesses, and the other confesses too, both will receive a suitably reduced sentence for having pleaded guilty, say six years. If he does not confess, but is convicted on the evidence of the other, then he will receive the full sentence of ten years. The prosecution lets each prisoner know that it has made the same proposition to the other. Each prisoner then has a strong incentive to confess: for if the other confesses, he will get ten years unless he does too, while if the other does not confess, he will get off scot-free, instead of doing one year for the minor offence. So, if they act according to their individual scale of values, they will both confess. But by so doing they will both end up worse off than if they both keep silent. If they both keep silent, they will each receive only one year for the minor offence; but by both confessing, they each receive the six years for having pleaded guilty to the major crime.

There are many Prisoners' Dilemmas in real life: tax evasion, fare-dodging, stealing, are all familiar instances, where, other things being equal, it would seem like a good idea to do them oneself, but a very bad idea to have other people doing them too. Hence the need for laws, backed by the sanctions of a state wielding coercive power. For our present purpose, however, the importance of the Prisoners' Dilemma lies not in its showing the need for the state, but in its revealing the inadequacy of static ascriptions of value to individuals. For there is a sense in which it is obviously in the prisoners' interests not to confess, and this rationality is occluded by the static schema employed by the Theory of Games. This point is often missed, because the prisoners are *ex hypothesi* wrongdoers, and hence presumed to be selfish. If only people were unselfish, and put others before self, then, so the argument runs, all would be well: the prisoners would not confess, the taxpayer would pay his taxes, the traveller would buy his ticket, and nobody would ever wrong his neighbour.

That all would not be well, however, is evident once we consider the dilemma of the altruistic couple where He tries to maximise Her pay-off, and She His, with the result that they both

He \ She	cooks	helps him mend the car
mends the car	good lunch, followed by pleasant drive 6 6	record journey, with meal in Transport Cafe 10 0
helps her cook	super lunch, but no drive 0 10	mediocre lunch, followed by mediocre drive 1 1

end up with something they neither want. Thus He might be keen on cars, and She on food. If He mends the car and She cooks, they have a good lunch, followed by a drive in the country. If He helps Her cook, instead of messing about in the garage, they have an absolutely super lunch, though no drive in the country, If, on the other hand, She helps Him mend the car, the car will go like greased lightning, but they will have to eat in a transport café. But if they each insist on doing what the other wants, He will try His hand in the kitchen, while She will wriggle under the car, and the result will be an indifferent lunch followed by a mediocre drive, much worse for both of them than if each had acted non-altruistically.

The Altruists' Dilemma is the mirror image of the Prisoners' Dilemma, and shows that the trouble lies not in one's being concerned to maximise one's own pay-off, but in being tied to just one pay-off throughout. In practice we are able to resolve or surmount the Prisoners' Dilemma because we modify our original preferences in the light of what we come to know about others', and are not confined to a single occasion. I conjugate over persons, and, knowing what you want, see that we shall both be better off if we follow a co-operative strategy, and for that reason come to want it. Although, other things being equal, I want to get off scot-free, and prefer a short prison sentence to a longer one, I do not want to let down my confederate. I identify with him, and begin to take his interests to heart, and consider what is best for us jointly, rather than for just me individually. I may not do so completely, and make his interests mine, as the utilitarians urge, but I do so enough to alter the balance of advantage so as to favour the co-operative strategy. Of course, in so doing, I

make myself vulnerable to being let down by him; but in real life
few situations are evidently and certainly one-off, and anyone
who lets me down on one occasion will forfeit my trust thereafter. In the long run I shall do worse if I let people down in
order to maximise my own pay-off on each occasion than if I
respond to each person as he did to me the last time we met, and
give those I have not met before the benefit of the doubt and
trust them to behave decently. Being reasonable seems reasonable
once we conjugate over persons, and proves to be the best policy
once we conjugate over time too. A completely static and purely
individualist approach is inadequate and demonstrably irrational:
if we are to be rational we must take the values of others into
consideration as well as our own, and must be prepared to
change our priorities in the light of them.

4.8. DYNAMIC

Reason is dynamic. We develop and refine our reasons in the
course of arguing with others, in deliberating by ourselves, and in
having to reach a decision in actual cases.

In arguing we first articulate our reasons as we face the chal-
lenge of others to justify our decisions. But we go further. We
need to meet their criticisms and counter their objections. In so
doing, we not only articulate further, but enter into their minds,
and appreciate the force of their contentions, if only to feel out
their weak points and fallacious reasonings. Unless we do this,
we shall often fail to justify, because we do not meet the actual
criticisms levelled or counter the actual objections raised. And we
have to go further still. Rational argument presupposes a love of
reason, and a general willingness to value an opinion more highly
for being true than for being one's own. If I am merely trying to
get you to hold my views, I am not arguing, but only propaganding, and you are justified in disregarding everything I say, with a
shrug 'Well, he would say that, wouldn't he?' To be taken seriously in discussion, I have to be a person who is willing to give
up his own opinions, if they are wrong, in exchange for the right
ones, and to see that not as a defeat but as a liberation and
benefit. Of course, we often fail to live up to this; and often,
more importantly, it is right to hold on to fundamental beliefs in

the face of criticisms and difficulties, acknowledging that they are indeed difficulties, but sensing that they can be overcome with the passage of time and given a wider view. Many trenchant criticisms were levelled against Darwin's theory of evolution, which the Darwinians were unable to answer satisfactorily at the time. They, rightly, stuck to the theory in its general outline, reckoning that in the fullness of time the difficulties would be resolved. And so they have. But Darwinism too has evolved, and is much more subtle and well worked out than when Darwin first formulated it. General physical and metaphysical theories are in the same case. They are not subject to easy refutation and sudden death in the way that less central hypotheses are. An undergraduate may not be able to refute phenomenalism, or controvert his tutor's arguments in favour of it, but is right none the less not to drop his belief in the external world. But he is not right to put the arguments he cannot meet out of mind. They are difficulties, and must in due course be either met or accommodated. The arguments may be fallacious—many arguments put forward by tutors are, just in order to give undergraduates the opportunity of discovering it for themselves—but if they are not, the realism which they criticize must be refined, so as to be less naïve and no longer open to those objections.

In arguing with others, our *amour propre* often obtrudes. Although I ought to welcome refutation, when, as a result, I exchange a false belief for a true one, often I would rather win the argument and show how clever I am, or vindicate my original judgement. I engage in what Plato termed ἐριστική (*eristike*), polemics, rather than διαλεκτική (*dialektike*), genuine discussion.[13] Nor is this always a bad thing. Freed from the constraints of reasonableness, I may explore, "for the sake of argument", a wider range of possibilities than a more sensible person would, and, egged on by competitive zeal, I may exert myself to think up more ingenious arguments than I would put my name too if I were being completely serious. Nevertheless, in the end, ἐριστική (*eristike*) is sterile, and we need to ratiocinate non-contentiously. This we do when we deliberate. In deliberating, I sometimes engage in an internal dialogue, but it is an internal one, in which I argue with my *alter ego,* with my *amour propre* not engaged on

---

[13] Plato, *Republic*, VII. 537–9.

one side rather than the other, and with seriousness of approach
guaranteed by the knowledge that whichever side I come down
on, I shall have to bear responsibility for what in the end I
decide to do. Since I shall carry the can, I want to get it right: it
is the judgement that counts, not winning the argument, and
therefore I am concerned not so much to be clever in my thinking as wise in the thoughts that finally emerge.

Deliberation ends with decision. We have to come down on
one side or the other: either to do or not to do some particular
action. And often it is hard, for there are weighty reasons on
both sides, and in deciding one way, we are rejecting the reasons
on the other side, and in deciding to do one thing we are forgoing the possibility of doing other things, also good. Each decision
implicitly expresses an order of priorities, as we have to decide
which considerations are to give way to which, an order of priorities which is being continually revised as we face new problems
and bite different bullets. It is not a simple, linear matter. Having
on one occasion decided to temper truthfulness with tact, and
not tell a lady what I really think of her new hat, or a colleague
my frank opinion of his book, I do not thereby commit myself to
always ranking charity above honesty, and may on another occasion vouchsafe my honest opinion in spite of the distress I know
it will cause. Circumstances alter cases. There are constraints of
rationality, which are as yet far from clear, on the judgements we
can reach, and some sets of decisions can properly be stigmatized
as mutually inconsistent, but the ordering of priorities is not linear, and it is perfectly rational in one case to rate freedom above
justice and in another to restrict freedom in order to ensure that
injustice does not go unchecked. All we can say is that the time
of decision is a moment of truth. As each person chooses
between the various possibilities open to him, he not only makes
reasons real, the effective causes of events in the public external
world, but also is determining which of those reasons are the
most real, and in discovering an order of reality among those
reasons, establishes the sort of person he is. Not only do reasons
emerge from the crunch of decision-making, but so do we.

Chapter 5

Shared and Collective Responsibility

5.1. THE LOGICAL SHAPE OF RESPONSIBILITY

Responsibility is not a material object. If I take a material object, I deprive someone else of it. But I can take responsibility for an action without depriving you, though sometimes with the intention of relieving you, of responsibility for it too. Often also I can be held responsible for an action you did, without your being thereby any the less responsible for it too. It is clear that the logic of responsibility is very different from that of material objects, and that we may be led into grave error if we unwittingly assume that it must have an essentially thing-like logic.

The different logic of responsibility is due to the different logic of reasons. Reasons, as we saw in Chapter 4, are not privative in the way that material objects are. My having a reason does not exclude your having it too, and one of the prime purposes of communication is to bring it about that we share reasons. Since reasons are inherently shareable, actions, which are the implementations of reasons, are shareable too. When we conjugate verbs, we have not only the first-, second-, and third-persons singular, but first-, second-, and third-persons plural as well. If we, ye, and they can be said to do something, we, ye, and they can be asked why they did it, and be required to account for what was done.

Of course, there is a difficulty. Though we can share reasons, we do not share bodies, and the bits of bodily behaviour which are the physical manifestations of an action are inherently individualised. But often our actions are concerted to form one coherent whole, and the action is described in terms of that whole, not of its individual constituents. If thou and I give a dinner party, it may be that it is by means of the movements of my body that the guests are invited and the drink brought from the shop, and by means of thy bodily movements that the food is cooked and placed on the table. But neither person's behaviour would be intelligible except in the context of the other's, and the description of us as giving a dinner party covers the actions of each for the purpose we both hold in common. Typically, therefore, actions of individuals which are intelligible only in the context of purposes shared by them all are described in terms of the common purpose which makes them intelligible, and responsibility for the actions taken all together is ascribed to each and all of those taking part.

5.2. COLLECTIVITIES

Reasons are not clear-cut. It is often not obvious what my reasons are for doing a particular action, nor whether I subscribe to some particular reason or not. We may both be acting so as to give a dinner party, but I may have caused great offence by the manner of my inviting a particularly prickly guest: is it then my doing alone or ours jointly? It is unclear whether my apparently brusque approach was a manifestation of ill will, or of inconsiderateness, or of the most courteous of intentions distorted by an ignorance of local customs. To ascribe any of these to my partner is to go beyond what the evidence warrants. Nevertheless we do: we regularly ascribe to members of a community reasons which we read into the actions of some one of them. For inasmuch as they were able to concert their actions at all, they must have established some rapport and common understanding well beyond the bare minimum needed for the giving and receiving of instructions. Shared reasons tend to extend themselves: for if there is some dissonance, we become aware of it, and articulate it, and try to resolve it. In the absence of explicit disagreement, therefore, we are entitled to presume a considerable measure of agreement, and hence to suppose that the reasons that activate one member of a community will weigh with others too. It is a presumption that can be defeated, but one that it is reasonable, in the absence of contrary indication, to make. Where people are doing things, or are in the habit of doing things, together, we naturally suppose that they constitute some sort of collectivity, who are collectively responsible, not only for what they collectively do, but for what is done in the general course of collective activity.

It is difficult to determine limits to collective responsibility. Indeed, it is impossible to draw exact limits, on account of the indefiniteness of reasons which we have just noted. But, exactitude apart, we feel uneasy at some extensions of collective responsibility. Can young Germans today be held responsible for the atrocities of the Nazis, all of them committed long before they were born? Many liberals in the north-east of the USA feel guilty about the treatment meted out to the Negroes by their compatriots in the South a couple of centuries ago. But their own forebears were largely in Europe at the time, and the culture of New England never countenanced slavery. Was Britain ever really responsible for the Amritsar massacre? In each case it is easy to deny responsibility absolutely, but that is to give the argument on the other side too short shrift. It may be that in each of these cases the ascription of responsibility is unjust, but it is not conceptually impossible. Responsibility is not a concept belonging to the natural sciences, where no later event can alter an antecedent state of affairs, but is concerned with meaning and significance, which are subject to "Cambridge change",[1] and may be reassessed and reinterpreted at a later date. As we enter into the inheritance of our predecessors, we undertake some responsibility for what they did in the process of producing those good things we now enjoy.[2] We cannot eat the fruits of their labours and wash our hands of the stains of their toil. At the very least we take on some civil liability to make reparation for what was done in the course of producing those benefits.[3] But often our responsibility goes further than that. We identify with our forebears, and make their values our own. In so far as we take pride in what our predecessors have done, and enter into their achievements, and make it a constitutive part of our identity, we identify also with the bad things they have done, and make their misdeeds our misdeeds for which we must answer, as much as we make their exploits our exploits for which we take credit. The

---

[1] See further, D. H. Mellor, *Real Time*, Cambridge, 1981, pp. 107–10; J. R. Lucas, *The Future*, Oxford, 1989, pp. 45–7. See also §6.4, p. 94 n. 9, and App. 1, p. 275.

[2] See §6.9 and §12.3, p. 262.

[3] For the distinction between civil liability and criminal responsibility, see App. 1, pp. 278–9.

more we preen ourselves and are proud, the more also we must shoulder the concomitant responsibility and take the blame.[4]

5.3. TAKING RESPONSIBILITY

The collectivities to which we ascribe responsibility in the ordinary course of events are diffuse and wide-ranging. But often there are much more specific interchanges between separate individuals which alter the burden of responsibility. I may order you, advise you, ask you, or put you up, to do something; I may be an accessory before the act, or after it; I may endorse what you did, and defend it and justify it; or I may simply carry the can in order to let you off the hook. In all these cases I become responsible for what you did, and in some of them you cease to be responsible for the actions which were effected by the movements of your own body.

In many cases it is evident that the reasons that activated your bodily movements were my reasons. If I tell you, ask you, suggest or recommend that you do something, I can be asked what the reasons for it were. I am often the originator, so it is to me that the questions can be most sharply addressed. There is no problem in ascribing responsibility to me, though that does not of itself exclude your being responsible too. It is more of a problem when I am not the originator of the action, but merely go along with it. If I am an accessory after the act, how can it be held to be my doing? Sometimes it becomes mine by own specific subsequent avowal. If you do something for reasons which I endorse, I may then endorse your action, and defend it and justify it. I am showing that your reasons are my reasons, and that I would have acted similarly had I been in a position to do so; hence it is entirely reasonable for anyone else to hold me to account for what was done by you. In other cases I am presumed to go along with it because I did not dissociate myself from it. If I come to know of what you are minded to do, and do not object, I am acknowledging the validity of your reasons simply by virtue of having knowledge of them and not pointing out their

---

[4] For a sensitive examination of the collective rights and responsibilities of the British and the Maoris in New Zealand at the present time, see R. G. Mulgan, *Maori Pakeha and Democracy*, Oxford, 1989.

invalidity. Reasons not only inherently call for action, but seek acceptance. If you have made me privy to your counsels, you have invited my comment on them, either to point out flaws and counter-arguments, or to acknowledge their cogency: I cannot just pass by on the other side, not noticing what you say, or silently suppressing my disagreement.

Of course, this is an idealized picture. Often our communications are less than fully frank, and we distance ourselves from another's plans, either because argument would be futile, or because it would be discourteous, or because we need to respect one another's spheres of decision-making, and it is no business of ours what is done by someone else. If you are bubbling over with your plans for a holiday in Majorca, I hold my peace rather than tell you how bored I should be with sunbathing on a tideless beach. It becomes my business to voice objections only if I know of some snag which you would, or should, regard as serious. If I know of a French air traffic controllers' strike, so that you will not get to Majorca, but will spend your holiday in the airport lounge at Luton, I ought to tell you. Equally, if the beaches are dangerously polluted, there is an outbreak of typhoid, or you are proposing to go to a place where the Shining Path guerrillas regularly murder tourists, I should be at fault if I did not let you know of these serious objections. But in the absence of weighty considerations, I may properly decide not to intrude on your deliberations, not participating in them, and not acquiring any responsibility for their outcome.

The same arguments apply both ways with regard to becoming an accessory after the act. Actions speak. If I come to know what you did, I thereby come to have some idea of the reasoning behind your deed. Hence, if I go along with it, and do not dissociate myself from it, I can be taken to approve. But again this line of argument is subject to severe qualifications. Not only is it none of my business to pass judgement on many things that you did, but often I shall reflect that it would not do any good anyhow. It cannot be undone, and it is no use crying over spilt milk. Life would be needlessly stressful if we were always remonstrating with one another over what had been done. Only in exceptional circumstances is there a call to pass judgement explicitly, and make it clear that we do not accept the reasoning behind some action that has come to our notice.

Two factors are relevant in ascribing responsibility. We need first to consider the closeness of association. Where people are associated in some common enterprise, or are close friends, or colleagues, or in a family, it is reasonable to reckon that they each have an obligation to speak out, and, in cases where they have not done so, that they approve of what is done. In the absence of some close association, we do not expect people to voice every disagreement, but only where some overriding objection needs to be raised. Legal and moral objections are such. If you tell me of your plan to do something legally or morally wrong, I owe it to you to point out the unwisdom of the project, and need myself to have nothing more to do with it if I am to escape responsibility for its being done. Similarly, though to a lesser extent, if I come to know what you did after you did it: if I help you complete the plan, or to get away with having done it, I thereby implicitly endorse the deed, by not, in view of the gravity of the objection, distancing myself sufficiently from it. It is your business how you spend your holiday, what career you pursue, whom you marry, and I properly hesitate to give advice unless asked, and am not answerable for the decisions you take. But for you to spend your holiday gun-running for a terrorist gang, or to make your living as a confidence trickster, or to commit bigamy, is not just your business: it is my and everyone else's business too, and I cannot acquiesce in your doing it on the grounds that it is for you alone to decide without reference to anyone else. Considerations of that gravity must be taken account of: either I dissociate myself altogether from what you have done, or else, by silently acquiescing and going along with it, I come myself to share responsibility for what was done.

5.4. THE BENEFITS OF SHARING

It is good to share responsibility. It not only flows from our being associated together in a community, but helps to create a sense of community. It is by taking pride in the deeds and exploits of my predecessors that I identify with them, and come to have an identity which makes sense of who I am. I cannot properly say who I am unless I can also say who we are. The alternative is alienation. I am alienated when I do not identify with my group, and feel that its decisions are not my decisions, that I have no lot or part in them, and so no shared responsibility for them. Inevitably most of the effective decision-making in any large group is concentrated in few hands—we do not have time or energy to consult everyone, and the exigencies of public life require that policies together form a coherent whole, and so must be overseen by a small cohesive group, which therefore excludes the majority of those affected. It is thus of great importance to have institutions which will none the less spread responsibility around, so that we do not feel that decisions taken in our name and affecting us all are decisions taken by "them", but are at bottom decisions taken by us. This, thanks to the non-privative nature of responsibility, is possible. We can endorse decisions *ex post facto* and accept responsibility for them, provided we know what they are and why they are taken. Mediaeval monarchs summoned parliaments to tell them what they were doing and why, so as to mobilise public support for their measures and induce a diffused willingness to carry their policies through. The same holds good today. We cannot all be active participants in the political process, but we can participate passively none the less by being informed about what is going on and the reasons for and against the decisions that are taken. We can metaphorically assist in French fashion.

But, as the development of Parliament shows, such participation is not completely passive, and carries with it its own logic. To be informed and invited to approve is also to be able to disapprove. Parliament cannot be just a chorus of yes-men but must have some potential to debate, and even to register disagreement as well. Communal bonds are strong, and constitute for many people a large part of their identity; but every community has to live with, and find means of accommodating, the possibility of dissent. The sharing of responsibility is thus important not only for securing identification with society but as leading to many political institutions.[5]

---

[5] See further §10.4.

5.5. DISCLAIMING RESPONSIBILITY

Responsibility is readily shared, less easily avoided. But often we want to disclaim responsibility, sometimes justly. Sometimes, although it is indisputable that it was I who did it, I can claim that I was only acting on orders, and that the question should be addressed not to me, but to the person who told me to do it. Sometimes it is a collective responsibility for someone else's misdeeds I am trying to avoid.

Although responsibility is inherently shareable and non-privative, sometimes one man's responsibility excludes another's. If you order a dish in a restaurant, and the waiter is asked why he brought it, he can simply say 'Because the customer ordered it'. Soldiers under discipline, employees generally, and many others in many other roles accept an obligation to do what they are told, and though they can be asked why they accept that obligation, they cannot be further questioned about the content of the orders they carry out. The letter I dictate to my secretary may be unwise, discourteous, even libellous: she may manage to give me pause for reconsideration, but if I tell her to type certain words, it is I, not she, who must answer for them. "I was only obeying instructions" is in most circumstances a complete answer to a demand to justify one's actions.

Acting on advice does not absolve from responsibility in the same way as acting on instructions.[6] If you did something on my advice, I certainly am responsible, but so normally are you too. You accepted the advice: it was up to you to evaluate the considerations I adduced, and decide whether they should or should not guide you. In some cases, however, where you sought professional or expert advice, it is built into the situation that you are not in a position to reach an independent judgement about the advice that is tendered, and then you can disclaim responsibility for actions undertaken on expert advice. If the doctor advises me to have an operation or take some medicine, and it proves highly deleterious, I am not responsible for damaging my health.[7]

---

[6] Though civil servants sometimes advise their minister to "put up an umbrella", that is, to appoint an independent commission to take a politically embarrassing decision. Although technically the commission only advises the minister what action to take, the fact that the commission advised a particular course of action will deflect much of the opprobrium from the minister himself.

[7] See further §9.6.

Indeed, we often indicate the abrogation of responsibility by talking of "doctor's orders". In constitutional practice we hold the Queen guiltless of actions done in her name on the advice of her ministers, and although now the language of advice is a transparent fiction, there was a time when the monarch exercised a real decision-making power, but could not be reasonably supposed to be seized of every situation, and was therefore obliged to be very largely guided by the advice he was given.

An important difference between advice and orders emerges when we consider the consequences of advice not being taken. If I give bad advice, I can be blamed: if I give good advice, which is not taken, I cannot be. An adviser can only advise, and cannot insist. If I have authority to insist, then even though I only offer advice, I cannot disclaim responsibility if it is not taken, because I could have insisted, and made sure that things were, or were not, done as I thought best. Responsibility goes with effective authority. In our age we often feel queasy about speaking of orders and authority, and are happier to talk instead of responsibility, not always realising that we are speaking of the same thing. The buck stops with him who has the final say—and having the final say should be seen not as a great extension of the ego, but as being often also a burden needing to be borne manfully, and not shuffled off on unwilling shoulders elsewhere. The traditional marriage vows have come under fire from feminists who feel it intolerable that the wife should promise to obey her husband, and husbands who thought of it as a right to subjugate deserve to be criticized; but it is a good, not a bad, principle that the husband should never blame his wife for decisions that turned out ill, and that if he did not insist on doing things differently at the time, should shoulder the responsibility himself, without recriminations, for the consequences that ensued.

5.6. THE LIMITS OF OBEDIENCE

The defence of superior orders is not absolute. As with more informal associations, I cannot disclaim responsibility for criminal or immoral acts. Although the spheres of responsibility are more sharply delineated, so that in normal circumstances the content of an order is exclusively the business of him who issues the order, and no business at all of him to whom it is addressed, it becomes the business of everybody once the bounds of morality or legality are overstepped. In that case the argument is the same as when I am privy to immoral or illegal deliberations. If I acquiesce or go along with them, I become an accessory before the act. It may sometimes be difficult, or dangerous, to refuse to obey orders, especially for soldiers in time of war, and this may be a faceable plea in mitigation of what one did. It mitigates, but it does not excuse. The duty of obedience is never unconditional. Even in the many cases where it is a valid bar to being asked "Why did you do it?", it still leaves us open to the question "Why did you obey him?", which can neither be evaded nor adequately answered when what he ordered was manifestly wrong.

Neither the criminal nor the moral law are absolutely clear-cut. It is one thing to condemn the enormities of the war crimes tried at Nuremberg, another to take seriously the finicky legislation and queasy consciences of the modern world. It is easy to present one's own predilections as fundamental moral principles. We are too ready to get on high horses about minor matters of little moment, and do not sufficiently recognise the possibility that we might be wrong, or that others, who have worked out their morality differently from us, might not be wrong. Some willingness to subordinate one's own judgement to that of others is an essential part of all social and political activity. Unless I sincerely believe that I am the only one who should have the final say, I shall sometimes be gainsaid, and required to act against my better judgement if I am to act at all. Not all my moral judgements, even on moral questions, can be fundamental moral principles, or I condemn myself to being a lone operator who can never act in conjunction with anybody else except on terms of their complete subservience to me. If I reject that form of moral egocentricity, I accept some obligation to heteronomy, to allowing that others may be right, and being willing to do as they will, not I. This is not to say that moral principles are not important. They are important, and ought to facilitate people being able to live up to their ideals. In particular, conflicts between what a man is told to do and what he believes to be right should be alleviated by provision for conscientious objection, so far as conscribed military service is concerned, and the general possibility of a dignified exit from civilian roles where unacceptable orders are given. But equally the disciplined obedience of the public servant, the loyal friend, or the monk do not derogate from an autonomy we ought all to strive to practise always, but witness to the converse truth that we may be wrong and others right, and that by doing as we are bidden and acting on their behests we make possible a continuing society in which imperfect men can live and work together.

5.7. DISTANCING

It is easy to share responsibility, but sometimes difficult not to. I am often put in the position of being an unwilling accomplice in something I know to be wrong or think to be inexpedient. Other people are busy sharing the responsibility with me, but I do not hold with what they are going to do or what they have done, and I want to have none of it; I am not one of them, or they are not one of us, at least so far as this action goes, and it cannot be laid at my, or our, door.

Distancing can take many forms. One can speak against the proposal, one can try and prevent it, one can disavow it, one can protest, one can resign, one can reprimand and discipline. Often it is the rationale of actions which have no serious chance of being effective.[8] A man may reckon that the chances of his being heard and heeded are nearly nil, but still he owes it to himself to witness to the truth and to stand up for things he believes in, even though ineffectively. He goes to public inquiries, writes letters to the papers, lobbies his MP, for if he did not, he would make himself an accomplice to the course of events he is in fact unable to prevent. He stands because he can no other if he will not go along with the bad things being done that would otherwise be done in his name. Distancing, only corporate rather than individual, also underlies the rationale of punishment, to which we now turn.

[8] See §3.6, pp. 47–8.

Chapter 6
Punishment

6.1. THE PROBLEM OF PUNISHMENT

Punishment is a problem. It involves the deliberate infliction of something unwelcome on a rational agent, and that seems hard to justify. Punishment need not be painful in the ordinary sense of the word—it may, as Mabbott points out,[1] be a deprivation of some good—but it is inherently unwelcome. When we punish someone we are doing to him something he would not, in the ordinary course of events, want us to do, and unless it is in some sense unwelcome, a punishment is not a punishment at all.

But if punishment is inherently unwelcome, it calls for justification. "Why are you doing this to me?" expostulates the person being punished, and often also the bystander may question "Why are you doing that to him?" We find it hard to answer these questions, but feel that we must try. Almost everyone has a concept of punishment, and on occasion thinks that somebody ought to be punished. Though sociologists and criminologists sometimes seem to be telling us that it is an outmoded concept that modern man ought to abandon, we are loath to drop it altogether, and we observe that those who profess disbelief in retributive punishment are none the less the first to demand punitive action when their own interests are infringed or ideals flouted. Punishment is a concept deeply entrenched in our moral and social thinking, difficult to elucidate, difficult to reconstruct according to modern principles, difficult to jettison altogether, and yet evidently in need of justification.

6.2. DEFINITIONS AND DIALOGUES

Punishments are unwelcome. You cannot punish me by increasing my range of options—offering me a holiday in France, say.

[1] J. D. Mabbott, "Punishment", *Philosophy*, 1955, pp. 3–33; repr. in H. B. Acton (ed.), *The Philosophy of Punishment*, London, 1969, pp. 117–18.

When the old lag commits a petty crime in order to be back in prison in time for Christmas, we sense that something has gone wrong. A punishment loses its point unless it is something that the person being punished would, at least at one level of thinking, rather not undergo. But there are many things that happen to us which we would rather not undergo, and few of them are punishments. If they just happen, and are not done to us by anyone, human or divine, they are not punishments. Only if they are done to us, only if they are done to us deliberately, can we raise the question "Why are you doing this to me?", and only if that question is answered in a particular way, can what is being done be construed as a punishment. For we often do things to people they would rather we did not, without its being a punishment. We give a child medicine for his own good, we turn down a candidate for a job because we think he is less suitable than another, we put people in quarantine for the good of others, and in lunatic asylums for their own good as well as that of others, we summon people to spend time on jury service, and in time of war conscribe them for military service, and we make people pay taxes. None of these are welcome; none of them would be freely chosen by the persons concerned. But they are not punishments. They may or may not be justified, but they are done for reasons of the wrong sort to be punishments. To be a punishment the question "Why are you doing this to me?" has to be met with an answer beginning "Because you did . . .", where what you are accused of having done is something you ought not to have done, something allegedly wrong.

Even when unwelcome things are done on account of previous wrongdoing, they are not always to be construed as punishments. If I perform poorly in an exam, and get a low mark, I am not being punished. Equally if I fail to get promotion on account of poor performance in my present job, I am not being punished. Although it is sometimes construed as a punishment if I lose my job as a result of dereliction of duty, it is not really so. If a butler is found tippling his master's port, he is sacked because that action shows him to be an unreliable custodian of alcoholic liquor; likewise the dishonest accountant or cashier loses his employment on account of what he has done, not in order to punish him, but in order to protect his employer from further defalcations. The fundamental purpose is not directed towards the person being punished, although his wrongdoing is relevant to the adverse action being taken. It is a ground for dismissal, because it is evidence of demerit—it shows him to be unsuitable for the job—but it is not the prime focus of concern. Punishment differs from other unwelcome actions on account of previous wrongdoing in that it is meant to be unwelcome, and understood as such. If I am punishing you, it is not enough for me merely to have an appropriate justification, and be ready to give it *if* the question is raised. If you do not ask me, then I must tell you why I am doing it. I cannot punish you without your knowing. I can dose you, quarantine you, restrain you, conscribe you, tax you, or pass you over for promotion, without your needing to know why I am doing it; I might, if I were a soft-hearted man, not tell the butler or cashier why I was sacking them—I might simply move them to another job, well away from the whisky or the till—and my action would be just as effective as if I had told them the unvarnished truth. But I cannot punish you unbeknownst to you. Punitive action is not a bare causal intervention in the course of events, but a communication, whose meaning must be understood if it is to be effective. The dialogues surrounding punishment not only occur naturally, but are constitutive of the concept.

Even when someone is being made to suffer the unwelcome attentions of another on account of some alleged wrong he has done in order to teach him a lesson, it may not be a punishment. It could be simple revenge. I can take vengeance on my enemies for insults or injuries they have inflicted on me, but it differs from punishment in being essentially personal and private. If I purport to be punishing somebody, I am not open to the argument 'I have not harmed you: you have nothing to complain about', whereas if I am seeking revenge, the one thing that is relevant is that I am an injured party, and unless I can make out that either I or mine have been wronged, my action becomes unintelligible: there can be no tit unless there was a tat, and a tat is essentially defined in first-personal, though sometimes extendedly first-personal, terms.

For the same underlying reason, if I am purporting to punish, I am open to the question "Who made you a judge over me?" To punish is to claim some sort of public, or social, or communal, *locus standi*. It does not have to be, as some thinkers have supposed,[2] a legal authorisation from the state. There are many other societies with shared values which may be upheld in the face of violations by some form of punishment, and families often have occasion to discipline wayward infants. It would be a mistake to adopt a definition which excludes many typical cases, though an understandable one, in that the person purporting to punish needs to have some *locus standi*, and the jurisdiction conferred by law is public and indisputable. But all that is essential if I am to punish is that I should be taking up some omni-personal stance, not an exclusively first-personal one, and lay myself open to further rational questioning, in a way I do not if I am simply retaliating for some injury done to me.[3]

Punishment is thus both a social and an individual concept. Punishment is imposed in the name of some community or society sharing some system of values which has been violated by a member of that society who ought not to have done what he did do. But the reason for which a punishment is imposed is essentially an individualised reason, although a reason individualised within a system of values held in common by some society. It can be understood only as being inflicted solely for reasons that are fundamentally directed towards the individual: even with vicarious and collective punishments, we have to hold the persons being punished responsible for wrong actually done by their subordinates, colleagues, or accomplices, and in the absence of such an ascription of responsibility, the punitive action would once

---

[2] For example, Hobbes, *Leviathan*, ch. xxviii: "a person is said to suffer punishment whenever he is legally deprived of some of his normal rights of a citizen on the ground that he has violated a rule of law, the violation having been established by trial according to due process of law, provided that the deprivation is carried out by the recognised legal authorities of the state, that the rule of law clearly specifies both the offence and the attached penalty, that the courts construe statutes strictly, and that the statute was on the books prior to the time of the offence." See also J. D. Mabbott, "Professor Flew on Punishment", *Philosophy*, 1955, pp. 3–33; repr. in H. B. Acton (ed.), *The Philosophy of Punishment*, London, 1969, pp. 117–18; John Rawls, "Two Concepts of Rules", *Philosophical Review*, 1955, p. 10, repr. in Acton, *The Philosophy of Punishment*, pp. 111–12; P. Foot (ed.), *Theories of Ethics*, Oxford, 1967, p. 150; J. Margolis (ed.), *Contemporary Ethical Theory*, New York, Cambridge, Mass., 1966; M. D. Bayles (ed.), *Contemporary Utilitarianism*, Doubleday, Garden City, 1968; J. J. Thomson and G. Dworkin (eds.), *Ethics*, 1968; K. Pahel and M. Schiller (eds.), *Readings in Contemporary Ethical Theory*, Englewood Cliffs, NJ, 1970; T. K. Hearn (ed.), *Studies in Utilitarianism*, New York, 1971.

[3] R. G. Swinburne, *Responsibility and Atonement*, Oxford, 1989, p. 94, n. 2, denies this.

again become unintelligible. So too with miscarriages of justice. It is, alas, possible to punish the innocent, and that fact has been seen by some as breaking the conceptual tie between punishment and guilt.[4] But although the innocent may be punished, they cannot be sentenced under that description. Unless I explain my unwelcome attentions as inflicted because of wrongdoing, they will not be construed as punishment. And further, since in this dialogue I lay myself open to further questioning and debate, I may need to make sure that the cap really fits the individual in the face of his denial that he did it, or protestations that it was not wrong: there is a germ of a trial in the very concept of punishment.[5]

Punishment, then, is something unwelcome, deliberately imposed on somebody by someone claiming to act disinterestedly on behalf of some society or community, on account of some wrong he or his has allegedly done, and understood as such.

6.3. JUSTIFICATIONS

It is difficult to justify punishment. There are many attempted justifications, and each has something to recommend it, but often there is a general unsatisfactoriness. In part it arises from the problematic way the demand for justification is raised. For already some justification has been given in describing the treatment meted out as a punishment: it is being imposed because of some wrongdoing. To ask for further justification is to ask either for more of the same type or for something different, and whichever is offered, it will fail on one count or another.

The justification for inflicting punishment on a particular person is his previous wrongdoing, and to many people this is justification enough. If asked why previous wrongdoing should entitle us to inflict unpleasantness, they will be at a loss how to answer, and will say, albeit in a grand manner, that it just does. Often they will invite us to view punishments as negative rewards. Just as good deeds deserve to be requited by good being

---

[4] A. M. Quinton, "On Punishment", *Analysis*, 14, 1954, repr. in H. B. Acton (ed.), *The Philosophy of Punishment*, London, 1969, pp. 55–64. A. G. N. Flew, "The Justification of Punishment: Postscript", in Acton, *The Philosophy of Punishment*, pp. 102–3.

[5] See §6.12 below.

done to the person who does good, so bad deeds deserve bad being done to the wrongdoer. But this argument fails to convince those who do not already accept the principle of retribution, and yields the counter-intuitive conclusion that, just as it is perfectly intelligible to pay someone before he does a good deed instead of rewarding him afterwards, so it should be all right for a malefactor to pay a fine or go to prison first, and then go and commit his crime afterwards, having already paid his debt to society. In fact, the argument is being used to argue in the wrong direction. There is indeed a parallel between the way in which it is appropriate to reward good deeds and punish bad deeds, but it illuminates the rationale of rewards rather than that of punishment. Punishments are not illuminatingly seen as negative rewards, but rather rewards as negative penalties.[6]

The justification of punishment by reason of previous wrongdoing is essentially backward-looking, and consequentialists, and in particular utilitarians, will allow only forward-looking arguments to weigh with them. Utilitarian justifications of punishment abound, and carry some weight. Few murderers who have been hanged murder anyone else, few drunken drivers mow down pedestrians while in prison. The prospect of losing their liberty or their licence has deterred many convivial souls from having just one more for the road. And while British prisons have not earned a great reputation as schools for virtue, some convicts have been brought to review their way of life while in prison, and have returned to the community as chastened and rehabilitated citizens. Punishment does sometimes prevent, sometimes deter, sometimes reform; and if only consequentialist arguments will be acknowledged as valid, these good consequences can be adduced to outweigh the evident disutility of the punishment itself.

But consequentialist justifications of punishment have an inherent weakness. If they are exclusively forward-looking, they cannot satisfactorily accommodate the essentially backward-looking orientation of the concept itself. If prevention is the real object of the exercise, I had better prevent people from doing wrong before, rather than after, the event; if deterrence, I need not worry too much about executing an innocent man, who just happened to be in the wrong place at the wrong time, *pour*

---

[6] See Ch. 7.

TABLE 6.1. *The Which? Guide to Punishment*

Account	Preventive	Deterrent	Reformative	Vindictive	Vindicative
Type	Utilitarian	Utilitarian	Utilitarian	Retributive	Retributive
Object of exercise	To prevent criminal from doing it (again)	To deter criminal from doing it again, and others from doing it at all	To reform criminal so that he is no longer minded to be antisocial	To pay people back for having done wrong	To vindicate the law and the victim by making the wrongdoer visibly not get away with it
Method	Incarceration, mutilation, confiscation, expulsion, execution, removal of licence	Adventitiously annex unpleasant consequences to the commission of crime	Compulsory subjection to rehabilitatory procedures such as boarding school or psychiatric hospital	Adventitiously annex unpleasant consequences to the commission of crime so as to restore balance	Adventitiously annex unpleasant consequences to the commission of crime
Merits	Effective (very few drunken drivers mow down people while in prison); recognises importance of effectiveness	Widely regarded; may work (who knows how many potential criminals have been deterred?)	Well-intentioned; might work in some cases; should not do any harm	Widely regarded; no punishment of innocent; no excessive punishments	No punishment of innocent; room for mercy

Demerits	Inapplicable in many cases (fraud, Official Secrets Act); manipulative	Does not work with actual criminals, most of whom continue to commit crimes; manipulative	No limit to amount or range of treatment that may be deemed to be necessary; manipulative	*Ruat caelum*; often inexpedient (uneconomic); no room for mercy; ultimate justification obscure	Excessive punishments not clearly ruled out
Advocates	Islamic fundamentalists, feminists, Conservative Selection Committees	Bentham, Smart	Protagoras, Plato, Lady Wootton, the former USSR	Kant, Bradley, Armstrong, Mabbott, Lewis	Feinberg, Cooper, Ewing
Critics	Bradley, Mabbott		C. S. Lewis	Most Modern-minded Members of the Chattering Classes	Walker

None of these accounts is conclusively ruled out; none of them is inconsistent. We cannot say of any of them NOT RECOMMENDED, and must allow that any one of them may be the most suitable for some particular argument. Nevertheless, we can give rational guidance for the general user on the strength of some of the features listed in the table, and conclude that
THE VINDICATIVE ACCOUNT IS THE BEST BUY

For a fuller account see Appendix 2.

encourager les autres, so long as the cost–benefit analysis shows that the loss incurred by his untimely demise is outweighed by a greater law-abidingness on the part of many others; and, as for reform, we are most of us in a far from satisfactory state, and could well be improved by a course of compulsory re-education.

Retributivists are quick to point out these unwelcome implications of utilitarian accounts, and utilitarians in turn complain that the retributivists offer no serious justification for the ill treatment they mete out to their victims, and accuse them of being simply vindictive. Each theory commends itself by emphasizing the demerits of its rivals, but singularly fails to meet the criticisms which they level against its own account.

The most satisfactory compromise is that first put forward by Hart, and worked out in detail by Ten.[7] A distinction is drawn between the general justifying aim of punishment, which is deterrence, and the principle of application in particular cases, which requires that it be restricted to actual wrongdoers in order to reassure the innocent. If enough weight is put on the latter consideration, a broadly utilitarian theory can be made to yield acceptable conclusions. But there is a suspicion of fudge. Utilitarian principles are often tailored to yield conclusions intuitively acceptable, but only by calling in aid some subsidiary considerations and giving them much greater weight than would normally be accorded them by those of a consequentialist turn of mind.

More particularly, there is a difficulty over the concept of punishment itself. What utilitarian arguments justify is the institution of punishment: it is like Plutarch's justification of religion—if we already have the institution, there are good grounds for keeping it for the sake of social harmony and well-being. But in neither case is there given a real rationale for having the concept or developing the institution. The institution is seen from the outside, as having a social utility, not from the inside with the concepts adequately grounded in the rest of our understanding, and with a vigorous life of their own. The Home Office official deals with punishment, much as his uncle in the Colonial Office used to deal with native religion, as something he has to manage for

[7] H. L. A. Hart, "Prolegomenon to the Principles of Punishment", *Proceedings of the Aristotelian Society*, 1959–60, repr. in his *Punishment and Responsibility*, Oxford, 1968. C. L. Ten, *Crime, Guilt and Punishment*, Oxford, 1981.

the good of society, but not as something that has any meaning for himself.

The concept of punishment can, however, be explicated, and the institution justified, in terms of responsibility, a responsibility for wrongdoing which the wrongdoer needs to disown, and which society is anxious not to share. Punishment is, on this account, a third-personal penance, needed as a token of an apology's sincerity, an emphatic disavowal of responsibility on the part of society, and a vindication of its values and the rights of the victim, if there is one, which have been flouted by the wrong done. It is an account in terms of communication rather than consequences, though consequences remain, as always, important, and it may be classified in general terms as retributivist. I shall call it a *vindicative* account, to bring out both the similarity with, and the difference from, the *vindictive* account, that is to say the standard retributive account.[8]

6.4. APOLOGY AND PENANCE

Sometimes I know I have done wrong, and own up to the wrongdoing, and admit my fault. I acknowledge it as my action, and acknowledge that it was wrong. In this case I both own the deed as my own, and disown it as a misdeed, that is, a deed I would not do now, were I to be deciding on it afresh. Contrary to the original sense of the Greek word ἀπολογία (*apologia*). I am not defending my action, but saying it away, no longer standing by it, but de-endorsing it. The misdeed no longer expresses what I am now minded to do, and no longer manifests an intention to flout our standards of right and wrong. If I apologize sincerely, I am altering my mind: I had been minded to do the misdeed, which my interlocutor deemed to be wrong, and could not accept as an action I would endorse. So long as I was minded to do it, and he was minded not to go along with its being done, we were at variance, and the action stood between us. We could not be of one mind on whether it should be done or not. But if I change

---

[8] The reader is warned that the argument given here and subsequently is not in line with prevailing philosophical fashion, and does not give other views the attention that they deserve. In App. 2 he will find a brief résumé of the main theories, explaining the "*Which?* Guide to Punishment" on pp. 92–3.

my mind, then we can be at one again. There is no longer a potential disagreement between us about what ought to be done. We are agreed that the action in question should neither be, nor have been, done. Since actions are not just events, but also means of communication, my actions can be construed as making a statement about my mind and values, and can therefore also be unsaid. We often withdraw statements by contradicting them: an apology is a sort of contradiction. If my apology is accepted as sincere, there is no longer a conflict between me, the agent, and those who hold that what I did was done amiss. We can make it up. They can forgive me, and I can be at one with them again.

The picture of apology, forgiveness and atonement is idealized: for one thing, actions are not just communications but also causes of consequences in the course of events, and what has been done cannot be undone;[9] moreover, in the real world people often cover up rather than admit to their misdoings, and apologies are often insincere, if, indeed, they are given at all. Nevertheless, the ideal pattern structures the conceptual framework within which punishment takes its place: punishment fills a crucial gap between the ideal and the all-too-real.

Many apologies are not sincere. Often we apologize merely as a matter of social convention, often also to avert wrath or penal consequences. Words slip easily off the tongue, and for that very reason are often less meaningful than deeds. If I really repent of my action, it is not enough simply to say 'sorry': I must mean it, and it may be difficult to make my words, without deeds, carry the message of genuine contrition. Sometimes I can unsay my ill-intentioned action by undoing its effects. Although what has been done cannot be undone in the easy way in which what has been said can be denied, sometimes I can undo, or make good,

---

[9] Aristotle, quoting Agathon, *Nicomachean Ethics*, VI, 1139^{b}10–11:

> μόνου γὰρ αὐτοῦ καὶ θεὸς στερίσκεται,
> ἀγένητα ποιεῖν ἄσσ' ἂν ᾖ πεπραγμένα
> (*monou gar autou kai theos sterisketai,
> ageneta poiein hass' an e$_i$ pepragmena*)

(Of this is even God deprived—the power to make undone what has already been done.) Compare Aquinas, *Summa contra Gentiles*, II. 25. 1023: *Deus non potest facere quod praeteritum non fuerit* (God cannot make the past not to have been). The unalterability of the past is constitutive of physical reality, but not of meaning and interpretation. See §5.2, p. 77 n. 1, and App. 1, p. 277.

the damage I did. I can give back the book I stole from you, I can mend the window of yours I broke, I can give you money to compensate you for the trouble or inconvenience I caused you. Though in many cases I cannot really restore you to the position you were in before my wrongdoing, sometimes I can, and if I do, then I am clearly cancelling my hostile or uncaring intention towards you, since I am putting myself out in order to ensure that you shall not be put out as a result of what I originally did.

In other cases the damage is irreparable. I cannot restore to life the man I have murdered, or call back the secrets I have betrayed. Not all wrongdoing is the infliction of harm on an assignable individual, and where there is no victim, no compensation can be paid to demonstrate the sincerity of contrition. In other cases again any compensation offered would be not so much inadequate as inappropriate. But tokens of sincerity may be needed none the less. Perhaps in theological contexts, when I am addressing God, to whom all desires are known and from whom no secrets are hid, my broken and contrite heart will be accepted for what it is, but for limited mortals, myself included, such transparency of motive is unattainable. I shall seem to have got away with it, if I have enjoyed the fruits of wrongdoing for a season, and then been absolved from them for free. The mirage of easy repentance and cheap forgiveness has led many sects astray in the course of the history of the Christian Church. For the sake of others, but even more for the sake of myself, I may need to offer tangible tokens of sincerity, if my change of heart is to be evidently genuine. Often in libel cases it is thought appropriate to make a contribution to a named charity. In the practice of some churches, the penitent does penance. Neither the donation to charity nor the penance does anything to restore the *status quo*, nor to compensate the injured party for the harm done to him, but they do in another way make amends: they purge the insult, even though they cannot make good the injury. They purge it by making the apology more real, more evidently meant, because indubitably costly. It is indisputably not easy to say goodbye to a large sum of money, or to submit to being beaten by the monks of some monastery. If I pay out, I make it clear to everyone that wrongdoing did not pay: my bad decision has cost me dear. No king would naturally and unconstrainedly submit to flagellation, and if a king does so as a penance, it is very clear to all his subjects that he would not now, in the light of these adventitiously annexed consequences, have made the same decision as he originally did. It is an emphatic disavowal of his deed, and its meaning, thus underscored, cannot be gainsaid by anyone.

The logic of penance is thus founded on a dissonance of values. I am re-expressing in terms of the unregenerate scale of values the value I now put on the action I did then. Originally it had seemed like a good idea to sleep around, fiddle the tax, betray confidences, stab a colleague in the back, and by so doing I reckoned to maximise my pay-off in life. These outcomes I now see for what they are, but I need to express their tawdriness in terms of the tawdry values of yesteryear, and need therefore to annex to them, adventitiously so far as the ordinary course of cause and effect is concerned, further outcomes whose pay-off is, on the old reckoning, such as to make the combined package a bad buy. My regretful self is seeing to it that my unreformed self would now regret having done the misdeed.

In our ordinary way of understanding, penance is a special case of self-imposed punishment. It is helpful, however, to reverse the connexion, and to view punishment as an externally imposed penance. In the limiting case, where the wrongdoer acknowledges his wrong and the justice of the punishment he is called on to undergo, punishment merges with penance, and has the same communication value. By being punished the wrongdoer expresses in terms of his old system of values the value that the community's system of values puts upon his misdeed, and thus espousing the community's system of values is once again at one with the community, and capable of resuming his membership of it as a member in good standing. In the much more usual case, where the wrongdoer does not own up to the wrong, and if found out, does not admit its wrongfulness, and is far from willing to accept punishment as his just deserts, the message is being forcibly impressed upon him. The penalties annexed to his wrongdoing by the community make it be the case that the whole transaction was a bad buy from his point of view and by his own system of reckoning, and the reason why it is being made to be a bad buy from his point of view is that it was a bad thing according to the community's system of values. The community's system of values is being vindicated by the violation's being shown to be manifestly inexpedient even according to other, more limited, systems.

But the idea of compulsory penance grates. When freely undertaken, it can have meaning as a token of sincerity, demonstrating that the contrition expressed is genuine. But typically the wrongdoer is not contrite, and the position then is that if he will not say 'sorry', we make him be sorry; but how far can we impose a meaning which the about-to-be-punished criminal emphatically disavows?

6.5. CONDONING AND DENOUNCING

We can understand better the significance of punishment by considering two alternatives, and how we would construe them. We could adopt a no-holds-barred approach, and reckon the wrongdoer outside the pale, and obviate the ill consequences of his action in any way we could—as we might, without compunction, fire a shell at a driverless runaway vehicle or a mad bull careering down a busy street. But we are rightly reluctant to regard a single lapse as putting a man *eo ipso* outside the community, to be treated simply as a means and no longer as also an end in himself. There could conceivably be public enemies to be warred against rather than punished, but we are concerned with those who are still members of the community. They may have broken the law or done some other wrong, but they are not outlaws, excommunicates, or disowned by the family; they have rights in spite of their wrongdoing; we are still in dialogue with them, and we are not prepared simply to bundle them around like a sack of potatoes. The response of the community when one of its members contravenes its values is a muted one, not a rejection of him altogether.

The other alternative is to do nothing. That also is not an option open to us. Always to do nothing as a matter of principle in the face of deliberate and open violations of rules is to acquiesce in their violation and to condone the action as not being really wrong after all.[10] If I tell you not to commit murder and

[10] Kant's famous passage makes it clear that this is the fundamental rationale of his retributivist stance: "Even if a Civil Society resolved to dissolve itself with the consent of all its members—as might be supposed in the case of a People inhabiting an island resolving to separate and scatter themselves through the

you commit murder, then if I do nothing about it, I am showing that I did not really mean it when I told you not to. Unenforced laws cease to be in force: rules which are regularly broken with impunity are no longer rules demanding to be observed.

The degree to which to acquiesce is to connive or condone varies very much with circumstances and the sort of society involved. The general form of the argument, however, is that the community has some authority over its members, and the actions of its members are therefore to be taken as actions of the community. For this to be so the community needs to have knowledge of what is being done, and an opportunity of disavowing it and showing it not to be an action it approves of; if then it does have full cognizance, and does not disavow the action, it has thereby given it tacit approval, and will be taken both by the member concerned and by others to accept the doing of that action as consonant with membership of the community.

It follows that if the misdeed is something the community cannot or will not tolerate, then it must say so, or people will get the impression from its acquiescence in the face of wrongdoing that it does not greatly care whether its members do it or not. Sometimes, contrary to what many retributivists have held, saying so is sufficient. In the armed services a reprimand and a severe reprimand are two of the penalties laid down, and entirely adequate ones. Often in civil life the mere fact of conviction is penalty enough. When middle-aged, middle-class women are charged with shoplifting, it would cost them far less to pay the fine than fight the case, but they fight it none the less in order to clear their name. The stigma of conviction is far greater penalty than any monetary loss. The values the courts uphold are widely shared, even by those who may have flouted them, who would therefore be humiliated by the knowledge of their wrongdoing becoming public, or insulted by the false supposition that they had done wrong being generally and authoritatively believed. But not all values are widely and unequivocally espoused. Some people do not accept some of society's values, and even if they do, it

whole world—the last Murderer lying in the prison ought to be executed before the resolution was carried out. This ought to be done in order that every one may realize the desert of his deeds, and *the bloodguiltiness may not remain upon the people; for otherwise they might all be regarded as participators in the murder as a public violation of Justice*" (my italics). I. Kant, *Philosophy of Law*, tr. W. Hastie, Edinburgh, 1887, p. 198.

is thought that they might not. For them mere verbal rebuke is, or might be, just water off a duck's back. If the rebuke is to be incontrovertibly telling, it needs to be one that cannot be simply shaken off with a toss of the head and an "I don't care": Don't Care must be made to care and the verbal rebuke must be given barbs that will indubitably penetrate the thickest skin.

Punishment is a message, primarily addressed to the person who did wrong, though also and importantly overheard by others, denouncing the wrongdoing in a way that will not be ignored. It is because you did wrong that we are punishing you, and were you to be fully of one mind with us, you would understand that what you had done was wrong, and acknowledge the justice of what we are doing to you. But since, in the typical case, you are not of one mind with us, we are having to tell you, in language you can understand, that what you did was something it would have been better for you not to have done, and the more we succeed in impressing on you the wrongfulness of your action, the more you will come to recognise the shared values of our community, and the closer you will be to being restored to full membership of it. At the time of your doing wrong you did not care that what you were doing was wrong; but Don't Care was made to care, and, in so far as he learns his lesson, he comes to know the values on which society is based, and, to the extent he comes to share them, he returns to being a full member in good standing.

With punishment as with penance, there is a dissonance between the value systems of the repentant and the unregenerate wrongdoer. For the whole-hearted penitent, mere reprimand is adequate. But since repentance is not always whole-hearted, and in the secular world of the civil courts the message will sometimes be addressed to a totally unregenerate wrongdoer in his possibly impenitent frame of mind, its thrust needs to be that crime does not pay. Although at the time of decision it seemed like a good idea to do the deed rather than restrain himself for the sake of some socially established value or precept, it has proved not to have been a good idea after all. No matter how little the wrongdoer shares the values of the community, doing wrong has turned out to be a mistake from his own point of view. In a manner of speaking we are retrospectively deterring him from crime, and so prospectively deterring him from doing it again, and others from following suit. There is thus an inherent deterrent aspect to punishment, and this is the truth the deterrent theory is trying to express. But, though inherent, deterrence is not central nor absolutely essential. Deterrence is forward-looking and general, whereas punishment is primarily concerned with a particular action that has been done. Nor is deterrence absolutely essential: the schoolmaster who confiscates the catapult, the highway authority that tows away the illegally parked car, the Privy Council that withdraws a doctor's licence to prescribe drugs, may or may not deter others from doing wrong too, but they are effectively preventing further wrongdoing or further ill consequences from the original misdeed. Forcible prevention negates the deviant intention as surely as effective deterrence.[11] Whether by retrospective deterrence or by prevention, the wrongdoer's decision to flout the values of the community is made one that he could no longer sensibly and successfully uphold.

6.6. THE OVERHEARERS

Although punishment is primarily directed at the person being punished, it is a public act, and will be noted by others, who will draw their own conclusions from what is being done. There may be others tempted to do a similar wrong; there may be a victim, who has had wrong done to him; there are those whose business it was to maintain law and order, and bring criminals to justice. In dealing with the wrongdoer, we have to consider also how our action will appear to these other important bystanders.

Although for some wrongdoers the mere fact of conviction or a mere reprimand is denunciation enough, often the courts reckon that in spite of their evident contrition, they must impose a further sentence, else others might be tempted, who were not yet abashed by being actually found out, or who might reckon they could weather the disapproval of the judiciary. They too must get the message, and therefore the ill consequences of

---

[11] The terminology of negating or annulling the intention of the wrongdoer is Hegel's. In his *Philosophy of Right*, tr. T. M. Knox, Oxford, 1942, §82, p. 64, §95, p. 67, and §99, p. 69, Hegel says that in punishing "coercion is annulled by coercion", and that to punish is to "annul the crime". All these passages are discussed and elucidated by David E. Cooper, "Hegel's Theory of Punishment", in Z. A. Pelczynski (ed.), *Hegel's Political Philosophy*, Cambridge, 1971, pp. 160–7.

wrongdoing must be such as to register according to the value scales of a less sensitive soul, who cares little for anything beyond his pockets and his skin. He too must see that crime does not pay, and that by the most tangible of reckonings, in terms of life, or liberty, or property, it would be better for him not to act in like manner. It is not just to the one man who actually flouted the law that punishment is addressed, but to anyone else who might be minded to pursue his own plans in defiance of the values of the community: he too needs to take in that he will not get away with it, and that if he sets his face against the community, he will not succeed in outfacing it, but will eventually come off visibly the loser. Hence what sometimes seems to be the needless severity of punishment. There are occasions where the accused has made a clean breast of it, and is clearly remorseful and extremely unlikely ever to step outside the law again, and yet the judge imposes a custodial sentence saying 'I cannot overlook the gravity of the crime', addressing himself not to the state of mind of the criminal, but to what might be the state of mind of potential criminals.

Often also there are victims. Victims suffer. Their rights were trampled on, their interests ignored by the wrongdoer, who was intent on getting what he wanted irrespective of the damage to them thereby engendered. They therefore have a fairly clear idea of the extent to which the wrongdoer was sensitive to considerations outside those of his own immediate interest at the time of the offence; and though it is possible that he has since undergone a sincere change of mind and change of values, they find that hard to believe. Almost inevitably they will impute to him the same scale of values as he manifested at the time he did them wrong, and so they will naturally construe his punishment by that scale too. Unless by that scale he has evidently fared badly, they will think he has been let off lightly, and the fact that the community is not prepared to avoid that impression will convey the further message that the community does not care for them, the victims, as much as for the offender, or the opinion of trendy opinion-formers.[12] They look to the punishment to vindicate

[12] In the new version of the parable of the Good Samaritan, the first passer-by is not a priest but a social worker, who goes over and, on seeing the man who fell among thieves, says, "My goodness, the person who did that is in need of professional help."

their rights, and to make it evident that he who trampled on them is not getting away with it. It is not exactly that they should have the last laugh, but that at least he should not.

Modern thinkers often fail to draw a crucial distinction between vindication and vindictiveness, and by refusing to allow a proper role to the former, actually encourage the growth of the latter. It is essential to identify with the victims, and the potential victims, of crime, as well as those who risk life or limb in bringing offenders to book. Society needs to express solidarity with them, and to make it clear that they matter, and that their point of view is recognised and respected. It makes a great difference to the victim whether the community takes his wrong seriously, or passes it off as of no consequence. If he sees the man who cared nothing for him go scot-free, he is given to understand that society cares nothing for him either. But if the wrongdoer is made to see the error of his ways, the man to whom the wrong was done sees his rights vindicated, and is assured that society cares for him, even if one of its members does not, and will uphold his rights in the face of assault and injury. The same is true of other bystanders, who may well see themselves as potential victims, and are to that extent in need of assurance that they too are prime objects of concern by society, which will see to it that nobody can harm them with impunity. Much modern criminology fails on this score. It shows great concern for the criminal, reminding us—and we may well need to be reminded—that criminals are human, and not outside the scope of our concern, but seeming to forget that their victims are also human, and that the community's first duty is to stand up for them, and only when it has effectively vindicated their rights, to concern itself with rehabilitating the criminal. Otherwise it beams to them a message that they do not really count, and that those who keep the law are of much less value in the eyes of the law than those who break it.

The same wrong message is mediated to another set of bystanders, those whose business it was to maintain law and order, and bring criminals to justice. They too need not to be told that their efforts were misdirected, and that society does not really care whether or not wrongdoers are brought to book. If society seems to care only for the wrongdoer, and not for the fact that wrong was done, then it is a waste of effort to try very hard to find out who did wrong, or to bring the case to court. In all of these cases, once cognizance has been taken of the misdeed, society's stance has been brought into question, and if it does not denounce the wrong with sufficient emphasis in terms that come across to those not already minded to abstain from doing that wrong, society will seem to be condoning rather than disavowing it, and saying that it does not really matter after all.

Punishment is an emphatic denunciation of wrongdoing. To the person being punished it is a reprimand; to those bystanders who might be tempted to do likewise it is a warning; to the victim it is a vindication; to potential victims it is an assurance; to those who brought the wrongdoer to book it is an endorsement of their efforts. It is a disowning of responsibility for the deed. The deed was a misdeed, and society dissociates itself from it, by deeds if necessary as well as words, in a way that cannot be ignored or overlooked, so that everyone shall know that the action, though an action of a member of the community, was his action alone, and not one that the community itself approves of, acquiesces in, or is in any way prepared to acknowledge as its own.[13]

6.7. VINDICATION

The vindicative account has only recently emerged, and is still largely misunderstood. Walker criticizes Feinberg's "Expressive Function of Punishment", which is its most authoritative formulation. He complains that Feinberg allows punishment to have other purposes besides that of disavowing the wrong done, and argues that since many criminals are not caught, the message of disapprobation cannot get through to offenders; he cites the

---

[13] This may be termed an "expressive theory of punishment". It is well argued for by Joel Feinberg, "The Expressive Function of Punishment", *The Monist*, 1965, pp. 397–423, repr. in his *Doing and Deserving*, Princeton, NJ, 1970, pp. 95–118. See also Hyman Gross, *A Theory of Criminal Justice*, Oxford, 1979; R. A. Duff, *Trials and Punishments*, Cambridge, 1986, chs. 9 and 10; Sir Walter Moberly, *The Ethics of Punishment*, London, 1968, pp. 212–22; E. Moberly, *Suffering, Innocent and Guilty*, London, 1978. esp. ch. 5. It has found legal expression in Law Commission of Canada, *Our Criminal Law*, Ottawa, 1976, and in *R. v. Sargeant* (1974), 60 Cr. App. Rep. 74, and *R. v. Llewellyn-Jones* (1965), 51 Cr. App. Rep. 204. It is criticized by Nigel Walker, *Why Punish?*, Oxford, 1991, to whom the latter references are due.

sparse newspaper coverage and general ignorance of what sentences the courts impose, and the general dissatisfaction with those that are known.[14]

These criticisms can be countered. It is inherent in the vindicative account that punishments will often be deterrent: if we generally seek to make it *ex post facto* a bad policy to have done wrong, people thinking of doing wrong will predict that it will turn out to have been a bad policy, and will therefore be deterred. Again, if we generally seek to prevent the bad intentions of wrongdoers from being effective, would-be wrongdoers who value their freedom of action will avoid incurring preventive measures. And if punishment is a forcible reminder of society's values, the message will sometimes go home, and result in an amendment of life on the part of the wrongdoer: we often speak of teaching him a lesson, and lessons are sometimes learnt, and lead to a reformation of behaviour. Communications often have consequences, and give grounds for consequentialist justifications. The only point at issue is whether these desirable side-effects constitute the whole rationale of punishment—and it is difficult to maintain that they alone can account for the individualised, backward-looking nature of the concept.

Walker argues that punishment cannot be seen as an effective means for expressing social disapprobation, because notoriously many offenders are not caught and so get away with it. But that says little about society's attitude. It is only when the offender has been brought to book that failure to do anything about it can be construed as acquiescence. Even then, of course, it is sometimes best not to notice peccadilloes, and the judicious practice of the blind eye has much to recommend it: children are often naughty in order to engage their parents' attention, and are properly dealt with by being ignored. But although failure to apprehend wrongdoers may weaken the deterrent effect of punishment, the fact that those who are caught are punished is evidence enough of society's attitude to what they have done.

Walker suggests that society could adequately denounce wrongdoing by merely seeming to punish the wrongdoer, while actually smuggling him away from the Old Bailey to live in freedom on the Costa Brava. It is difficult to see how the wrongdoer

---

[14] Nigel Walker, *Why Punish?*, Oxford, 1991, pp. 21–33.

himself would understand this as a denunciation of his action. For a utilitarian advocate of the deterrent theory such a deceit would make reasonable sense, but if we regard punishment as a tangible token of disapprobation, a reprimand that cannot be brushed off, which makes it evident even to the thickest skin that it was not a good idea to flout the values of the community, the one person who cannot be deceived is the putative recipient of the message. A similar consideration bears on some empirical evidence Walker adduces to the effect that the public do not derive much satisfaction from newspaper reports of sentences. Newspaper reports, though widely read, are not much regarded. What matters to most people is what happens in cases in which they have some personal interest, not what takes place in ones that concern them little: if they, or members of their family, or friends, or neighbours, have been attacked, or defrauded, or harmed, they are angry and upset if the courts are soft, and let the wrongdoers get away with a light sentence. They look to the authorities to uphold their rights, and are indignant if they fail. And this has nothing to do with newspaper reports and reactions to them.

Actions speak. What they signify can be understood by considering how inaction is construed. If a society in full knowledge of wrongdoing on the part of one of its members does nothing, it acquiesces in the wrong done. Its not doing nothing indicates its non-acquiescence, its repudiation of the misdeed. The misdeed meant that the wrongdoer did not care sufficiently for society's values to abide by them: he was, among other things, making a statement, a statement to the effect that society's values were not, so far as he was concerned, values at all. And, in imposing punishment, society is in turn making another statement to him, and telling him that on the contrary their values are valued, and are not to be violated with impunity, and thus vindicates them.

6.8. FORGIVENESS AND MERCY

It is a great defect of the standard theories of punishment that they leave no room for mercy. It is clearly wrong on retributive principles to remit any penalty due; equally, on the various consequentialist theories, our duty is simply to calculate what measures will best deter others, reform the criminal, or prevent him from being able to commit another crime, and apply exactly those: to impose anything less would be sub-optimal, and so a dereliction of duty. On the vindicative theory, however, there is room for mercy, because we are operating with actions whose significance has to be construed according to many different canons.

In some cases the offence, although an offence against society's values, was motivated by other values, also recognised by society, so much so that the action is seen not as a simple flouting of society's values but as manifesting an integrity that deserves respect, though not an endorsement of what was actually done. The conscientious objector is not just being selfish. Gandhi's sentence under the British Raj was the least allowed by law. So too those who commit crimes under provocation are treated more leniently than those who fully intend to do wrong, and mercy-killers are often shown mercy as not really being murderers at heart. In most cases, however, the exercise of mercy is a response to repentance, and has the same underlying logic as forgiveness, but subject to the constraint of being an official act which may be misunderstood by bystanders as well as by the wrongdoer himself.

If a man genuinely disclaims his previous intention, he removes the barrier which had stood between him and his fellows. He is, so far as what he is minded to do goes, at one with them again, and they can make it up. But it does not follow that they will. They can continue to nurture a grievance, and it is not a conceptual mistake for them to do so. They have suffered, and the injury remains. The mother whose daughter is murdered by a rapist will forever be bereft; maybe the rapist will be converted to Christianity in gaol, but that will not bring his victim back to life, or restore the shattered happiness of her family. Some people may be able to transcend their grief, and forgive those who have destroyed their happiness, but 'I can never forgive him' is an entirely understandable stance.

Christians are none the less told to forgive. In part it can be argued for as a precept of wisdom. Many wrongs done were done for reasons we can understand and come to respect. As we come to comprehend more the personalities involved, we see the action less as a manifestation of an ill will, and without condoning the deed can bring ourselves to pardon the doer. In part it can be argued for as a counsel of prudence, psychological prudence. To nurse grievances is unhealthy.[15] There is a sufficiency of evils in the current day, without need to treasure them up from the past. Bad things happen—people die—without any one bringing them about by ill will, and we have to make the best of the situation as it actually is, without forever repining about might-have-beens. The hatchet can be buried in oblivion, and often in the course of life we find erstwhile enemies valuable allies in some new battle, and forge links with them in spite of their hostile behaviour hitherto. Often also apologies are tacit. People, men particularly, are shy about saying 'sorry' on the occasions when they mean it, but indicate in other ways that they no longer stand by what they once did. To hold out for the ultimate grovel is to erect barriers on one's own side of the fence and to make it that much more difficult for relations to be restored. Even where a great wrong has been suffered, although it is abrasively harsh to say it insensitively or too soon, at some stage it is right to urge a partial amnesia of what was done, and, forgiveness being an aid to this partial forgetfulness, forgiveness can be urged on the victims of wrongdoing in those cases where the wrongdoer is indeed disowning his deed, and genuinely would undo it, were that possible.

The Christian injunction to forgive is not, however, grounded on our psychological health, but on a lively awareness of the barriers created by our own actions and attitudes. We are naturally self-isolating creatures. It is the reverse side of our autonomy. We are independent agents, capable of making up our minds for ourselves, and as each does his own thing, he is likely to implement values of self-aggrandisement that are naturally not shared by others. Not only in particular actions, but in the whole course of our decision-making, we are inclined to be guided by self-regarding concerns, which set each one of us apart from others and at odds with them. This being our nature, whose natural outcome of autistic loneliness is fearsomely unwelcome, we are not only wise to practise forgiveness as a useful discipline, but impelled by gratitude to make it up with others as others have made it up with us.

[15] See Joseph Butler, *Fifteen Sermons*, Sermon VIII, "Upon Resentment", and Sermon IX, "Upon Forgiveness of Injuries", ed. J. H. Bernard, London, 1900, pp. 112–24.

Forgiveness presupposes repentance, and repentance is unfashionable. It is currently thought that there is an unconditional duty to forgive, without any antecedent requirement on the part of the person forgiven to admit that what was done was wrong. But that is a confusion. Where there is no repentance, no change of heart, no apology, there is no possibility of making it up. The wrongdoer is prepared to resume relations, but on his own terms, that he was right to do what he did and the man wronged accepts that. But there is no reason for him to accept that: the passage of time does not require him to accept that what was done by the might of the wrongdoer should now be deemed to have been right too. The duty to forgive is not a duty to condone. Forgiveness cannot be granted where it is not sincerely sought, and though we are bidden to pray for our enemies, we are not supposed to pretend that they are actually our friends. There are occasions when we conceptually cannot, and morally should not, forgive. But they are far fewer than we think, and we do well to remember how damaging, psychologically, resentment is, and how often we, too, are in need of being forgiven.[16]

The case of mercy is comparable, but complicated by the fact of its being public, and in danger of being misconstrued by others, and in particular by the victim. Although occasionally a victim forgives the wrongdoer, it is not for us to exercise an easy forgiveness on a third-party basis. Sometimes there are exceptional circumstances which justify accepting the criminal's expressions of regret as genuine and letting him off more lightly than the gravity of the offence would normally warrant, but these occasions are rare, and when they occur, need to be clearly marked out as exceptional. Provided the exercise of mercy is clearly exceptional, other potential wrongdoers will not be encouraged to count on their also being able to plead successfully for mercy should they be found out. If the victim also asks that mercy be shown, he too will not be let down by the punishment being remitted. Other bystanders too can be assured in some circumstances that the judge is not being soft if he shows mercy. What is essential is that all are convinced that the change of heart of the wrongdoer is genuine. The penitence commonly professed by those convicted of wrongdoing is much more a sorrow

---

[16] For a fuller discussion, see Jeffrie G. Murphy and Jean Hampton, *Forgiveness and Mercy*, Cambridge, 1988, esp. ch. I, "Forgiveness and Resentment".

at the likely results of their wrongdoing than a genuine repudiation of it apart from the penal consequences now likely to ensue. We do not readily believe what wrongdoers say, and rightly are ready to impute to them, even when they profess the contrary, a strong attachment to the old Adam, who originally sinned, rather than to the new man, who has put all wrongdoing behind him. Hence the difficulty in not transmitting the wrong message if we treat wrongdoers leniently, and the general need to discount repentance and demonstrate the unwisdom of wrongdoing according to the unreformed reckoning. But this general need is not absolute, and mercy can operate in the interplay between the imputed original system of values of the wrongdoer and the actual system of values of the genuinely reformed character.

6.9. COLLECTIVE AND VICARIOUS PUNISHMENT

A communication theory of punishment argues that its prime purpose is to "negate" the intention of the wrongdoer to flout, or "negate", the standards of the community. It presupposes that the wrongdoer had that intention, what the lawyers call *mens rea*. We cannot sensibly unsay something that was never said. 'I didn't mean to' is an entirely apt rejoinder to a criminal charge. It is natural, therefore, to draw a distinction between penal responsibility and the more general notion, with the former focused on individual, positive intention, the latter admitting a wide range of shared and negative responsibilities.[17]

But we sometimes punish people for things they have not done. The employer may be fined for the negligence of his employees, even though it is shown that he had no knowledge of what they were doing, and had indeed given explicit instructions to them not to do it. The sins of the children are laid at the fathers' door, and the sins of the fathers have often been visited on the children. The whole class is kept in after school on account of some misdemeanour that only one of them did. These are clearly counter-examples to the principle previously laid down.

---

[17] See §5.2, p. 77, §12.3, p. 262, and App. 1, pp. 276–7. For a legal account, see Glanville Williams, *Criminal Law: The General Part*, 2nd edn, London, 1961, pp. 266–86.

They are. But the very way they are glossed constitutes support none the less for the principle itself. In order to make the punishment intelligible as punishment, we have to extend the 'do' or the 'you' of the wrongdoer. Under certain conditions the principal is held responsible for the deeds of his agents: by employing someone an employer takes on a negative responsibility to see to it that in the course of his employment the employee keeps the law, and fulfils all statutory requirements. Fathers can keep their children in order, and have a duty to do so, and if they fail, can be brought to account for them. Families are communities, and what is done by some members is the business of all, who share responsibility for what the rest of them do. Even a class at school can be regarded as a community. Perhaps it is unfair—in some cases it certainly is—to punish someone for what another did, on account of some imputed responsibility. It is a matter for detailed argument in each case. But sometimes at least, the person being held responsible for the misdeeds of another could have taken action to restrain the other from wrongdoing, sometimes the values of a community to which we belong and from which we have benefited are values that lie behind the wrongdoing: although we did not actually do the deed ourselves, we may have countenanced it, or retrospectively endorsed it, and for that reason have responsibility ascribed to us.

Such ascriptions are not always conceptually impossible, though often unjust. But they need to be made if punishment is to be in point. I can fine an employer because *his* employees have failed to observe safety regulations, but not because the employees of the Standard Oil Company of New Jersey have misbehaved; the IRA may "execute" me as a punishment for the wrongs they imagine the British to have committed, but not on account of alleged misdeeds by the Russians, or because the weather has been bad. The link between the wrong done and the person being punished may be stretched, and may sometimes be tenuous, but it has to be made out, or the punishment ceases to be intelligible at all, and is seen either as some other sort of adverse decision-making or as gratuitous malevolence.

Even when some identification can be made, we are extremely chary of punishing anyone vicariously. Unless we can pin on him some definite failure or breach of duty which contributed to the wrongdoing being done by someone else, we think it unfair to punish him, even if he is responsible in some wide sense. He is liable for a tort, rather than guilty of a crime. Punishment for crimes deemed to have been committed according to the canons of strict liability stick in our throat, because they purport to negate bad intentions that were, in fact, never held by the person being punished.[18]

6.10. STRICT LIABILITY

In some cases, our qualms notwithstanding, the law, for reasons of public policy, deems people to be vicariously responsible for the wrongdoing of others, and punishes them for misdeeds they knew nothing of, and were in no position to prevent. "Strict liability" holds a man responsible for what is done even though he had no part in the doing of it. A farmer can be convicted of watering his milk, even though he did not do it, or know that it was being done; indeed even if he had given specific instructions to prevent its being done: Parliament has enacted that a landlord is vicariously responsible for drugs being consumed on his premises, even though he has no means of preventing, or even knowing of, the offence.

Strict liability is popular with legislators and administrators, unpopular with judges, juries, and ordinary citizens. It is easy to impose, and leaves no room for excuses, and therefore makes people take redoubled precautions not to fall foul of the law. If I am in danger of being done for watering my milk, I shall not rest content with merely telling my employees not to add water to the milk, but take extra care to make sure they really are carrying out my instructions. But, expedient though it is as a means of manipulating people, it is unfair, and in the long run counterproductive. Beyond a certain point, we reckon a person to have discharged his duty of care, and if then an enemy or disgruntled employee adds water to the milk in order to get him into trouble, we know that he is not responsible, and are not prepared to hold him responsible, whatever the administrators may say. This is what happened in Miss Sweet's case. Miss Sweet was a schoolmistress who let her house in Woodstock to a number of

---

[18] See further §6.10 below.

young people; while she was on holiday in Spain, the police raided the house, and found drugs being taken, whereupon Miss Sweet was prosecuted and convicted by the magistrates for permitting her house to be used for drug-taking. She appealed, and the House of Lords "interpreted" the statute to mean the opposite of what its wording naturally meant, because it was manifestly unjust to convict her of a serious crime she had no part in and could not have known about.[19] It is, of course, bad that the House of Lords should fly in the face of the express intention of Parliament—that way lies the subversion of the constitution, as practised in America by the Supreme Court. But it is bad also that Parliament should instruct the courts of justice to condemn innocent people. Legislatures have a clear and present duty to avoid the easy option of strict liability, and to make sure that all ascriptions of vicarious responsibility are properly considered and judicially assessed.[20]

6.11. THE CONSTRAINTS OF LAW

Many thinkers have reckoned punishment by legal authorities to be the only proper type of punishment, and have often written such a requirement into their definition.[21] Although an understandable mistake, it is a mistake none the less, not only because it excludes many typical cases, but because it distorts our understanding of the concept itself, importing extraneous constraints which are not inherent in punishment, though they may be appropriate to the operations of the law, which is governed by considerations of practicality and utility, and arouses deep fears of possible abuse.

We are rightly awed by the law. The punishments imposed by legal authorities are nearly always the most severe we are likely to encounter. Many people feel frightened if they find a policeman calling at their door. In our own century we have witnessed again and again the horrors of the police state. We cannot do without the law, but we want to circumscribe it as much as possi-

---

[19] *Sweet* v. *Parsley*, All England Law Reports, 1969, I, pp. 347–64.

[20] For the sorry state of English law, in which strict responsibility has largely ousted the requirement of *mens rea*, see Glanville Williams, *Criminal Law: The General Part*, 2nd edn, London, 1961, ch.6, pp. 216–65; see, in particular, his §89 in which he evaluates the arguments in favour of strict responsibility and the requirement of *mens rea*. [21] See above, §6.2, pp. 89–90.

ble, to ensure that it remains our defender and does not become our oppressor. We lay down many requirements of due process, standard of proof, and limitation of judicial discretion, to prevent the extreme sanctions available to the law being used to tyrannize over us. These often are proper restrictions, but they are practical restrictions imposed on a developed legal system, not conceptual restrictions on the nature of punishment.

Some tags of the jurists are deeply embedded in the concept of punishment. *Nulla poena sine crimine* follows from the definition of punishment, though, as we saw in the previous section, it has sometimes been flouted in current legal practice. *Nulla poena sine judicio* is also, as we have seen,[22] almost a conceptual requirement. *Nulla poena sine lege* and *Nulla crimen sine lege* do not stem from the nature of punishment, but have been argued for on the basis of what the law ought to be, and have been adopted as principles in some fully developed legal systems.

6.12. FAIR TRIAL

The principle *Nulla poena sine judicio* is almost as fundamental as the principle *Nulla poena sine crimine*. It follows from the dialogue which confers on punishment its meaning. I cannot punish you without telling you that this is what I am doing, or it will not be a punishment at all. I have to tell you that it is a punishment for something you have done wrong, and therefore you have an opportunity of protesting that you did not do it, or that it was not wrong at all. Because punishment is an individualised communication, the person to whom the message is addressed has the logical opportunity to deny the presuppositions of the message, and though his denials may not be believed, they have to be rejected for the punishment to make sense, and we are under deep intellectual pressure to make sure that the rejection is well founded before proceeding to deliver the punitive message itself.

Where the punishment is not great, I may ignore your protestations. The childish 'but' is often obliterated by the maternal slap, and no great harm done. But the punishments imposed by law are severe, and we need to be very sure that the accused

[22] See above, §6.2, p. 90.

actually is guilty before we punish him. Hence the requirement in criminal cases that the case be proved beyond reasonable doubt. Often in practice, however, the requirement has been made unrealistically stringent. Although the burden of proof is rightly placed on the prosecution, once a prima-facie case has been established, the dialectical nature of argument throws the burden on the other side, to show how the prima-facie case may be rebutted. The Anglo-American right to silence arose originally as a protection for those of scrupulous conscience who might otherwise be put on oath and asked whether they had committed the crime. That is a proper protection. But once it has been established that there is a case to answer, a refusal to answer it strongly implies that there is no answer. Our present rules are needlessly restrictive, and counter-productively so: it is because of artificial barriers to proving guilt that strict liability laws have been enacted, and often juries assume that the police must have evidence of guilt they are not allowed to produce in court, and convict people on the grounds of their having been charged.

The elaboration of procedures leads to unconscionable delays. Justice delayed is justice denied. In England a criminal case is often not heard until more than a year after the alleged crime. Memories fade. The accused, who is in some cases innocent, has been all that time living with the charge hanging over him. And for the guilty the intended connexion between crime and punishment is attenuated by the elapse of time. If society wishes to contradict the wrongdoer's violation of its values, it should do so promptly, or its ministrations will be misinterpreted as gratuitous malevolence.

In minor matters elaborate procedures, with personal attendance and cross-examination of witnesses under oath, are in any case out of place. A more informal mode of adjudication, by letter or telephone, would be appropriate, with appeal to the ordinary courts only in cases of great dispute. The present system not only clogs the courts, but actually results in injustice, since many of those wrongly accused reckon it cheaper to pay the fine than fight the case.

Two other principles, forbidding double jeopardy and double punishment, are often cited. We do not put people on trial for the same offence again and again because we need legal decisions to have an assured stability which would be lost if a question could be reopened after it had been settled. Also, in the case of criminal charges, it would expose a man to being perpetually hassled by the authorities if he could be repeatedly charged with the same offence. These are sound practical reasons for laying down that once a man has been acquitted, he cannot be charged again, but they are not conceptual requirements, and indeed are not, in practice, always just. If at one stage a man has denied an accusation, and we have not been sure enough of our ground to overrule his denial, and later evidence emerges which shows he was lying, it would be perfectly intelligible and on occasion quite reasonable, in the absence of a legal provision to the contrary, to proceed to punish him.

Double punishment is different. It does not make sense for a society to punish a man twice for the same offence, because the punishment, being a compulsory penance, constitutes also a forcible atonement, whereby the wrongdoer is purged of his wrongdoing, rehabilitated, and restored to full membership of the community. Once done, there is no room for it to be done again. But there are qualifications. The same bit of bodily behaviour can constitute a breach of more than one injunction: my passage down the road may constitute exceeding the speed limit, dangerous driving, drunken driving, and driving while uninsured, and I may be punished for each of these misdeeds. Also, and more importantly, the same action may contravene the rules of more than one society, and the fact that I have been punished by one is no bar to my being also punished by another. If I deal in dangerous drugs, and am sentenced by the courts as a pusher, I am not thereby protected from being disciplined as a doctor and struck off the register. It is very common, and entirely right, that professional bodies should have higher standards than the criminal law, and often charges that cannot be proved in court are none the less shown convincingly to be true. In such cases the complaint of double jeopardy or double punishment is out of place, and it is reasonable for the other jurisdiction to take cognizance of the violation of its values and to signal its emphatic dissociation appropriately.

6.13. *NULLA POENA SINE LEGE?*

A person may only be punished for a wrong he is taken to have done: but how was he to know that it was wrong? In families and other close-knit societies, where the values are very fully shared, each member can be expected to know what is right and wrong, and the same holds good for many primitive legal systems. The judge judges on the basis of shared values, and has no compunction in punishing the wrongdoer. To the plea "I did not know it was wrong" he retorts, "Well, you do now". In more developed legal systems, however, we hesitate to be so brusque, and articulate a legal code of what may and may not be done, and tend to confine punishment to transgressions of that code, and to lay down *Nulla poena sine lege* as a ground rule.

Four different lines of argument support our adopting that principle: the fear of judicial tyranny, the need to give the citizen breathing space in which to make his own decisions, the difficulty of drawing precise lines, and the opaqueness of some regulations. In the first place we are wary of judges. They are not to be trusted with unfettered discretion. Under the cover of public morality, they may feather their own nests; or, more insidiously, they may propagate some idiosyncratic ideal they have and father it on the shared values of our society contrary to our convictions. We garb Leviathan with legality not only to legitimise his powers, but to restrain them, and to protect each of us at our most vulnerable, when we stand before the judgement seat awaiting sentence, to ensure that sanctions shall be exercised against us only for misdeeds publicly specified as such.

The argument from fear, though all too justified in this century, is often muddled with another, more benign, consideration. We need to distance the state from the individual, in order to leave him room to be himself. Small cohesive societies, though highly supportive, can be suffocating. I cannot take over all of society's values wholesale without examining them for myself, or I cease to be an autonomous rational agent, and begin to suffer from *mauvaise foi*. However much I am identified with my own *polis*, I am not purely and simply a member of it, and may come to espouse values different from those it maintains. There is always some possibility of disagreement. And this possibility not only exists, but is recognised and legitimised by civil society. Civil society values its citizens, and sees them not simply as members of itself, as ants are of their ant hill, but as independent agents with minds of their own, minds which could be made up differently without thereby being guilty of some sort of treachery. It is not that every sort of disagreement about values can be accommodated, but only that complete agreement is not insisted on. Individuals, therefore, are not expected to internalise completely the knowledge of right and wrong, and have the right, at least in some cases, to be told where they stand. The principle is not so much *Nulla poena sine lege* as *Nulla crimen sine lege*. The code may be Draconian, but it gives guidance about what will not be tolerated without expecting the citizen to agree wholeheartedly with all its provisions. It allows some liberty of thought, if not much liberty of action.

It is often thought that a legal system needs to be fully articulated as a code, and that nothing can be said to be legally wrong unless it is specifically forbidden by some explicit law. Hart criticizes Lord Simonds for developing the common law to brand offences against public morality as criminal.[23] But that presupposes a wrong view of the nature of law. Law is not just the positive enactment of an effective enforcing power, but the common property of rulers and ruled alike, which enshrines some shared values they generally hold dear. Although citizens are not required to identify completely with them, they are, and must be, if law is not to rest on force alone, expected to identify with them by and large. The law against murder does not create the legal wrong of murder, but only defines its boundaries. Although the citizen should not be expected to know of himself all the law's requirements, he may be expected to have a fairly clear idea in many cases, and to know many things to be wrong without recourse to the law books. No code covers all eventualities, and judges in practice have to interpolate and extrapolate to bring new cases under existing legislation. Whether the judges stretch the meaning of some law already laid down, or appeal directly to some values underlying the whole legal system, makes little difference in practice. Judicial interpretation merges into judicial innovation. Rather than insist on *Nulla poena sine lege* as an absolute requirement of a developed legal system, and then

[23] H. L. A. Hart, *Law, Liberty and Morality*, Oxford, 1963, pp. 8–10.

stretching the available *lex* to cover new cases, it is clearer and better to see it as a general desideratum, encouraging the law generally to move towards greater explicitness rather than relying on citizens' internalising all its values.

In those legal systems in which the law is fairly fully articulated, it is sometimes thought of as the minimum morality which society expects all its members to observe and which it will enforce by coercive sanctions if need be. But actually it is a sub-minimal morality.[24] Society would soon break down if its members observed only the requirements laid down by law. Before making some rule of behaviour a legal requirement, we have to consider not only whether we want all members of society to abide by it, but also the costs of enforcement, and whether it is really necessary to enforce it. Often, we reckon, the costs are great, and social pressure alone will suffice to ensure its general observance. We are reluctant to bring to bear the cumbersome machinery of legal enactment, unless the consequences of a single breach would be disastrous for someone—we do not rely on social opprobrium alone to dissuade murderers from making a habit of killing people—or there is some Prisoners' Dilemma so that if defaulters could get away scot-free, others would be tempted to follow suit. Commercial life depends on a much higher standard of honesty than that required by law; similarly professional codes of behaviour are much more stringent than the legal minimum imposed on everyone. What the law does is to put up No Through Road signs, so that those tempted to cheat know that though they may get away with it on some occasions, they cannot consistently, and that sooner or later they will be found out and brought to book.

Two other considerations lead us towards making laws explicit. Though the fundamental principles are based on values we share, the exact line between cases falling under one—the right of privacy in one's own home—and those falling under another—the duty not to disturb or annoy one's neighbours—is not universally obvious. Specific knowledge of precedent and case law is called for, and that knowledge is necessarily more external than an understanding of values. More important is the fact that many legal provisions are not articulations of some underlying values,

---

[24] See §8.14, pp. 172–3.

but practical measures designed to secure some practical ends by uniform means we could not work out for ourselves without being told. It is quite reasonable to have parking restrictions, speed limits, safety regulations, and to enjoin everyone to obey them. But I cannot know what is required of me except by being told, and the obligation to obey arises solely from the ordinance of the legal authority, and not from the inherent rightness of regulation. If the Queen-in-Parliament tells me that I must wear a seat-belt when driving, then I ought to do so, but only because she has told me, not because it is inherently right. It is a *jus quia jussum* rather than a *jus quia justum*. Many laws are of this type, particularly those intended to overcome some Prisoners' Dilemma. I cannot be expected to conclude that I ought not to park here on the grounds that if everyone did the road would be blocked:[25] but if in order to secure free access there is a rule that nobody may park, then in the light of that rule it would be wrong for me to park, and if I do I may be held to have done wrong.

Some thinkers draw a distinction between crimes, in which a serious wrong has been committed, and violations of regulations, which justify the imposition of some penalty, but carry little moral stigma. It is a useful distinction. In the latter case the penalties are simply retrospectively deterrent, enough to make it generally a bad policy to violate the regulations, but not denouncing it with any great fervour. It may be inconsiderate, but it is not very reprehensible, to park on double yellow lines. It needs to be effectively discouraged, or motorists in a hurry will ignore the prohibition implicit in the yellow lines altogether. We need penalties as deterrents, not punishments as denunciatory disavowals, and then, since the persistent parker is not going to be branded as a criminal, we do not need to protect him from being unfairly saddled with the charge in the way we do where serious crimes are alleged, and can adopt the less cumbersome procedures outlined in the previous section.

[25] In such cases also the principle that ignorance of the law is no excuse is clearly inapplicable. See further Glanville Williams, *Criminal Law: The General Part*, 2nd edn., London, 1961, §102, pp. 201–2.

6.14. VICTIMLESS CRIMES

It is a common view that there cannot be a crime unless there is a victim, and that the only reason why force should be exercised against a man is the prevention of harm to someone else. It is certainly not a general truth. Wrongdoing is possible without there being anyone who is wronged. The child who will not say 'Hullo' to a visitor, the schoolboy who talks in the dormitory after lights out, the scientist who fakes experimental evidence, are not harming anyone, but they are doing wrong, and may be punished, and have sanctions imposed on them, sanctions that ultimately depend on force. If I am expelled from a learned society for dishonesty, it is in the end the policeman and the bailiff enforcing the orders of the courts that will prevent my frequenting the society's premises as I had done previously. So, too, more obviously for the schoolboy made to write out a hundred times 'I must not talk after lights out', or the child not given a chocolate biscuit at tea. All sanctions, whether those of the civil authority or those of other bodies or voluntary associations, depend ultimately on the enforcement of the law, by physical coercion if need be.

The criminal law, likewise, punishes wrongdoing even when there is nobody harmed. In the United States people have been punished for disrespect to the Stars and Stripes, in Britain for blasphemy, and in almost every country there are laws protecting the sacred symbols of their culture and national identity. In modern times, however, some influential thinkers have maintained that a state ought not to legislate morality, and ought not to make any action criminal unless it causes harm to others.[26] The argument is based on a certain view of the state, which is seen as a minimal association for the maintenance of peace and order, rather than a natural community founded on values held in common. Historically there has been good reason to be wary of the pretensions of the state, and to seek principles which cut it down to size, but the minimalist view of the state is untrue to the facts as they are, and is impracticable anyhow. States do enshrine shared values, and unless they could inspire loyalty and devotion

[26] See J. S. Mill, *On Liberty*, 1859, ch.1; Everyman edn. pp. 72–3; and H. L. A. Hart, *Law, Liberty and Morality*, Oxford, 1963. For criticism, see B. G. Mitchell, *Law, Religion and Morality*, Oxford, 1967.

so that men were prepared to die for them, they would not survive long.[27]

If the minimalist doctrine of the state is rejected, it will not follow from the nature of the state that we should not brand any action as criminal unless it causes harm to someone. Even in the absence of a victim, we may want to dissociate ourselves from something done by a compatriot. We do not think that God is harmed by a blasphemous celebration of the black mass, but we want to dissociate ourselves from it. More recently the feminists have quite rightly protested at obscene publications and advertisements, which degrade women. The actual damage to women —or men, for that matter—is open to dispute, and pornographers regularly make out that their products exercise a cathartic effect on their consumers. What is indisputable is that if our society countenances women being publicly represented as mere titillating sex-objects, we are endorsing a message which we ought to dissociate ourselves from.

There are other arguments for not making actions criminal, unless we have to, arguments of practicality, of respect for individuals' autonomy, of the need to encourage authenticity and free debate.[28] These often carry the day. But the argument that if something is wrong there ought to be a law against it is not broken-backed, even though not conclusive. So far as the concept of the state is concerned, there is no reason why a nation should not have laws requiring citizens to abide by certain standards; and if those standards are flouted, punishment is their appropriate vindication.

[27] See §6.13, p. 119 above, or, more fully, J. R. Lucas, *The Principles of Politics*, Oxford, 1966 and 1985, §67.
[28] See §6.13, pp. 118-9 above.

Chapter 7
Doing and Deserving

7.1. DOING WELL

I am responsible for what I do. If it is bad, I am blamed, reprimanded, and sometimes punished: if it is good, I am praised, honoured, and sometimes rewarded. Intuitively we regard good deeds as appropriate grounds for reward, and in the case of co-operative enterprises as the—though not the only—just basis for distributing the fruits of co-operation. But the arguments are complex, and we need to draw finer distinctions than are enshrined in the ordinary use of ordinary language.

7.2. DESERT AND MERIT

Desert needs to be distinguished from merit. It is a difficult distinction to make, because they often overlap, and the words are often used interchangeably—the Latin word *mereor* from which 'merit' is derived is standardly translated by 'deserve'. Nevertheless, there is a distinction. Merits are features of any appropriate kind which constitute grounds for a rational decision. The merits of the case are the facts of the case, undistorted by any extraneous considerations or imposed rules of relevance (for example, some rule of interpretation imposed by statute). My merits are facts about me which make me worthy of selection: height, if we want a look-out; weight, if we want an anchorman in a tug-o'-war; knowledge of Greek for a Hellenic cruise. Merit corresponds to the Greek ἀξία (*axia*). If the decision is one that ought to be guided by merit and merit alone, it is unfair if I am passed over because my merits have not been taken into account, or because extraneous factors have been taken into account. These merits may, but do not have to be, the results of my own decisions. My knowing Greek is the result of having given thought to it, but not my stature. If you are born with a

beautiful face you may win the Miss World contest, and it would
be unfair if you were passed over for a less comely lass, but it
would be straining language to say that you deserved to win,
because you have not *done* anything: your beautiful face is a
God-given gift, not anything you have worked for or earned.

Deserving is tied to doing. 'What have I done to deserve this?'
we exclaim after some stroke of good, or ill, fortune. We can
then be told that it was merely fortune, and that there is nothing
we have done to deserve it; but we cannot be told that we
deserve it on account of something that Peter did, nor even on
account of something we did, unless what we did can be represented as something that it was good, or bad, to do. In this
desert has the same logic as punishment, except that we can
deserve to be well done by for what we have done well, as well as
to be ill done by for what we have done ill. That desert is tied to
doing can be seen if we consider cases where there is no question
of our allocating any good things to those who have deserved
well, since the good outcome was entirely their own doing. When
we say of someone that he deserved his success, we are saying
that it was not due to luck or favour that things turned out well
for him, but that it was the result of his own efforts. Often, but
not always, there is some suggestion of its having been hard to
achieve.[1] Certainly where someone had to work hard, or take
risks, or forgo other pleasures or activities to achieve something
good, we say that he deserved his success; but if there were a vir-
tuous undergraduate, who liked reading the books his tutor set
him, and much preferred reading Ovid's *Ars Amoris* to going out
with girls, and von Neumann and Morgenstern's *The Theory of
Games* to playing them, we should still say he deserved his First,
even though it had not been at all hard for him to do the things
needful for getting a First, and he had not had to overcome any
temptations in order to concentrate on his work.

Desert and merit evoke different responses. I admire you for
your merits, for what you are: I praise you for your deserts, for
what you have done. I admire you for your good looks, your
athletic prowess, your neat turn of phrase: I praise you for having got up early to go down the river, coped with a friend having

---

[1] James Griffin, *Well-Being*, Oxford, 1986, ch.XII, pp. 255–6, suggests that one
has to do better than par to deserve anything.

a nervous breakdown, kept yourself free from the permissive habits of your contemporaries. But, though different, they are easily confused because it is often through doing things that we acquire those desirable qualities of mind or character which are grounds for choosing us in preference to rival candidates for the good things that are going. Although my height and your pretty face are desirable features neither of us has done anything to bring about, and so cannot be said to deserve, my ability to do formal logic and your skill as a cox have been acquired by much practice, so that inasmuch as a decision in our favour is based on those features it is both based on merit and one we deserve. If we say "He merits careful consideration", we mean that he has the right qualities for the job, and may prove the best candidate; it is a statement in the present tense: if we say "He deserves to get the job", we mean that he has earned it by what he has done; it is a statement with implicit reference to the past. If the world were created five minutes ago, it would still make sense to use the former locution, but not the latter. Nothing having been done, nothing can be deserved. We talk of the deserving poor: they are not the same as the needy poor. There are many people who need our help: drug addicts, criminals, the feckless and inadequate. Their circumstances are such as to merit our pity and our help. The deserving poor are different, in that they have become poor through no fault of their own, indeed in spite of their efforts to make ends meet and to make proper provision for the future. In view of what they have done, they deserve not to be poor, and have a quite different claim on us, as against the needy, who may, for all that has been said about them, be the authors of their own misfortunes.

7.3. DESERT AND RESPONSIBILITY

Since desert is connected with doing, it is connected with responsibility. If someone is responsible for what he did, then we assess his desert in line with our assessment of his deed: if what he did was good, he deserves well, if bad, then he deserves ill. There is a corresponding link between desert and praise and blame. If I reckon that you have deserved well, then if you had sought my advice before you did the deed, I should have counselled in favour of doing it, and if it had been for me to decide whether or not to do it, I should have decided to do it. Similarly, if I reckon that you have deserved ill, then if you had sought my advice before you did the deed, I should have counselled against doing it, and if it had been for me to decide whether or not to do it, I should have decided not to do it. There would be an inconsistency if I now did not come down in favour of your having done then what I would have done if I were you, and correspondingly against what I should have counselled against and decided against if my advice had been sought or the decision vested in me. To say that you have deserved well is to praise you, and to blame you is to that extent to say that you have done badly and on that score deserve ill.

We can now see more clearly the way merit and desert stand with respect to each other. Your merits constitute grounds for a favourable *choice* on my part: your deserts constitute grounds for a favourable *attitude* on my part. What count as your merits depend on the choice I am making and the purpose for which it is made. If I am casting for amateur theatricals, I should regard as merits features that would be quite irrelevant if I were conducting an academic examination, or electing a Member of Parliament. But though the criteria of relevance vary from case to case, and though there may be good reasons for considering further, and even extraneous, factors,[2] there is a close conceptual link between merit and choice: it would be prima-facie irrational not to base choice on merit. With desert the link is less immediate. Although there are very strong feelings that desert ought to be rewarded, it is not inconsistent to deny it, and to maintain that virtue is its own reward, and that there is something demeaning in annexing adventitious advantages to having done well. The corresponding irrationality in the case of desert is to think that someone has done well and not to think well of him. It may be that to think well of him implies, at least sometimes, on suitable occasions, and in the absence of countervailing factors, deciding in his favour, but it is not self-evident that it must. Some leading thinkers of our own time have denied it, without lapsing into incoherence.

---

[2] See §9.5, pp. 191–2, and §9.8, pp. 197–8.

7.4. RAWLS AND RANDOMNESS

Professor John Rawls argues that desert is not an appropriate basis for the just allocation of benefits.[3] He asserts that such a principle would not be chosen in the original position. It is not clear why not. He admits that there is a tendency for common sense to suppose that the good things of life should be distributed according to desert; and if the original position is one in which people are not guided by common sense, it becomes one we may be loath to occupy even hypothetically in our speculations. Rawls points out that the criteria of deservingness do not admit of precise definition, and that there are other bases of distribution, such as entitlement and need. He also points out that in a market economy people are not in fact rewarded according to desert: other factors, such as demand for scarce skills, determine what a person actually receives. "The distributive shares that result do not correlate with moral worth, since the initial endowment of natural assets and the contingencies of their growth and nurture in early life are arbitrary from a moral point of view."[4] And finally he maintains that even conscientious effort is not a proper basis for a just distribution, since the effort a person is willing to make is influenced by his natural abilities and skills and the alternatives open to him. "The better endowed are more likely, other things being equal, to strive conscientiously, and there seems no way to discount for their greater good fortune."[5]

These arguments carry little weight. Since Plato we have known that moral concepts cannot be precisely defined in terms of non-moral ones, but that has not stopped us using them. Again, it is true that there are other bases of just distribution besides desert, but this shows only that desert is not the only basis, not that it is not one at all. The fact that the market economy does not reward people according to desert is beside the point: critics of the market economy will see it as another of its demerits, and those who defend it, urge other considerations in its favour to outweigh what is generally seen as a defect. And the market is not everything. If I were economic man I might have

---

[3] John Rawls, *A Theory of Justice*, Oxford, 1972, §48, "Legitimate Expectations and Moral Desert", pp. 310–15.
[4] Ibid. pp. 311–12.   [5] Ibid. p. 312.

to buy in the cheapest and sell in the dearest market, but I am not economic man, and in allocating the good things that are in my gift, I may well wonder whether desert should be a ground of distribution, alongside status, merit, need, and entitlement.

Rawls' final criticism of desert is that men's initial endowments are arbitrary from a moral point of view. It is not at all clear what the moral point of view is, nor why from this point of view men's endowments should be arbitrary. We seem to be invited to take some ultimate metaphysical stance, and then draw great conclusions from what cannot from that stance be justified. But in the ordinary course of life we do not judge everything from that point of view alone: the initial circumstances and consequent needs of men are also arbitrary from the moral point of view, but we do not deny the relevance of need to our decision-making on that account; we do not ask how it is that people came to be ill, and argue that unless we can give some moral reason why they ought to be ill, we ought not to give them medical care. Equally with desert, we need look no further than what people have actually done in deciding how they should be rewarded, without enquiring how they came to make the contribution they did. Only if they become Pharisaically self-righteous, and maintain that as they deserve well on this occasion, so they are overall deserving, should we take some loftier standpoint, and remind them that they were indeed fortunate in their natural endowments and early nurture, and have much to be thankful for rather than to be pleased about. Even from a high theological standpoint, we need to be careful. Rawls' final argument teeters perilously on the brink of determinism and a complete denial of human responsibility altogether. It is right to remind those fortunate in nature and nurture that they have much to be grateful for, wrong to insinuate that they had no choice in how they used their talents. The better endowed may find it easier to strive conscientiously, but they do not find it that easy, and many people fail, it seems, to make good use of their natural talents. In the end there are only two possibilities: either a man's decision to strive conscientiously is completely determined by his heredity and environment, and it is not in the least up to him whether he tries or does not try; or it is partly up to him, and depends on his choice whether he tries or does not try. If the former, then, indeed, desert is not a basis for distribution, but since the distributive decisions we take are determined by factors ultimately outside our control, no argument about which bases are relevant are in point: if the latter, the argument is, indeed, well worth carrying on, but desert cannot be discounted altogether on the score of people not being in any way the masters of their own fate. Desert follows on responsibility, and Rawls' discountenancing of desert subverts responsibility too. I all too easily excuse my failings with a general disclaimer of responsibility:

It is not my fault that I was born lazy, I say. The fact that I don't like work is neither here nor there: it does not mean that I do not like other things, like food and drink and theatre tickets. In fact I need them more, since I do not get a kick out of work. It is quite wrong that the game should be played according to the rules of self-righteous meritocrats, who award themselves extra brownie points for doing what they like doing anyway. Some people are made that way; they have their reward: others are not, and should not be penalised for being the way they are.

Rawls' attack on desert fails. But that does not mean that desert is completely vindicated as a basis for distributing good things in the way that merit is. Desert is not to be dismissed as irrelevant, at least not on the grounds that Rawls gives. But the conceptually appropriate response to desert is praise, and what we have to confer is honour, not any more tangible goods. It may be that the conferring of honour ought to carry with it, on appropriate occasions, the grant of money, but it is not obvious that it should; and indeed in many cases it would be inappropriate, as reducing to a pecuniary level what is essentially non-pecuniary.

7.5. THE TWO SCIENTISTS

We can sense what is wrong with Rawls' approach, and the conditions under which pecuniary rewards are appropriate, if we consider two cases of two scientists.

The first case is that of two medical scientists who research into life-saving drugs. One is dedicated to the relief of human suffering, and works long hours for low pay, and finally produces an anti-viral equivalent of penicillin, which he does not patent, but makes available for all mankind: the other insists on having all the extra money available, often threatening to abandon his research and take a job with an arms manufacturer, and when he finally achieves his breakthrough, rushes out to obtain effective patents, so that he can exact a full royalty on every batch produced. Our normal moral intuition is that the former is more deserving: while the latter has behaved entirely within his rights, the former has shown great public spirit, and is eminently worthy to be rewarded with some *ex post hoc* grant of public money. Not so, says Rawls: desert is not a basis for a just allocation of money, though incentive payments are. If the first scientist had behaved like the second, then it would have been right to pay him, but since he made it clear that this was not a necessary condition of obtaining his services, it would be wrong to give him money that could be given to more pressing purposes.

Such reasoning repels us. We believe that we should take into account, when we are deciding how good things are to be allocated, not only forward-looking considerations about which rules will conduce most to our future advantage, but past actions and the attitudes of people too. A just decision looks at the case from all points of view, both temporal and personal. It seems quite wrong to exclude an action from consideration merely because it is past, and can no longer be undone. If an incentive payment would have been reasonable before the moment of decision, then it is reasonable also to make an equivalent payment in respect of an action after the moment of decision too. It is wrong also to trade on people's good nature. We need to consider not only the actions people actually did, and the bargains they actually struck, but the actions they might have done and the bargains they could have struck, had they been so inclined. If we take an omni-temporal point of view, we are no longer required to discount past actions merely because they are past, as we are if we take the more limited view of corporate self-interest. And if we take seriously the fact that people are free agents, we see each actual action not as our sole datum, but set in the context of the choices open to the agent at that time, and thus not solely as the cause of subsequent events but also as the manifestation of his mind. The one scientist manifested altruistic devotion to our well-being and it is fitting that we should respond to his benevolence: the other manifested a great concern for the well-being of number one, and, having done well by number one, has had his reward, and there is no call on us to go beyond the terms of the bargain he drove with us.

The case is altered if the scientists' labours did not materially benefit us. If they were cosmologists, extending our understanding of the Big Bang, or pure mathematicians, whose researches could not conceivably have any practical application, we should think them worthy of honour, but not feel so insistently the need to reward the one who had disinterestedly laboured to our advantage. Suppose there were two brilliant mathematicians, the one content with the moderate stipend his university paid him, the other making sure that his mathematical talents received their full market return. Both were mega-stars, one having proved Fermat's Last Theorem and the other Goldbach's Conjecture. We should praise them both for their contributions to mathematics, but might well think more highly of the one who was loyal to his university, and did not regularly visit his Dean with an offer from another university in his pocket, to make sure the President and Trustees realised that they could count on his staying with them only so long as they matched the best offer their rivals could make. It might be appropriate to arrange things so that any available funds came to the one rather than going to the other, who anyhow soaked up money like a sponge. But it would not seem wrong if we merely honoured him, without annexing any monetary reward. The reason is that we had not been benefiting in a financial, or any other material, way as a result of his efforts, and were not in any sense trading on his ungraspingness. The medical scientist had done good to us in a fairly tangible way: the mathematician had done well, but had not done well particularly by us, and there was therefore no call upon us to express our appreciation in a particularly tangible way.

The issues are complex. On the one hand there is a distinction between the case where the person has done well by me, or us, personally, and the case where he has done well in some general and impersonal way, which seems to be the mirror image of the distinction between revenge and punishment; on the other there seems to be a range of considerations affecting the appropriateness of expressing our appreciation of the well-doing in some particular, possibly monetary, form. The underlying thought is that reward is a negative punishment, a tangible token of esteem; it is praise that says it with flowers. But the details need considerable further elucidation; and in the first place we need to compare and contrast it with gratitude.

7.6. GRATITUDE

If someone has done me good, I should feel grateful. Gratitude differs from praise in much the same way as resentment from blame, and correspondingly vengeance from punishment. I cannot feel impersonally grateful, whereas to praise someone and to recognise his desert is to claim an omni-personal appreciation of the deeds done. In expressing gratitude I identify myself as, or with, the recipient of the good rendered: my son, my family, my college, my country, or even, grandiloquently, the whole of humanity. I may be speaking on behalf of them, or, if they have already spoken, I may be just associating myself with the sentiments already expressed. But always, if I am saying thank you, I am saying it, if not for, then with, those to whom the benefit was rendered.

Gratitude is primarily a feeling, an attitude, a state of mind, an awareness of a good done to oneself or one's own, construing it as a manifestation of good will, and being well disposed in return. Although in itself only a state of mind, it is one that calls to be expressed; and then I may be moved to express it in deeds as well as words. Words are cheap, and it costs nothing to be polite, so that nice things trip easily off our tongues, and for that reason often seem to mean little: if I say 'a thousand thanks' when someone opens the door for me, how can I express real gratitude? Clearly I could not disburse a thousand pounds with equal abandon, so that in putting on a money tag I am at least stopping the coinage of gratitude being inflated to vacuity. Furthermore, I have to consider not just what I mean, but what others may think is meant. Since words are often insincere, they may seem so even when they are not, and even when not actually seeming so, I may fear that they are. Deeds speak not necessarily louder, but more convincingly, and are more incontrovertibly meant. So I want to do something, something good, something good in return for the good that has been done me. But then there is a danger of gratitude descending into a mere *quid pro quo*. Griffin sensitively explores the difference.[6] In the latter case,

---

[6] James Griffin, *Well-Being*, Oxford, 1986, ch. XII, p. 260: "Certainly, if you, as depressingly many people do, turn the help I give you into a debt which I can collect, then you destroy gratitude. You transform it into an exchange. You destroy my act as a favour, and you destroy your response as thanks. Repayment

once I have made an adequate return, we are quits. Once I have paid the butcher's bill, I do not need to go on being grateful for life. But gratitude cannot be discharged. It may be forgotten—too often indeed it is; it may be overlaid by subsequent disfavours, so that where once I was grateful to someone, now I remember only the wrongs I later received at his hands; but it cannot be discharged, as a debt can be, and any attempt to discharge it spoils it. It is the attitude of mind, not the actual action, that is important. The attitude is often most naturally and fittingly expressed in action, but is not constituted by it. The action when done is done, but the attitude has no natural term. I remember for good those who have done good to me, and though in the course of time I may forget, I do not ever deliberately put them out of mind. For this reason a continuing, though less costly, response is often more expressive than an immediate one. A costly gift in return immediately makes the original gesture to have proved a good move in terms of narrow self-interest, and so calls into question its status as a disinterested expression of good will; but after the lapse of years, it could no longer be thought to have entered into any prudential reckoning, and is simply and solely evidence of a continuing sense of gratitude. It need not have any monetary value: it is a personal communication, not a commercial transaction. Sometimes a willingness to put oneself out is an indication of how much one appreciates the benefit received; sometimes a careful consideration of the needs and wants of the benefactor, so as to give him some service or object he particularly likes. But always there is a sense that the feeling of gratitude should be something that persists: we remember for good those who have done good to us, long after we have said thank you, and shown by any appropriate means that we mean it.

Sometimes, in fact, it is best simply to say thank you, and to go on meaning it, undemonstratively and unembarrassingly. There are many good turns for which no return can be made: if you save my life, it is unlikely that I shall ever be in a position to

is certainly not gratitude. And duty does not look much like it either." Griffin quotes J. Gross (ed.), *The Oxford Book of Aphorisms*, Oxford, 1983, quoting Anon, *Characters and Observations*: "Gratitude is a debt, 'tis true, but it differs from all other debts, for though it is always to be paid, yet it is never to be demanded."

save yours, or render any commensurate return, and you might be embarrassed if I wrote a letter of gratitude every week. Also we may have a sense of not presuming to press our tokens of esteem on another's attention: as the Book of Common Prayer puts it: "Although we be unworthy . . . to offer unto thee any sacrifice . . ." Sometimes no return can be adequately made for a benefit received, and then any attempt to make a return mars the relationship. All we can do is to say thank you on occasion, and continue to keep in mind the good we have received at another's hands.

7.7. PRAISE AND HONOURS

If a man has done well, I think well of him. I may praise him to his face, or I may speak well of him behind his back. And as on occasion we need to express our reprimands in some more tangible way than mere words, so we may want to express our approbation in the form of public honour or monetary reward. We can set up a general schema of responses to well- and ill-doing: if a man has done well by me, then the appropriate response is gratitude, if ill, resentment, which may be expressed in deeds of revenge; if a man has done well, though not particularly by me, then the appropriate response on my part is approbation and praise rather than gratitude, and if ill, disapprobation and blame, leading sometimes in the one case to honour and reward, and in the other to reprimand and punishment.

If I think well of what someone has done, it is natural to communicate this thought to others, and sing his praises, perhaps even to his face. I recognise his contribution to the course of events turning out well, and I see his good deed as a manifestation of his good will. The two are not quite the same. Some good deeds did not actually contribute to the course of events, though they might have done. The sentry who was vigilant when no enemy was in the locality did not actually ward off a surprise attack, though he might have done had circumstances been different; and the one who was vigilant at the crucial moment may have been motivated by some unworthy motive—he may have been looking out for a camp-follower he was hoping to consort with. But the doer and the deed are typically linked, and in praising one we are usually right to praise the other. We are endorsing them, associating ourselves with the values they exemplified, not taking responsibility or credit for them, but giving them the credit, because the values embodied in them are values we espouse.

As with gratitude, we often find it difficult to make words mean all we want them to mean. A simple 'Well done', like a simple 'Thank you', slips easily off the tongue, and may seem a mere conventional courtesy, not a sincerely serious sentiment. Some public ceremony—investiture with a medal, conferment of a title, grant of honorary citizenship—may widen the circle of the endorser and make it more evidently meant. Honours are formal and public expressions of the esteem in which we hold someone on account of the good he has done.

7.8. REWARDS

As with gratitude, a good opinion naturally needs to find expression, and often words and even ceremonies seem inadequate, and something more tangible is called for. If we merely praise and honour those who do well, our words may seem empty. Even honours may suffer from inflation. But if we add to them tangible tokens of esteem, we make it indisputable by anyone that they are really meant. A reward makes an honour more evidently meant, and in many cases it means, not exactly more, but something none the less, to the recipient. For most of us money talks. It is a normal, though not universal, human condition to be short of money, so that for most people more money is something they could do with. A dinner out, a new suit, a holiday abroad, a fax machine, or a word-processor seldom come amiss, so that if we annex a pecuniary reward to an expression of regard, we ensure that the whole transaction comes across as something good. Rewards as tangible tokens of esteem make perfectly good sense, on occasion, as a means of communicating to the recipient, in a way which he, and everyone, can understand, how much we endorse the decisions he made and appreciate the actions that flowed from them.

Here the view of rewards as negative punishments is illuminating. Just as punishment is an emphatic dissociation from doing something bad, so reward is an emphatic association with doing something good. It is a form of retrospective endorsement. We were not, as a matter of fact, in on the decision to do the good deed, but if we had been, we should have voted in favour. What we can do, retrospectively, is to merge the individual's good decision in a corporate one, making it part of a set of decisions whose joint outcome is both the good deed and the good assigned to the individual. Since the good assigned to the individual *is* a good, it is one that can be ascribed to him without a positive choice on his part: we can take it that he may be reasonably deemed to accept it. The joint outcome, therefore, is one that he can be deemed to have wanted, and is made possible not only, though chiefly, by his unaided action, but also by ours. So we become, late in time, participators in a good enterprise.

We can reach a similar conclusion if we project ourselves into the position of the agent at the time he decided to do the good deed, and seek to ensure that it was wise from his point of view, even if he had not been swayed by moral or altruistic considerations. Just as we want to see to it that crime does not pay, so we are inclined to make it the case that virtue does. Although we feel in part that virtue should be its own reward, we also want it to be the case that if a man were to assess the costs and benefits of virtue in purely prudential terms, it would turn out to have been a good policy even from that limited point of view. The good man who does good things may seem a mug to the wise according to the wisdom of this world, but turns out to be wiser than the worldly wise, and to have done better than them even according to their standards of judgement; they had the first sneer, but he has the last smile.

These arguments have weight, and often justify our adopting desert as a ground for the allocation of good things. Often, but not always. Though money may emphasize, it may also distort, the meaning of what we say: in the first place it invites comparisons where none are needed and any are invidious. My reward of £1,000 is either more than, or less than, or the same as, yours, and altogether rules out the possibility of our both being appreciated incommensurably more than others. It is like the Order of Lenin (Fourth Class) which makes me wonder how I failed to make it to the Third Class. The logic of the nicely calculated more and less destroys the open and wholehearted endorsement that praise suggests.

Again, though money is, by and large, nice to have, it is not all that nice. The dedicated scientist might be embarrassed by being given the many millions which would represent the cash equivalent of the good he had conferred on mankind. It would depend on his circumstances. If he had been living in penury, honours which did nothing to relieve his need would seem insincere, but if he already had enough, it might seem almost insulting to give him money which he had not deigned to acquire. Although it is quite proper for us to want to see to it that he shall not suffer through his high-mindedness, we owe it to him to respect his decision about what is really important in life, and not to imply that he would have chosen to make money out of his discoveries if only he had been financially competent. A man may be a willing mug, knowing that he is being made use of, and accepting the readiness of others to trade on his good nature, as part of his calling in life. But then he does not have to accept the reward. Rewards, unlike punishments, can be declined. More naturally he might accept the money and pass it on to charity, so that although it is not a self-interested good, it is still disposed in accordance with his wishes, and thus helps him to further his own ideals.

Again, a man may be proud. He may resent our muscling in on his good deed, and trying to associate ourselves with it. To accept a reward is to accept a certain non-individuality, that his own values are shared by other people, and that they would like to associate themselves with his own good deed. He may say "It was all my own work", and insist on leaving it at that. Or he may be modest, and reckon that too much is being made of what was only, after all, his bounden duty. Or he may be shy. These and other considerations constitute good reasons for not insisting that desert be the main ground for allocating goods, but not for denying that it should be a prima-facie one. There are occasions where the mere mention of money would spoil the honour being conferred, and contexts where, as with gratitude, it is in fact inappropriate. But for the most part rewards are a natural way of associating ourselves with good deeds, as punishments are a way of dissociating ourselves from bad ones.

7.9. THE FRUITS OF CO-OPERATION

Thus far we have distinguished two sorts of good deed: where the good is done to me or mine by some other benevolent being; and where the good is a general good, done disinterestedly by an independent agent. But many good deeds are in neither case. They are done in the course of a co-operative undertaking, in which someone who is one of us contributes to our overall success. In that case the good was done neither out of pure benevolence nor disinterestedly, but in pursuit of some corporate interest, in which both he and we share. Often the corporate interest is in the promotion of some non-material good, and the appropriate recognition of individual contributions is non-material too. If I was the man of the match, taking seven wickets and scoring half a century, I may be given a clap, or even carried shoulder-high from the pitch, but not a cheque for £24.45. But where the fruits of co-operation are financial, or can be measured, more or less, in monetary terms, then questions of distributive justice arise, and they should, in the absence of other considerations, be shared in accordance with the contributions made. We judge what each person did in accordance with the values of the joint undertaking. Just as each individual acting on his own deserves to reap the rewards of the actions he undertook with the intention of bringing about those consequences, so each is naturally entitled to the fruits of collective action, and if they are fruits which need to be distributed, then the contribution each has made is relevant to the share that is assigned to him. Indeed, in such cases the presumption is that desert ought to be *the* basis of apportionment. It would be conceptually incoherent in such cases to try and sever the link between doing and deserving: for we all have to decide what to do, and each decision-maker has to make up his own mind in the light of his values what course of action to undertake. His pay-off is for him the relevant criterion. It need not be a self-interested set of values, but it is *his*. To try to make him ignore his own scheme of values is to deny his status as an independent agent. He is no longer an individual, but a mere tool.

Justice requires that we address ourselves individually to each person concerned, and consider things from his point of view. We need, therefore, to consider his decision in the light of his values. If thanks to his co-operation we have done well by our standards, we need to make sure that he has done well by his. These do not have to be purely selfish ones: sometimes individuals identify themselves with some communal or impersonal good to a great extent, and are sufficiently rewarded by the progress of the cause or the prosperity of the community. But this should not be taken for granted. Where there are tangible proceeds of a joint enterprise, the presumption should be that he, too, would like a share, because most people, quite naturally and properly, have a concern for their own good. If someone waives all claims to a share of the proceeds, that is his business, and does him credit; but the offer should be made, because it recognises the individual's separate identity, and witnesses to the fact that he could have chosen otherwise, and not joined in the enterprise at all. We want to make it clear that his joining in was not to be taken for granted as though he had no independence of action at all, by making it be the case that it was, from his own self-interested point of view, had he been solely concerned with that, none the less a rational option.

There is thus a presumption that desert is the prime basis for the just distribution of the fruits of co-operative enterprises. The presumption may be defeated by some other antecedent agreement—the deserving party may have contracted to do his bit in return for a wage—or it may be defeated by reason of the nature of the enterprise—a voluntary society to help the needy—or it may simply be waived. But in the absence of some special condition it would be unfair not to recognise desert in distributing the fruits of a collective enterprise. For in that case what is being given is not just a token of esteem but a share of what his action helped to achieve.

Chapter 8
Money

It is good to have a vote. As we shall see in Chapter 10, it enhances the ego, encourages participation, and may make the government more responsive and responsible. But the trouble with having the vote is that other people have it too, and one is always in danger of being outvoted. Perhaps we should not mind too much—perhaps we ought to reflect more on the truism that if one is to be a member of society, one cannot expect always to get one's own way—but often such comfort seems slick, especially where what is at issue is some central concern of one's own life. Other people may think I ought to become a monk, or give my body for medical research, or donate my heart and kidneys to some more deserving fellow human being; but even if everybody else agrees that this is what I should do, I still think it is for me to decide, not them. Even if there is a public debate followed by a democratic vote, I still think that my opinion on the matter ought not to be overridden by the views of others, who may well have not given the question much thought and who are anyhow much less intimately concerned with the outcome. My view ought to count for much more than theirs; indeed, in most circumstances it ought not to be overridden by theirs, no matter how numerous they are. On some questions at least—those that most closely concern me—I ought to have not just a vote but a veto.

Clearly there are limits to the vetoes that may be conferred on every member of a society. A society which can decide to do only those things that are agreed to by all its members is likely to be extremely indecisive. In a world in which decisions often have to be made, we cannot confer on everyone an unlimited right to veto every sort of decision. If there are to be vetoes, they must be limited in scope. My veto must be confined to matters that concern me more than anyone else, or we all shall be in perpetual deadlock while I insist that you should wear a tie and you insist that you should not. But provided the scope of the veto is suitably restricted, it is feasible to give each of us a veto within wide limits over decisions about what he should do and what should be done to him.

We can go further, and confer on each person not only a negative veto but a general entitlement to take positive decisions about his own actions. Not only may I forbid others to dictate to me what I shall do, but I may decide for myself what I shall do and expect my decision to be respected and facilitated by society at large. Of course, there are limits: I do not have the right to move my fist to where your face is. Moreover, the exact delimitation of my rights may be a matter of dispute, because often my freedom of action may impinge on someone else's security of not having his affairs interfered with; nevertheless, within these limits I enjoy a very considerable liberty of action, not only with regard to the movement of my body, but over the use and disposition of some material objects and small areas of the earth's surface as well.

8.2. DECENTRALIZATION

If we confer on individuals not only some sort of veto but a limited right to take positive decisions which will be respected and upheld by society at large, we are adopting a decentralized system of decision-making. Because it is based on individual rights, it has an importantly different rationale from other decentralized systems. It recognises that we have different values. I may attach more importance to my liberty, my health, my prosperity, or my projects than you do, or than I do to your liberty, health, prosperity, or projects. The difference can be sharpened by a comparison with Rousseau. Rousseau held that each individual might have his own opinion about what ought to be done, and cast his vote accordingly, but on finding himself outvoted would conclude that he had been wrong, and that the true values were those endorsed by the General Will; a more robust voter might reckon that it was the majority that was wrong, though he ought to go along with their decision none the less. In either case the assump-

tion is of there being one system of values we are all trying to
discern, and of any disagreement being due to a failure on someone's part to apprehend the practical truth about what ought to
be done. In contrast to this, a system of rights allows for our
having different values—not totally different, but differing in
some systematic respects. It is because of this that we cannot be
happy with dissidents being simply outvoted, but want to give
them both some sort of veto and a positive entitlement to make
decisions in the light of their own values, and not just to have a
say in the articulation of ours.

No man is an island. Traditional rights theorists have assumed
that it is a feasible model of social life to assign to each individual a sphere within which he is king, with an absolute right to
decide everything within it just as he pleases. That view is pervasive and attractive, but fails on three counts. In the first place,
not every right is absolute. My decisions may be wrong, so
wrong that they ought not to be respected by others. In time past
parents were thought to have an absolute right over their children, and could sell them into slavery, as in some parts of the
world they still do. Even today feminists hold that mothers have
an absolute right to terminate the life of the foetuses they are
carrying, and many people, both in ancient Rome and in the
modern world, believe that everyone has the right to commit sui-
cide. Such views can be argued for, but they can also be argued
against. They are not necessary or incontrovertible truths. We
can believe in rights without holding that people are entitled to
do absolutely anything they like within their own particular
sphere.

The second difficulty is that people's spheres are not spherical.
They do not have any determinate shape, but interpenetrate one
another. My using my vacuum cleaner in my own house may
interfere with your television across the road. What I do in my
bed may land you with having to pay extra taxes for education
or social security in time to come. We may be able to reach a
view as to who should, and who should not, have a say in these
matters, but it is often a difficult and controversial question, not
something simple to be read off from the facts of the case without more ado.

Quite apart from the difficulty of delimiting such spheres of
sovereignty, there is, thirdly, the much deeper one that social life

involves interacting with others, and what any individual can do on his own is much less than what he is likely to want to do. Most of the things I want to do, I may do only with the consent of others, and they may withhold their consent. The choice is theirs, and they are entitled to make it according to their system of values, not mine. But, happily, often their values sufficiently coincide with mine for us to be able to concert our actions to our mutual benefit. Jack wants to dance with Jill, and Jill with Jack, so they dance together. Almost all our life is constituted of doing things with one another which we all find worthwhile. Although each is entitled to decide for himself according to a set of values that is not the same as everybody else's, it is not utterly different either, and in fact for most people is very largely the same.

8.3. FROM WHERE I SIT

The fact that each party to a business transaction is a separate decision-maker, making up his own mind for himself as he thinks best, has led many thinkers to suppose that they must be selfish, each seeking to maximise his own economic advantage. That is a mistake. We need to distinguish the two questions: Who makes the decisions? and How does he arrive at his decisions? The essential feature of economics, as opposed to politics, is that decision-making is decentralized. It does not follow that the decision-makers must be guided by self-interest. A mother buying Black-Forest gâteau, which she abominates, for her children, who relish it, is not being selfish; nor is a civil servant arguing the Treasury case against a pay rise for civil servants; nor the bursar of a charity getting a good rent from a prospective tenant. Once we think of real examples, we see at once that not all economic decisions are governed by self-interest; but as soon as we stop thinking, we revert to supposing that they must be. We are evidently in the grip of a powerful fallacy.

The fallacy stems in part from the extendability of the self. The children are the mother's children, and their happiness is her happiness; so, it is argued, in promoting their happiness she is merely promoting her own. So, too, the Treasury official, though suffering in his own pocket from his successful efforts to block a pay increase, is enjoying an enhanced ego, as the Really Effective

Spokesman for the Top Department. The bursar likewise identifies with his school, or college, or hospital, and having made its interests his interests, is promoting his interest in securing its.

It is a powerful argument, and, as often in philosophy, is best controverted not by making it out to be invalid, but by showing it to be too strong. Undoubtedly people do identify with their social groups and institutions, and undoubtedly sometimes infuse some personal *amour propre* into their corporate activities. But if every sacrifice of individual interest to the good of the community is to be deemed selfish, then the word 'selfish' must lose most of its opprobrium; and if every action is sufficient ground for supposing there to be some extended self-interest to motivate it, then to say that an action is selfish is to say no more than that it is an action. We face the cynic with a dilemma: either his claim is an empirical one, based on observation and examination of human actions, in which case we cite counter-examples—not only those of people subordinating personal interests to group interests, but instances of purely disinterested action, undertaken, as it seems, for the love of humanity, the love of justice, the love of truth—which count against his purported generalisation; or his claim is a necessary one, based not on observation but on some deep understanding of the way things are, in which case he is entitled to discount apparent counter-examples, but can no longer use the word 'self-interest' to condemn some actions rather than others. If his claim is simply that as a matter of fact all actions *are* motivated by self-interest, we shall cite facts to show that this is not always so: if his claim is that all actions *must be* motivated by self-interest, we point out that in that case there is nothing special about being motivated by self-interest, and that to say of any particular action that it is motivated by self-interest is to make no criticism of it.

The fallacy is made more compelling by the language of economists. They find it very useful to characterize each agent's preferences by an ordinal ranking, and define a rational agent as one who seeks to maximise his pay-offs. Properly understood, it is a useful analytical tool: so long as it is understood that I may perform an act not as a means to bringing about a pleasurable state of affairs but out of gratitude or in order to manifest solidarity with an oppressed group, then we can accommodate these cases by assigning a suitable ranking to gratitude or solidarity. But it is easy to forget the elasticity needed to accommodate our actual reasons within this framework, and to assume that all the actions of a rational agent are in order to bring about the consequences he happens to desire, and that we necessarily set no store by doing what others want. We seem to be rigidly constrained by the definition of rationality to act only so as to maximise our own interest, and to perform non-consequentialist or altruistic actions only when lapsing into irrationality. But it is an imaginary constraint that comes from our applying in Procrustean fashion a definition which would not be plausible at all unless it were taken in an elastic way.

Although decision-makers do not have to be selfish, the underlying rationale of decentralizing decision-making, with each person having some right to take decisions in his own sphere, is that each decision-maker has his own values, not necessarily the same in all respects as those of other decision-makers. I may not be selfish, but my values are mine, not yours. Economics is, in Wickstead's term, "non-tuistic".[1] It is not my responsibility to mind your, or other people's, business. Whereas in reaching a common mind about what we should do collectively as a social or political group we ought to take into account what others want, and not try to railroad our preferred solution without considering their criticisms or objections, in reaching a bargain, we are more limited in our responsibilities. The mother's business is to find food for her children, not to provide custom for inefficient shopkeepers; the bursar's business is to make good use of the endowments of the college, not to provide housing at uneconomic rents. Once we recognise that we have more than one decision-maker, and hence need a separation of offices and a division of responsibilities, we are committed to those responsibilities being limited, and its not being incumbent on the holder of an office to do all those things that, abstractly considered, it would be desirable that they should be done. Much as it is better that drivers simply keep to the Highway Code rather than each act so as to further the greatest happiness of the greatest number, so in the larger pattern of social life it is better that mothers do the

---

[1] See Philip H. Wickstead, *The Common Sense of Political Economy*, London, 1910, Bk. I, p. 174; I owe this reference to F. A. Hayek. Hayek makes this point himself in his *The Constitution of Liberty*, London, 1969, pp. 78–80.

best for their children and bursars the best for their charities than that each should seek to maximise human happiness as circumstances seem to require. None of us can be responsible for everything. And that implies not only that for each one of us there are some things outside our respective spheres of responsibility, but that we need to confine them so that other people can rely on our each doing his own job properly, and not being distracted by other, perhaps admirable, calls to action.

The non-tuistic nature of economic transactions is easily mistaken for selfishness. As I try and do business with you, I find that you are not primarily concerned with me and my interests, and that I am not so much an individual in my own right as a unit, which could well be dispensed with and replaced by another. I find this woundingly impersonal, and suppose that since you are not concerned to further my concerns as I would like, you are just pursuing your own. Since I am often selfish, and from where I sit self-interest usually looms large in my calculations, I ascribe a similar partiality to you, and construe your non-devotion to my affairs as a selfish concern with your own. But that is only my construction, and I may well be misconstruing your actions. The essential point is not that you must be selfish, but that you can take only a limited view, one that does not make your own all my values and priorities. It is a fundamental limitation depending on our each being unique individuals, and is expressed by Wicksteed's use of the second-person singular, *tu*, rather than *vos* or *vous*. Economic transactions can be, and, as I shall argue, should be, '*vos*istic", taking into account what the other party, not as a unique individual but as a standard type of person, may reasonably be presumed to want. A trader may need to take into account the standard needs of the standard customer, and provide what would be a fair bargain for him, but he cannot enter into an intimate assessment of the exact values and preferences of each individual. I can, on your behalf, reckon that you want your eggs uninfected with salmonella, and your trains to run on time, but I cannot enter into thy mind, and decide on thy behalf that thou preferrest eggs to bacon, or wouldst rather spend thy holidays in Bournemouth than Brighton. To that extent *caveat emptor* is a necessary truth: only the lady herself can make up her mind whether she actually likes the hat.

8.4. *CAVEAT VENDOR*

The doctrine of *caveat emptor* has been much abused. It has been adduced to justify offloading on to each party to a transaction not merely the ultimate responsibility for determining priorities but the sole responsibility for assessing every detail of the transaction. Economists often picture the two parties as engaged in a one-off, purely peripheral transaction, a trader and a South Sea islander exchanging beads for copra,[2] in which they have minimal contact or shared background, and can consider only their own point of view. But most transactions are not one-off, and take place in the course of well-established and widely understood patterns of life. I buy milk every day. I am a *customer*, accustomed to buy milk, and the milkman would not be a milkman unless he had customers, whom he was accustomed to provide with milk, and from whom he was accustomed to receive payment. His job, and mine, and the baker's, and the candlestickmaker's, are integrated, so that we can each work effectively, relying on the other to do his bit adequately. If the milkman misses me out, I am inconvenienced far more than the South Sea islander who decides that the trader is not offering pretty enough beads, for I had had a reasonable expectation that he would leave me a pint, and had arranged my affairs—invited you to coffee—on the assumption that there would be a pint available. The mere fact that we use money—qualitatively identical, conventional tokens of value—indicates that the transaction is not inherently one-off, and takes place within some conventional understanding of the roles of the parties involved.

These considerations give rise to important "*vos*istic" constraints on the way responsible economic decisions are to be made. Business transactions presuppose certain minimum standards of honesty and fair dealing. Often also there are legal requirements that goods be of a merchantable quality and other quality controls. More than that, many businessmen see themselves not simply as money-makers, but as ministering to others by providing goods and services: they want to see what they do as something that, seen from the other side of the table, would be seen as good. Nor is this merely a pious aspiration on the part

[2] F. A. Hayek, *The Constitution of Liberty*, London, 1969, p. 136.

of the thin-skinned. Although I can, intelligibly if not very hon-
ourably, see myself merely as a money-maker, I cannot think of
other people wanting to do business with me under that description alone. It must be because I hold myself out as able and
willing to provide them with some goods or services, that they
come to me and are prepared to part with money in order to
have me do something for them. Although the adage 'The customer is always right' is as untrue as '*Caveat emptor*', it encapsulates the important insight that any account of business activity
must see it as depending essentially on customers, whose
demands it seeks to satisfy. The customer's point of view is ineliminable. It is my business therefore, as a vendor, to view what
I have to offer from the standpoint of potential purchasers, and
see it from their general point of view.

It is sometimes held that we cannot, sometimes that we ought
not to, put ourselves in another's position, and assess things from
his point of view. Each man, we are told, is the best judge of his
own interests. But that is not necessarily, nor always, true. The
main point of the concept of *interest* is that it can be ascribed
vicariously to third persons. Other people's interests are what I
can take into consideration in their absence. Often, of course, I
do not do it very well, and they can stand up better for themselves if they are present. But we can ascribe interests to them,
and our ascriptions may sometimes be more correct than their
actual avowals. The boy may say he wants more chocolate, but
mother knows best; the wino judges that his interests are best
served by consuming a bottle of sherry; the pensioner believes an
investment in an offshore company offering a marvellous rate of
interest is just the thing to secure his future: they are all wrong.
Their interests are not what they actually want, but what we
judge a reasonable man in their position would want. Nevertheless, they may have a right to be wrong, and we hesitate to
displace the wino's and the pensioner's misjudgement of their
own interests by our less mistaken one; but, contrary to the doctrines of the libertarians, we are not always hesitant, and are
properly prepared to be "paternalistic" and protect people from
doing themselves grievous harm or destroying their future ability
to take sound decisions. Even though at the present moment the
housewife genuinely wants to enter into a hire-purchase agreement to obtain the marvellous double glazing the salesman has

on offer, she should be protected against her present inclinations in order that later she shall not find her liberty of manœuvre restricted by the onerous terms of the hire-purchase agreement. Although the ascription of interests is only rough and ready, and may be overridden by the sustained, informed judgement of the person concerned,[3] it is perfectly possible to know what the customers' interests are, and to take care that the goods or services I offer are suitable from their point of view.

I may be tempted not to, sometimes out of short-sighted selfishness, sometimes because of a defective theory of economics. But then further constraints come into play. "You can rip off anybody once, but then he won't come back" is a counsel of prudence that many traders adopt, which leads beyond prudence to a minimal standard of business ethics. The defective view is not only defective, but, even by its own defective standards, inconsistent. Just as consequentialism, we saw,[4] leads to bad consequences, so dishonesty is not only bad ethics, but bad policy too.

We thus see that the non-tuistic nature of economic transactions, though fundamental, should not be overstressed. There is an analogue in politics. It is a fundamental feature of political life that I may be outvoted or otherwise required to act against my better judgement. But although the stark alternative of either going along with others or else going it alone is a recurring theme in all political argument, it is, happily, not often an actual choice. We try to reach consensus. When we cannot reach complete agreement, we seek some compromise that all can live with. We do not push our opponents too far, and will settle for only three quarters of a cake rather than leave them with nothing. Similarly with economics. Although the other party to a bargain is not primarily concerned with my concerns, he does not have to be totally unconcerned. He has some idea of what my concerns are from the mere fact of my wanting to do business with him, and in accounting for his actions, should justify them under the description of addressing the concerns that the sort of person would have if he engaged in the sort of transaction that I did.

---

[3] See further §9.8, p. 198.   [4] In §3.6.

8.5. SELF

The argument thus far has been with the economists who make out that since business transactions are non-tuistic they should take no account whatever of the interests of others, and can only be governed by purely financial considerations. But we are inhibited from thinking responsibly about economics also by the moralists, who preach an absolute altruism which seems quite impracticable. We are told to deny ourselves, to take no thought for the morrow, to sell all we have and give to the poor, and then, having failed to do that, we cannot bring into the equation a proper concern with self alongside due consideration for others.

A decision-maker does not have to be selfish, but very often we expect him, if he is responsible, to have some concern for his future well-being. At the least, we do not want to be lumbered with looking after him as a result of his high-minded neglect of the ordinary dictates of common sense. The world would not be a better place if we were all altruists minding everybody else's business but our own. Conflicting desires to do good to others can, as we have seen,[5] create an Altruists' Dilemma just as intractable as the dilemma of completely selfish prisoners, which shows that the root of the problem is not our having self-interested values, but our not being ready to modify our choices in the light of the values that others espouse. Self-interest *per se* is not the problem. Once it is recognised that interests are not inherently bad, it is sensible, since each person is in an exceptionally good position to know what his interests are, to charge him with seeing that they are reasonably well looked after, and not to deprive ourselves of that source of information, or rely exclusively on others to see to it for him. More generally, we ought not to take the low view of the self that some moralists would wish on us. If my self is bad, then so are the selves of others. I cannot universalise a principle of absolute altruism, and hate the self that others ought to cherish. The biblical injunction to love one's neighbour as oneself comes to nothing unless one has some love for oneself. Christian theologians, notably St Augustine and Joseph Butler, speak approvingly of self-love, so long as it is within the context of our love for God and our fellow men.

[5] See §4.7, p. 71.

Although we should moderate our natural inclination to care for ourselves to the exclusion of everybody else, we should continue to value ourselves, along with other people, and see self-fulfilment as a proper object of endeavour. Indeed, not to do so would be to deny the creative purpose of God.

We need to make a distinction between unselfishness and selflessness. Both are opposed to selfishness, the unbridled pursuit of one's own interests regardless of others, but in different ways. Plato and many other moralists were right to see πλεονεξία (*pleonexia*), self-aggrandisement, as the prime cause of dissension and injustice, but wrongly concluded that the remedy was complete selflessness, with the individual entirely merging his identity in the community. For communities are as vulnerable as individuals. They too can be guilty of group selfishness, as we in the age of nationalism know only too well; and a wrongly based pursuit of communal self-fulfilment can be as empty as the individual's solipsistic search.

An individual's decision, in economic as well as in other affairs, can be criticized on the score of selfishness, but it does not follow that only selfless decisions are morally pukka. Each individual is responsible for his own well-being, and can properly cite that as a reason for his actions. It is only if he fails to accord due weight to the well-being of others that he is open to criticism. What constitutes due weight, and the extent to which he ought to give up his own good for the sake of others, is often a matter for dispute, and depends on the circumstances; but it is not in principle wrong for a decision to be taken in furtherance of the decision-maker's own interests.

8.6. THE TEXTS

We remain uneasy. The self is an unlovable object, and we have a long tradition of admiring self-abnegation. The Authorised Version has imprinted many texts deep in our consciousness, and we are uncomfortable at the easy speaking of those who tell us that it is after all right to look after number one. Such doubts are proper, and need to be articulated and answered. In part they are due to a misreading—perhaps even a mistranslation—of the texts, in part they reflect different levels of personal aspiration and moral discourse.

We are told to take no thought for the morrow, and to consider the lilies of the field. But we are also urged not to build a house on sand, nor to engage in war with a foreign power without doing our sums and making sure we shall have enough troops to win. It is difficult therefore to read the New Testament as commending imprudence. The message is, rather, against our being *over*-anxious. We are, many of us, too ready to mortgage the present to the future, and to forgo the real benefits of jam today under the illusion of securing jam tomorrow. Many housewives need telling to be at peace as they survey the faces round the table, and not to disturb themselves with worrying whether the turkey will be enough for the in-laws on Boxing Day: μὴ μεριμνᾶτε τῇ ψυχῇ ὑμῶν (*me merimnate tei psuchei humon*), enough unto the day are the worries thereof.

Since English has lost the distinction between the second-person singular and the second-person plural,[6] we are in danger of interpreting specific injunctions to individuals as general instructions to us all. The Rich Young Man was told to go, sell all that he had, and give to the poor. But this was addressed to him individually: ὕπαγε, ὅσα ἔχεις πώλησον, καὶ δός πτωχοῖς (*hupage, hosa echeis poleson, kai dos ptochois*);[7] he had already been keeping all the commandments and had found mere observance of the moral law not enough, and was seeking something further. Jesus told him that there was something further if he would be perfect, to set his heart on heavenly rather than worldly possessions; he was being called to a special vocation, and did not take up the opportunity of being a proto-St Francis. It was a great loss. But not all of us are called to the Franciscan life—life could not go on unless many were filling much more humdrum roles—and we need to distinguish vocations, which give rise to first-personal reasons adopted by the individual concerned, from omni-personal reasons, which ought to be adopted by everyone. The thrust of the New Testament is to point out the inadequacy of merely keeping the moral law, and to stress the importance of first-personal commitments.[8] But Jesus is insistent on the importance of

[6] See §4.6, p. 65, n. 8.
[7] Mark 10: 21; cf. Matthew 19: 21 and Luke 18: 22.　　[8] See further Ch. 12.

the law, and at that level of discourse it is perfectly proper on occasion to justify one's decisions by reference to one's own interests. It is not wrong to be rich, though those who set their heart on riches are worshipping an empty idol, and are likely to discover in due course the vanity of what had been their heart's desire.

We are told to deny ourselves. But the injunction was not the simple negative one that negative moralists like to quote at us: rather, it was the prelude to a positive command, ". . . and follow me".[9] The sacrifice is not just a sacrifice, but the necessary means to a greater good. It is a hard truth we all have to come to terms with. Our ideas of the good develop, and often go beyond the aspirations of conventional wisdom. There is nothing wrong with that. But in making new choices, we need always to keep in mind the inescapable fact that to choose is to reject, and that as we decide to do one thing we are deciding thereby not to do an alternative which may also have much to commend it. There are costs involved in the pursuit of the good, and great achievements require great sacrifices. It is well to remember this when giving up the freedom of the bachelor in order to be married, the prospect of a large income for the rewarding life of a teacher, the security of a safe job in order to be able to do one's own thing. In each case the sacrifices are real and constitute a cross which must be borne by anybody following that path. But it is not an exercise in negativity. We are not denying ourselves good things simply for the sake of doing without, but only forgoing a lesser good in order to obtain a greater. If decision-making is decentralized and decision-makers have their own values which may develop in different ways, we need to be reminded that hard choices will need to be made, and that some decisions are costly.

8.7. GUILT-EDGED CURRENCY

Thus far we have been considering the responsibility a man has in his day-to-day dealings with his fellow men, where they are collaborating for their mutual benefit, but with each having separate responsibilities and separate powers of decision-making.

---

[9] Mark 8: 34; cf. Matthew 16: 24 and Luke 9: 23.

These transactions are immensely facilitated, but our moral understanding of them greatly complicated, by the use of money. Money is like sex. We feel bad about it. We respond usually by not liking to talk or think about it seriously, sometimes by flaunting it with an air of bravado. We are aware that it is a powerful, pervasive drive, difficult to control, dangerous if out of control, not only in an obvious way to others, but, more insidiously, to ourselves. Although it can be a means of personal fulfilment and creativity, it has the odour of sin about it. It is difficult to handle money and keep one's hands clean, and it is not surprising that those who would be pure in heart have embraced poverty with as much fervour as celibacy. Even those who have not felt a call to renounce the world prefer not to think about business ethics or the responsible use of money. They recognise some obligations in practice, and are quick to spot unethical behaviour in others, but prefer to keep their thinking in two separate pockets, being moral on Sundays, and reckoning that business is business on working days of the week. The two-pocket expedient, however, never really works. Ideas filter across, but below the threshold of conscious scrutiny, and induce inhibitions, which, because they are not properly thought through, contaminate subsequent thought with a general fuzz. If we are not to be paralysed in our thinking, we must articulate difficulties and solve them, not put them to one side. We need to understand the nature of money, why it is valuable, and the way in which it facilitates business activity, and see why we are torn between incompatible models of proper behaviour.

8.8. THE VALUE OF CHOICE

Money has value because it encapsulates choice. Other things have value—love, honour, knowledge—but these do not of themselves confer on us the power of choice. Money, so long as it is valued, does, and so long as it does, is valued. It extends choice both over circumstances and over time. I do something to help you further your purposes now, and in return you enable me to choose what I want requiring the co-operation of some other person at some future date. If I were in a very high-minded society where everybody else did only what he thought was right and never did anything for money, then money would be no use to me either. Conversely, if I were in a kingdom where everyone was pleased and proud to do the king's bidding, then the king could recompense me for my help by writing a letter instructing his subjects to carry out my requests as though they were his. As things are, many people will do things for me in exchange for money which they would not otherwise do, because they think that they in turn will be able to use the money to induce others to do what they want. It is valued by them because it facilitates their choices, and it facilitates their choices because it is valued by others, whose choices it will in turn facilitate.

Money not only facilitates choice but extends the possibilities of co-operation. It extends the possibilities of co-operation by being a transferable token of interpersonal value that enables settlements to be made at the end of each joint action and provides those to whom the co-operators' surplus did not naturally accrue with benefits none the less, avoiding a Battle of the Sexes,[10] and thus creating the possibility of multilateral transactions. It enables us to bargain more closely, more widely, and over extended periods of time. I can price goods to the nearest p., thereby making them available to those who could not have afforded a greater price, and would have been unwilling to accept them at the cost of taking on some ill-defined obligation to do me a good return in some unspecified way. I can provide you with my specialist services, and use the money you give me to buy groceries from him. And I can sell you my car today and wait until next year before deciding what I want in its place. Money, for all its impersonality, and in spite of its bad effects on the character, enables us to live far richer and more effective lives, and quite largely liberates us from the tyranny of time and circumstance.

Money carries information. It shows what people's actual priorities are. Although we would like to have many things, we can afford only a few of them, and have to decide which ones to buy and which to do without. Money is in that way a vote, a vote which may be outbidden by others, but less in danger of being simply outvoted than the ordinary political vote. Moreover, the things people buy bear on the prices they com-

[10] See §3.5, pp. 42–3.

mand in the market-place, and signal to third parties what the demand really comes to, and what supplies are most called for. Market mechanisms are subtle and sensitive, and enable some sorts of information to be coded and passed on in an effective form. They are not, as some free-marketeers make out, perfect, nor is theirs the only sort of information that is relevant. But, for all their faults, market economies are less bad than controlled ones.

Four facets of money are relevant to its moral evaluation: it increases choice; it introduces an adversarial aspect into all business transactions; it is impersonal, and imparts a facelessness to everyday life; and it gives rise to fallacious economic doctrines which lead good men to suppose that they have no choice but to do evil.

8.9. THE BEST OF THE BARGAIN

Money is often defined as the medium of exchange, and traditionally the exchange of goods is taken as the paradigm of a commercial transaction. In reality, however, the exchange of goods is only a special case of collaboration, which includes also the rendering of services and many joint enterprises, that benefit all those engaged in them, but some much more than others. Nevertheless, it is the exchange of goods that has dominated our thinking about economics, and often distorted it. It is easy to think, as Aristotle did, of the cobbler exchanging shoes for a house, and to think of each of these as having some definite real value.[11] Each exchange then becomes a zero-sum game in which, provided goods are valued correctly, neither party loses out. The relative permanence of material goods imputes a static set of values and a static theory of exchange, which makes people fearful of parting with their possessions at less than their true value, and obscures understanding of the dynamic nature of economic activity. If possessions have inherent value, there is no point in exchanging them. It is only because one thing is of more value to me and another of more value to you that the exchange is worth making. But once this point is taken, no static account of

---

[11] See App. 1.

economics is plausible, and we should cease to think in terms of zero-sum games and states of equilibrium, and think instead of our all being better off as a result of economic activity, and our always being in a state of disequilibrium, moving from the present position to some other that is taken to be better.

Although economic activity is not fundamentally a zero-sum game, there is, none the less, a competitive aspect to it. In bargaining about the division of the co-operators' surplus, we find ourselves in an adversarial situation. Once we have money, with a large range of outcomes possible in which the benefits of collaboration are differently distributed, we sense that, on top of the non-zero-sum game arising in the course of nature from our collaborating, there is a zero-sum game in which those benefits are divided between us. As far as the latter game is concerned, those benefits are fixed, and if any one person gains, it will be at the expense of someone else.[12] Hence, as we haggle over the price of a house, we come to feel that we are engaged in a basically adversarial exercise, in which your gain is my loss, and that business relations are fundamentally unfriendly.

This double focus—of the non-zero-sum game which underlies all economic activity on the one hand, and the zero-sum game which we cannot but play in determining the actual price on the other—leaves us subject to awkward tensions as we try to work out where our economic responsibilities lie. It gives substance to the obstinate feeling that getting money is tainted, because there is inevitably some element of exploitation, inasmuch as the division of the co-operators' surplus is a zero-sum game, so that, as Plato and most subsequent thinkers have supposed, if I have more, πλεονεκτέω (*pleonekteo*), others must have less; and hence that it is bad for me to have more or seek my own good. But that is not an argument that business associates, employers, customers, or clients may use on us. Their not taking our interests to heart precludes them also from taking it upon themselves to tell us what our ideals should be. It may be that you are called to a life of self-renouncing poverty, and often treat the sick for free, and give all the money you do earn to medical missions in Africa; but that is your business, not mine, and I (who am quite

---

[12] I owe this point to R. B. Braithwaite, *The Theory of Games as a Tool for the Moral Philosopher*, Cambridge, 1955.

well off, thank you) am in no position to suggest that you should
treat me at cut-price rates. So far as I am concerned, I wanted to
see a Harley Street surgeon, and should expect to pay Harley
Street prices. And quite generally the non-tuistic nature of economic transactions imports a certain universalisability, and
debars us from suggesting to any one person that he ought to
forgo his fee and do business at substandard prices. Indeed, not
only is there no generally available argument that anyone should,
but there is some argument against, in that the price does serve
to indicate to all and sundry the cost of the goods and services
provided, and to provide them at a lower price sends a signal
that they are freely available at that price, and invites their mis-
use. The communists used to subsidise necessities as a matter of
principle, but then discovered that boys were using loaves of
bread as footballs, and families were buying it to feed to their
chickens. Similarly, where clergymen, or schoolmasters, or social
workers, or nurses, are underpaid, administrators use them
instead of typists, or caretakers, or cleaners, as a cheap form of
unskilled labour. Whatever responsibilities a person undertakes in
the use of his money, and whatever limitations there are in the
way it may legitimately be obtained, it is not inherently wrong to
obtain it, whether as a profit on a business enterprise, or as a
wage, salary, or fee, or as some other form of reward.

8.10. RESPONSIBLE GETTING

Many tender-hearted thinkers who would like to engage in the
business of the world while remaining no man's enemy have
sought to resuscitate the mediaeval doctrine of the just price, the
just wage, and the just business deal. Economists are apt to
mock. At one level, certainly, mockery is justified. There are no
monetary values laid up in heaven for the philosopher to discern
and communicate to his brethren in the world: it is only because
both sides are better off than they would have been otherwise
that the transaction takes place. But since there is an adversarial
aspect to bargaining, it is reasonable to want to avoid bargaining
as a means of arriving at a price. There are whole ranges of
different prices or wage levels at which both parties would be
worse off if the deal fell through than if they settled on those

terms, and, as in the Battle of the Sexes, there is a games-theoretical premium on intransigence. If there were a just price or a just wage, it would enable both to collaborate without any adversarial element, transferring goods or rendering services at a price determined independently of either's bargaining skill or power. If the just price does not exist, we should like to invent it.

In fact we can. Although there is no price laid up in heaven for all time and all circumstances, there are ways of determining a price, a wage, or a fee, which is not arrived at by bargaining and has many of the marks of a fair deal. Often the nature of the deal will give guidelines. Since business deals, though not tuistic, are vosistic, each party can view it from the sort of position the other can be deemed to take, and thus weigh considerations on both sides of the case, and strike some sort of reasonable balance, which, being reasonable, is likely to converge with that struck by the other ratiocinator. Instead of an adversarial I–thou conflict, painful to me as much as to thee, we have a we-argument considering in general terms one party's interests and contributions as compared with another's. Often this is made easy by there being many people similarly situated to either party, so that there is a going price, which I could have obtained if I were dealing with some other you than thee, and thou wouldst have had to pay if thou hadst dealt not with me, but with someone else. If I want to sell my car to my brother, we can get a valuer to name a price "as between willing buyer and seller", and for very standard goods and services there is at any one time a fairly precise market price which is effectively independent of both parties, and at which in many cases neither side can be said to be doing the other down.

8.11. BUSINESS IS NOT BUSINESS

The market price, although effectively independent of both parties, is not necessarily just, but has often been made out to be by economists. Economists err by overgeneralising. They put on long-distance spectacles, and posit conditions of perfect information and perfect competition, and view the abstract economic man as engaged in an abstract business enterprise. Real life is not like that. I never have been in possession of perfect information:

indeed, it is characteristic of decision-making that decisions are made under conditions of imperfect information. Nor for the most part is competition anything like perfect. Nor am I an economic man: I have much better things to do than buy in the cheapest and sell in the dearest market. The greater part of my life, like that of most other people, is occupied with concerns which are at most only partly economic. Almost all of family and social life and much of professional life is guided by considerations of which the economist knows nothing.

Current doctrines emphasize the value of information mediated by the market, and it is true that the market does convey important information that decision-makers ignore at their peril. But it is not the only source of information, and the non-market sources are of great importance in influencing the way we characterize our work-time activities and justify the decisions we take. We are not confined to the straitjacket of market indicators and economic motives. There is no reason, therefore, why we should be confined to strictly financial considerations in explaining our actions. Indeed, once we recognise that nobody would do business with us if all we were doing was to make money for ourselves, we see that it would be incoherent to characterize our activity in terms of money-making alone. There must be some other view of what we are doing, and this view will make relevant other facts and other sources of information. For most people these are far more important than purely financial considerations. The doctor, the teacher, the research worker, the priest, the academic, all see themselves primarily in terms of their profession, and are guided in the decisions they take by professional standards, which often enable them to determine what the responsible action on their part is, over and above a purely financial assessment. Although doctors seek salaries and charge fees, they are predominantly guided by medical, not financial, considerations in arriving at decisions, and are esteemed by their colleagues for their medical, not their financial, success. Similarly in the academic and educational world. Colleagues co-operate, colleges and universities work together in planning syllabuses or conducting examinations. They manage for the most part to reach agreement without there being any authority set over them to decide contentious questions. Occasionally money changes hands, but making money is not a dominant motive, and the esteem in which individuals or institutions are held depends on their meeting criteria appropriate to the work they are trying to do, not their balance sheet. The guild structure of many professions generates a certain consensus about the etiquette that members of the profession ought to observe, and the standards they should apply in their professional work, while leaving each practitioner free to use his best judgement in the service of his clients. We have many such models of decentralized but consensual decision-making, and would do well to take more note of them.

Economic theories also import a spurious determinism into economic affairs. Once we start viewing ourselves as economic men, we readily suppose that we have no choice but to buy in the cheapest and sell in the dearest market. We think that we are obliged to grind the faces of those we employ, because in a state of perfect competition we should put ourselves out of business if we did otherwise. We think we must maximise profits, because we should be acting irrationally and contrary to our nature if we did not. We would like to take on a crippled employee, to sell a house to a particular purchaser who would treat it well, to dispose of industrial waste carefully instead of polluting the environment, to invest in an ethical drug company rather than one selling armaments to Third-World dictators, but somehow feel that we have no choice but to be guided by financial considerations alone. We are enthralled by theories of economics which seem to determine a market price that leaves no room for a just—or unjust—price, or for any other behaviour than that attributed to economic man.

But once again we are being misled by abstractions. The perfect market of the economists has been idealized beyond all actuality. We do not actually have perfect information; transaction costs are a considerable brake on seeking alternatives; the market is not in equilibrium. With most transactions there is not one and only one price at which it will take place, but a range of prices bounded at one extreme by the price at which it is not worth it to me, and I will either look for another bargain or give up the idea of making that transaction altogether, and at the other extreme by the price at which it is not worth it to you, and you will either look for another bargain or give up the idea of making that transaction altogether. At prices near the one extreme I shall feel that you are driving a hard bargain with me, but still reckon that I should do better to accept than go elsewhere or go without: at prices near the other extreme you will feel that I am driving a hard bargain with you, but still reckon that you would do better to accept than go elsewhere or go without. Between these are others, one, or some, of which, not necessarily that half-way between the extremes, will be acknowledged as fair. Similarly with taking on employees, dealing with industrial waste, investing our savings: we do not have complete liberty of action, and are often constrained and unable to do all we should like to do; but we have some freedom of manœuvre, within which we can exercise responsible choice.

Economic textbooks often make out that profit-making is the prime motive in business, and that profitability is the sole criterion of success. Both views are mistaken. Many firms are concerned not to maximise profits, but to stabilise them. That makes good sense. If I am a manager of, say, a chemical firm, it will not do me all that much good to make enormous profits for the next five years, which will then create expectations among the shareholders that it will be difficult to live up to. Better to have a reliably rising trend over the next fifteen years, until I have garnered my pension, and let the next chap go for the jackpot, if he wants. Having found a comfortable niche in the market, it may well be best to stay there rather than expose oneself to the risks of moving into unknown territory and taking on extra liabilities. Again, I may find one line of business—say, antiquarian books—congenial, and another—pop music—uncongenial, though much more profitable; in such a case it would be perfectly rational to reduce the singles counter to make way for a new section on old maps. Why get headaches from unwanted decibels, when I can manage on the custom of interesting bibliophiles?

Economists who consider only monetary motives are like legal theorists who consider only what the bad man gets told by his solicitor. Each offers an important insight we do well not to ignore, but each gives a distorted view of his subject if that is all he considers. The extreme case marks an important boundary, but it is a boundary, not the region where most of us live and have our being. Accountants are like solicitors. They set financial guidelines, just as solicitors set legal ones: I must make sure that ends meet if I do not want to end up in queer street, just as I must get my conveyances and contracts properly drawn up if I do not want to end up in court. But these are outside limits within which I must work, not the be-all and end-all of the whole enterprise. The headmaster listens to the bursar, and has to choose between putting the fees up and doing without a new pavilion or a new classics master, but what he is really proud of at the end of the day is not the school's balance sheet but its A-levels results and Oxbridge successes, and the tenth-wicket stand that gained it the Southern Counties Schools Cricket Championship last year.

Political economists in modern times have tended to assume that there are only two alternatives for reaching decisions: either by means of collective, authoritative allocations, as in communist countries, or by reference to financial considerations alone, as in a market economy. It is worth reflecting that we know of many walks of life in which neither of these patterns applies; and then we may free ourselves of doctrines which distort our understanding by leaving out important sources of information, and by importing a spurious determinism into economic affairs.

8.12. EXTERNALITIES

Economic transactions do not affect only those who are party to them. Other people also may be affected, and there may be consequences not taken into account by the price mechanism. Advocates of the all-perfection of the market make out that these can be safely ignored, but give no cogent reason for that conclusion. A responsible operator does not ignore information because it is not mediated in a particular form.

In recent years we have been much concerned with the environmental effects of economic activity. Farmers burn straw, and dirty housewives' washing in neighbouring towns; motorists spew out poisonous fumes, destroy the peace and quiet of the countryside, and make the roads unsafe for other users; manufacturers pollute the atmosphere, and dump toxic waste into our water supplies. In each case, again, the hard-line economist is inclined to say that these matters are none of his business, and he will look after the environment only if he is paid to do so. But the fact that economic transactions are non-tuistic does not mean that no account should be taken of any consequences that may result, other than those with a price tag. As I do business with you, I am not negatively responsible for everything, and, in particular, I am not completely and ultimately responsible for evaluating the proposed deal from your side of the table. But neither of those limits on my responsibility relieves me of responsibility for the actual consequences of my actions. In the extreme case, if I discharge prussic acid and kill people, I shall be guilty of manslaughter. The damage I do by letting out sulphur dioxide is less spectacular, and more difficult to lay at my door, but the fact that I did it by way of business activity is no defence.

Bilateral transactions are inherently exclusive. If you and I do business together we are not doing it with anyone else. Often it is of no great moment, as there are others willing to do business with others, but this is not always so, and it could be that we are leaving somebody out in the cold. If at a dance we all pair off, except for three girls who are left as wallflowers, I ought to forgo just the odd dance with my attractive partner in order that their evening shall not be utterly spoiled. Nozick denies this.[13] He is right in resisting a general claim that we are negatively responsible for everything we fail to avert. But often bilateral arrangements are made within a more limited institutional frame, for whose general working we do have some responsibility. It is one thing to make sure that nobody is completely excluded at a private dance, where we are all members of the same party, but quite another at a disco or a pub, where there is no call on me to chat up unaccompanied females. In the economic case, if once I have established a dominant position in the market, I ought not to be choosy about further customers. Because everyone else in the village comes to my shop, Mr Grumpy has no alternative to me, and if I refuse to serve him, he will have to do without. In some cases common carrier obligations are imposed by law, but even where they are not, a responsible businessman will recognise that he should observe them.

[13] Robert Nozick, *Anarchy, State, and Utopia*, New York, 1974, pp. 262–5, disallows any argument from the point of view of those who are excluded by the voluntary transactions of others. But often in practice, as with "common carrier" obligations, we insist that people should not be unreasonably excluded by the otherwise legitimate choices of others, and it is hard to see that our concern for potential losers is wrong.

Other people may suffer as a result of my business activities. The result of a takeover bid may be to put many people out of work; certainly if I compete successfully for a contract, my rivals will suffer. Most economists advocate complete unconcern: a few thinkers, by contrast, commend total soft-heartedness. Neither is correct. We cannot be totally soft-hearted without falling down on the job assigned to us. If my job is to make steel, I have an obligation to make steel efficiently, not to maintain employment in Sheffield. Nor is it a kindness to featherbed people. Not only is it not treating them as responsible individuals, capable of taking stock for their own future, but it prevents them and others from making the necessary changes to adapt themselves to new circumstances. But it does not follow that I should show a ruthless unconcern. There is no need to make hard truths harsh. Often it is possible to phase out outmoded techniques gradually, giving old dogs time to learn new tricks, and often we can, at no great cost, temper the wind to the shorn lamb. Once we recognise that we do, in many cases, have some room for manœuvre, and are not precluded from taking any, save hard economic, factors into account, we can no longer duck responsibility for the decisions we take, which we are in a position to have taken differently, and for which there are reasons available to indicate what ought to be done.

8.13. FACELESSNESS

The third parties who suffer as a result of my business activities are typically difficult to identify. We do not meet them face to face, and often they are remote and unknown. My efforts to invent a new machine may put thousands of artisans in the north out of work; my discovery of a new synthetic fibre may deprive plantation workers in some Third-World country of their means of livelihood. Even if I take the other chap's point of view into consideration in arriving at a business deal, and am admirably vosistic, I am operating an impersonal market mechanism, and am part of a faceless fact dominating other people's lives.

The impersonality of the market is often felt to be morally undesirable: it is dehumanising; people are not regarded as ends in themselves, but merely as means; my transactions with the booking clerk, the ticket collector, and the telephone operator are merely instrumental, when I ought to be regarding them as persons in their own right, and engage in meaningful face-to-face dialogue with them. It is a serious charge, put forward by many people, but none the less misconceived.

The very impersonality of the market, paradoxically enough, enhances some aspects of personality, by conferring a limited, but morally unrestricted, freedom of choice, thus enabling us to exercise, and hence also to discover, our own particular individual predilections. The opposite often seems, at first sight, to be the case: if we did things simply to oblige our fellow men without thought of any reward or any expectation, and they likewise were guided solely by a concern for our well-being, they would return the favour and would come to our aid whenever we needed it. But then we should feel inhibited in asking people to do non-necessary things for us. If I am evidently ill, I can accept the services of doctors and nurses with a good conscience, but I hesitate to take up the time of a great expert with my non-necessary inclinations—I should like to see the museum of modern art, and you are a great art expert, but have better things to do than show strangers round. If, however, you hold yourself out as being willing to show people round for a fee—perhaps you want the money to pay your son's school fees or buy a pony for your daughter—then I need have no qualms in taking you up on your offer. Money is not just the fruit of human selfishness and evil: it is also the means whereby we can come to terms with our not being the only pebble on the beach, not the only focus of concern for other people. However much I recognise a duty to meet other people's needs, I know that I could not possibly meet all the wants that other people happen to have, and therefore realise also that they cannot be expected to make all my concerns their concern. If I am to go beyond the close circle of family and friends where my wanting something is a strong reason for trying to bring it about, I need to have some means of addressing other people in terms of their set of values, and not just trade on their good nature to include me in. So strong is this feeling that we are often embarrassed to receive services, and especially goods, free, and want to make a contribution in return, and look to market prices to give us a rough guide as to what an appropriate contribution would be. Sometimes, no doubt, it is pride that makes us want not to have to be grateful, but often it is a dim sense of the necessary otherness of other people, and the unsustainability of their always and indefinitely putting themselves out for us. We want them to treat us as we should like to treat them, as somewhat separate entities rather than close friends, so that we can make clear-cut choices within our own budget about what we most want without entering into a nebulous web of indefinite obligations to feel grateful or make some return for benefits received. Only so can we really choose freely; only so can we discover and develop our own individual personalities.

The impersonality of the market also takes the sting out of disappointment and unsuccess. I am disappointed if someone buys her hat at another shop, but it does not carry the same message of disapprobation as if thou, my hitherto friend, preferrest my rival. In a world in which not everything can go my way, it is good to have decisions not always loaded with meaning, and to be able to accept the knocks of life, if not philosophically, at least as being only injuries and not also insults. We have learned to regard nature as inanimate, where causes are followed by effects regardless of our moral deserts, and we import a certain degree of impersonality into the law and the administration of justice, in order to secure both the impartiality that justice requires and the reliability and predictability that we desire. The impersonality of the market should be seen in similar light. It is not altogether bad, and has much to recommend it even from a moral point of view.

The analogy with the law should make us wary, however, of cultivating impersonality too much. The law is impartial, but does need to listen to interested parties, and take due account of their rights, arguments, and interests. So too the market, being like the law a human institution, needs to take cognizance of the fact that money was made for men, not men for money. Although I cannot, and should not be expected to, enter into a deeply personal I–thou relationship with the booking clerk, the ticket collector, or the telephone operator, there is no need for me to be impersonal, or to avoid making the conventional acknowledgements of their status as human beings. And though I should not attempt to force on them an intimacy they do not desire, I am under no institutional obligation to rebuff their conversational advances. More generally, but equally importantly, although I individually cannot be negatively responsible for the unknown third parties who lose out under our economic system, we collectively cannot similarly shrug off responsibility for their fate. It may be that we cannot do much—Marxist meddling mostly makes matters worse—but we cannot put the question completely out of mind on the grounds that the operations of the market are as impersonal as those operations of nature that give rise to famines and earthquakes.

8.14. THE WAY OF THE WORLD

Often we feel qualms about what we do in the course of business, but then reckon that we have no alternative. The system dictates our choices. We are enmeshed in wickedness that requires us to harden our hearts and turn away the widow from our door, sack the secretary with the nervous breakdown, and block our ears to the cries of the poor. We would like the widow to be housed, but we need the rent to pay the repair bills. The secretary needs a lot of patient care and counselling, but we just have not the time, and cannot risk our correspondence going astray again. The poor need food and clothes, but we need money to pay our suppliers. We should like not to send women down the mines or children up chimneys, but our competitors do, and we cannot afford to lose our competitive edge; if we were to install plant to clean up our emissions, we should have to pass the cost on to our customers, and they are not prepared to pay for it. We should like to invest our money in housing associations for the poor and in ethical pharmaceuticals, but we shall get a much better return from tobacco or armaments manufacturers and South African gold-mines, and need the money for our children's education, or for the charity of which we are trustees.

These are serious arguments, but they do not extend quite as far as is made out, and the problems they raise, though difficult, are not irresoluble. It is neither the case that we are completely trapped, nor that we are subject to irreconcilable obligations. The feeling of helplessness can be dissolved by careful thought.

We feel that we have no choice, because we feel pressured by economic considerations. The sense of being pressured stems ultimately from the fact that each of us has some effective say over what happens, and power is inherently costly to exercise. Those in positions of great power are constantly bothered by people getting at them, wanting them to decide one way rather than another. In the decentralized decision-making system of the market, each of us has a veto, and is therefore under pressure not to exercise it in certain ways, and to go along with what other people want. A vote may be cast secretly and freely because it is only one of many, and may always be outvoted. A veto, because it is by itself effective, is of more concern to others, who will therefore be readier to bring pressure to bear in order that it be not interposed. And since our vetoes are limited to particular spheres of responsibility, it cannot be concealed who is exercising it. People will know if I refuse to go along with their projects, and will be ready to retaliate by interposing their vetoes on my projects until I change my tune. I do not have to work in a free society in the way I do in a communist labour camp, but other people will not give me food if I exercise my right not to work. The very security which protects me from having to do what others want frustrates me when others refuse to do what I want.

I am pressured by dogma. I am mesmerised by the doctrines of the economic man.[14] Because I really am under pressure, I too readily construe my situation as precluding any freedom of action on my part. But in most cases we are not living on the margin, where the slightest deviation from market behaviour will land us in queer street. We often think we are, and therefore need every penny, and cannot afford to forgo any income. But though we are often poorer than we like, or indeed than we deserve, we are not just on the brink of bankruptcy. The marginal man, the marginal business, is only just making ends meet, and would go under if he made the slightest concession to non-economic imperatives. But most operators are not minimally successful, and could make some sacrifice, could carry some disabled employee, adopt some environment-friendly procedure without teetering over the edge into bankruptcy. Even quite poor people can buy biodegradable washing-up liquid. They may not be able to do anything very spectacular, and certainly not all that is required, but something none the less.

Often I am pressured by law and conventional understanding

---

[14] See §8.11 above.

of my role. If I am a trustee, I am legally obliged to get the best price I can, irrespective of other considerations, even moral ones. The Church Commissioners feel impelled to destroy village after village, as they sell the glebe field to speculative builders who will make a quick profit out of selling desirable residences in Vicarage Close, even though it will entirely destroy the character and amenities of the village that the church was intended to serve. The story is told of an Oxford don at the beginning of this century who every year went to Scotland for the Long Vac with a trunk-load of books, sent passenger's luggage in advance. One year the railway officials queried the weight and the rate, and after some altercation persuaded him that the correct charge was some 50 per cent higher than he had been accustomed to pay. Reluctantly persuaded of this, he wrote a cheque not just for the difference demanded but for the amount owing for the previous twenty years as well. In due course he received back a letter from one of the directors returning the amount he was paying for previous years, as the board had decided in the circumstances to waive the charge. Whereupon he wrote back curtly, saying that the money was not for the directors but the shareholders.

We can understand the reasoning, but now also see the fallacy. The non-tuistic nature of business transactions leads us to ascribe to incorporated businesses and trusts only those values that can be explicitly read out of their articles of association or trust deed. Whereas an actual person may have moral commitments that may moderate his seeking the greatest possible profit, a corporation has no soul, and no implicit morality. But in practice things are different. The directors of public companies do sometimes waive payments they are legally entitled to exact; they make contributions to charities as well as to political parties; they give grants; they promote good causes; they establish pension funds, and give employees share options. In all this they are careful to make out that they are merely seeking the company's good, and in a real sense they are. But it is not simply a profit-maximising good. Rather, it is a long-term good, taking account not only of the company's financial position, but also of its position in the community, and its good name as a good employer and public-spirited organization.

We can make sense of this, if we work through the implications of business being non-tuistic, but not thereby non-vosistic.

Companies, and likewise trusts, exist for different purposes, and these are to be respected, and not set aside by the directors' or trustees' moral judgements, however sincere. However much I happen to think the poor ought to be housed, I ought not to divert trust funds to Shelter, when they were intended for the education of deserving sons of the inferior clergy. Shareholders rely on me to earn them dividends, and my judgement that the money would be better spent on famine relief is something that should not weigh with me as I go about the company's business. But whether or not stated in the articles of association or the trust deed, there is an implicit commitment also to the common standard morality of the time, because it is only on that basis that business can be conducted. It is the same as with the implicit legal constraints on the directors' freedom of action. Whatever the articles of association, I am obliged to keep within the law. But the law, of necessity, constitutes a very minimal standard of behaviour,[15] the standard that will be enforced by the coercive sanctions of the courts. There are many loopholes in the law, many pieces of sharp behaviour that a trustee or director could get away with were he to try it on. But we should not hold them to account for not having tried it on. Although we do not allow them to be very generous with other people's money, we do expect them to act honestly and reasonably. They should deal well with deserving employees, and even generously, within reason, to them and to circumambient good causes around their main area of enterprise, acting in the same way as a reasonable, but not idiosyncratic, individual would, were he sole owner of the enterprise, or sole beneficiary of the trust.

It is not just that we have failed to recognise the importance of the customer's point of view in a business transaction. We are also chary of admitting moral considerations into decision-making, because we are worried by the claims of the moral sceptics that moral judgements are purely subjective and arbitrary. If they were, we should be on a slippery slope once we allowed any sort of moralising, for there would be no saying what moral judgements might be reached by a sufficiently idiosyncratic individual, and we should have no way of holding trustees to account. The law, by contrast, would seem objective and definite, and if we

---

[15] See §6.13, p. 120.

allowed only legal constraints on their pursuing the main purposes of their trust, we should know where we were. But in fact the law is not only often unclear, but is inevitably too minimal for this task. Business requires a higher standard of morality than that enjoined by law, and takes for granted a principle of fair dealing which anyone acting on behalf of someone else, whether shareholder or beneficiary, is expected to adopt. And this standard, being the common morality of the reasonable man, is sufficiently objective and definite, and not a mere exercise in arbitrary whim.

Although we are, when we undertake some office as director or trustee, indeed under pressure, from our understanding of our role and from the law, to carry out the commission entrusted to us, rather than to act simply as we think fit, the pressure is not as immoral as we sometimes suppose. Always when undertaking an office we are subordinating our freedom of choice to the duties of the station we occupy, but it is a limitation rather than a complete abdication of responsibility that is implicit in taking up an office. The bursar is primarily responsible for the welfare of his school or college, the trustee for the beneficiaries of the trust, the director for the shares paid to his shareholders, and they ought not to put these aside in pursuance of some other moral ideals they happen to have; but in the discharge of their official duties they should be sensitive to moral considerations just as they are to legal ones.

All in all, we are under pressure as we operate in the world, but not so much as to leave us no room for choice or no freedom to exercise it responsibly. We do not have as much freedom of manœuvre as we would like, and often we are under obligations to conform to the common morality of our time rather than our own personal ideals. But we do have some freedom, and are entitled to take responsible decisions.

But will they do any good? The little that any one operator can achieve single-handed is too little to signify, so he might as well go along with the rest, and enjoy the fruits of sin for a season, waiting until the public conscience is at last aroused, and legislation is passed to enforce responsible action collectively. Against that defeatist attitude, it is important to argue that we are not concerned to do only consequentially effective action, and to point out that often exemplary action is effective. Sometimes, rather than engaging on consequentially effective action, we are simply witnessing. No doubt, if I refuse to let my house for immoral purposes, somebody else will; if we do not sell arms to a Third World dictator, the French will. But to refuse, though ineffective as a means of ensuring that an undesirable state of affairs is not brought about, is none the less valuable: it makes a statement; it shows what sort of people we are—and even in business integrity is something we should be ashamed to ignore. Often also there are direct consequences of value. If I will not employ minors in dangerous procedures and insist on all my employees taking safety precautions, I may not shame other employers into doing likewise, but shall not be the cause of a foolhardy boy being maimed for life, or a careless operative suffering grievous harm. I show that such precautions are practicable, and pave the way for their being made mandatory. I may not affect the attitude of the cowboys, but I alter perceptions of what the best practice is, and may by my example as well as my advocacy secure some improvement in general standards. Often in economic affairs we are in a Prisoners' Dilemma; but Prisoners' Dilemmas can be escaped from if only someone will make the costly first move. And it is not necessarily the case that we cannot bear the cost of a small first step.

The way of the world does not constrain us as much as we sometimes think; but still it does contaminate us. We do make hard, non-tuistic decisions, and instead of entering into an I–thou relation with the widow, the secretary, and the poor, distance ourselves from their personal needs, and treat them generally, not indeed as *its*, but as *them*. The world treats people unintimately, not necessarily unjustly, but without the commitment and tenderness we all of us crave. And those who come off badly in the world may tax us, who are of the world, with lacking kindness in our dealings with them. Individually, we may disclaim responsibility, and point out that there must be limits to the responsibilities that can be landed on any one person; but corporately we have something to answer for. It may be that we can answer adequately. Life, quite apart from the system, is not a bed of roses, and our system is less bad than others we know of. The poor in the West have something to be thankful for: they are not liable to summary imprisonment, torture, or execution, like those under communist or Third World regimes. But still they are poor, and sometimes homeless and hungry: we, individually and collectively, need to be mindful of their plight. Although individually we cannot be held negatively responsible for those who lose out in market economies, we can, sometimes even individually, do something to make things better for someone, and collectively take steps to ensure that the sharp edge of competitive endeavour does not cut the weaker brethren to the bone.

The way of the world is not necessarily as bad as we are inclined in our gloomier moments to suppose. Although it frustrates our occasional impulses to live up to the high standards we would like to set ourselves, it also guides others away from the low courses they would otherwise be inclined to follow. If you refrain from murdering me for fear of the law, or from cheating me for fear of losing my custom, you have not exercised the Kantian good will, but, quite apart from the bad consequences averted, you have been encouraged to overcome your baser urges and form good moral habits. Although we are not absolutely the creatures of habit—perhaps less so than Aristotle made out—we are very largely so, much more than Kant and his followers acknowledge. Most people are very largely the creatures of their age and social environment, and only occasionally make autonomous choices uninfluenced by the heteronomy of the done thing. And if the done thing is a good thing to do, they will become, by heteronomously doing it, nearer to being autonomously good. By playing his part in the world, a good man may make the world a better place, and other worldly people better in consequence. Although we should honour those called to practise a cloistered virtue in monastic isolation from the world and all its wicked ways, we ought not to feel obliged to follow their example. If we renounce the world, we may also be abandoning the world: if we are responsible for the moral, as well as the material, well-being of our fellow men, we may need to go along with ungood people seeking ungood things, in order not only that unbad consequences may ensue, but that bad people may become less bad.

8.15. THE ETHICAL INVESTOR

The conflict between economic and moral values has in recent years often presented itself most sharply in the investment decisions we are called on to make, either individually or vicariously on behalf of some corporate institution. In time past the Ecclesiastical Commissioners were regularly lambasted in the popular press because their properties were being used for prostitution, and many universities and colleges are under pressure now to disinvest from South Africa.

Once again, there is an aura of guilt, deriving from biblical texts, which inhibits moral ratiocination. Of course, Old Testament injunctions are evidently inapplicable to modern circumstances. It is one thing to lend to a neighbour to tide him over a bad harvest, quite another to lend to a joint stock company so that it can extend its sphere of operations: in the former case usury is properly forbidden, and such loans, if made at all, should be made free of interest; in the latter an economic service is being rendered, for which payment in the form of interest can quite properly be charged. But what about the money-lender who lends money to a poor man to enable him to buy a wedding present for his daughter, to be repaid, at a high rate of interest but with no security and heavy transaction costs, over the next two years? If we discountenance such loans, as we traditionally do, we are paternalistically taking from him the control over his own life that we give to the Yuppie mortgaging his future earnings to buy a house. It may be right to restrict the poor man's freedom of choice in this instance: though people generally are, they are not necessarily nor always, the best judges of their own interests. Although thou mightest now sincerely and wholeheartedly want to borrow money from me to buy a present for thy daughter—or a drink for thyself—it is not in your long-term interest to saddle yourself with repayments over the next two years. And if that be the case, I ought not to lend you the money, any more than I should rip you off over the sale of goods.

Investment is in the same case as other profitable activity. It is not inherently wrong, but it is not necessarily all right. It is not wrong to make a profit from financial transactions—on the contrary, that is a sign that they are valued by our fellow men. But the fact that activities are valued by our fellow men is not conclusive evidence that they are morally acceptable—as every woman knows. Market indications of value may be overridden by evaluations based on fuller information or more general principles.

The actual problems of the ethical investor are much more ones of application than of principle. It is fairly easy not to buy shares in armaments manufacturers or tobacco firms. It is quite difficult to decide whether investing in South Africa does more good or more harm than not investing. It is exceedingly difficult to determine how far responsibility extends: is a bank bad because it provides banking facilities for bad firms? Is a chemical manufacturer bad if it sells chemical substances which are then used by others to make poison gas? There is a partial veil of ignorance, and even more of unconcern, which blocks the attribution of responsibility for the remote effects of our business transactions.

The veil of ignorance can be penetrated, and the veil of unconcern is not absolute. In time past it was a common tactic to inform landlords if one of their houses was being used as a brothel, so that they could invoke the relevant clause in the lease, or insert one and let to a new tenant when the lease came up for renewal. A shareholder is more than entitled to apprise the board of directors of any shady business on the part of their firm. The standard response of directors is to tell the shareholder to mind his own business, to which the proper reply is that it *is* his business. Beyond that, if the last word of the directors is, as it all too often is, to get lost, there lies the annual general meeting, when the directors are legally obliged to listen, and will be, provided that the press have been briefed in advance, deeply embarrassed at having to do so in public.

British financial culture, by contrast with American, is deeply passive and apathetic. Most shares are held by institutions, often insurance companies, who do not want to know of the failings, even obvious economic failings, of the firms they invest in. Rather than intervene, they sell. It is less trouble. It is also intellectually and morally lazy. It is for this reason, along with the increasing dishonesty and sharp practice of recent years, that the City has been falling in public esteem. It is failing in its responsibilities for the investments it controls. By concentrating exclusively on short-term profits, it jeopardises long-term profitability and social acceptability, and invites ham-handed regulation by incompetent governments.

The responsible investor ought on occasion to raise his voice, but should not realistically expect it to be effective. He is witnessing to important principles, rather than altering the course of events. The most he can hope for is that he will help alter the general climate of opinion, so that in time to come managers will follow more enlightened principles. In practice, the only way to escape responsibility for dubious enterprises is to sell the shares, making public one's reasons for doing so. Although the actual effect will be minimal, the message may be picked up—and is one that both the board and other shareholders fear—and it does relieve the erstwhile shareholder of responsibility for what is being done.

It is difficult to strike a balance between the good and the harm done by a firm's activities, between the virtue of retaining shares and continuing to needle the directors, and of getting out of the business and being shot of it altogether. It is important to be humble in one's own moral judgements, and to remember that in a market, as in any society which takes other people seriously, a lot of things are not my business: though I ought not to let my house for immoral purposes, I should do wrong as a bus driver if I refused to pick up a prostitute on her way to the West End.[16]

8.16. RESPONSIBLE GIVING

Money is disposable. We can give it away. And sometimes we feel that not to give it away is wrong, and that to spend any money on ourselves is selfish wickedness. More often we compromise, and take out some covenants to the National Trust and a few favoured charities, and eat, drink, and consult our accountant about what to do with the rest.

Although money is highly disposable at the margin, it is not indefinitely so in large amounts. I can give £10 to Oxfam without difficulty, but if we were to try and redistribute £10 million from our admittedly well-heeled neighbours, we should certainly disrupt the local economy, disappoint legitimate expectations, and might well paralyse the goose from laying golden eggs. Money lubricates existing patterns of co-operation, and only if that co-operation is maintained, is there any co-operators' surplus to distribute. We cannot extrapolate from small acts of generosity to large ones, or argue that since money is disposable, it can be

---

[16] For a much fuller discussion, see Richard Harries, *Is There a Gospel for the Rich: Christian Obedience in a Capitalist World*, London, 1992.

redisposed on a large scale. Moreover, once we acknowledge that our negative responsibilities do not extend without limit, we need not feel obliged to respond to all calls on our generosity. Sometimes it is an adequate answer to say "I have already bought a flag" or "I subscribe to another charity in that field". More generally, we need to recognise that we are persons, that is to say selves, who are able to operate in the world only by virtue of having bodies, and that we are properly concerned with our selves as selves and with our bodily needs. Too often we have been misled by Plato's assumption that since selfishness is a vice, selflessness is a virtue. But it is not. If I am completely selfless, I am denying my humanity, and destroying the basis of fellow feeling with my fellow men. Although there are some goals—the discovery of mathematical truth—which can be pursued without benefit of humanity, most—even most academic ones and certainly those that concern us in social and political life—require some measure of human understanding on our part. We need to be men if we are to get on with and understand our fellow men, among whom we live and move and have our being.

As men we have particular needs, particular ties, and particular ideals. Although my money is inherently transferable, and could be given to anyone or any good cause, I am not a donative unit, but an individual person, whose life is necessarily lived among family, friends, colleagues, and compatriots. Money spent on distant good causes is effectively anonymous: money spent on local festivities carries a message as well. For most of us, our contribution lies not only in our donations to charities, but in our work and social life. They need money spending on them. It is different in primitive economies, where money is peripheral to the daily life of most people, but in a world of trains and taxis and telephone calls, money is used at every stage to facilitate the ordinary business of life, and a person without it is unable to be fully a person, support a family, do things with friends, or make a meaningful pattern of his life. But these are good purposes. Once we accept that we are persons, we should aim to fulfil ourselves as persons, living a meaningful life among friends and with our families. Spending money on them is not something we should feel bad about.

It does not follow that we should always turn a deaf ear to charitable entreaties, or that all self-sacrifice is foolish. On the contrary, we all ought to acknowledge the claims of humanity, and for some self-fulfilment is to be found in austere life-styles with few material possessions. It is difficult, indeed misleading, to attempt to lay down guidelines. The biblical tithe has been raised to 17.5 per cent in VAT, and 25 per cent for most personal incomes, but the analogy is misleading, since much of our tax revenue is used to finance activities from which we benefit, and should be seen as a sort of payment rather than redirection of our earnings to the needs of others. Some people are hard put to it to find further funds to give away, but many are visibly spending money on unrewarding purchases. Few of us err on the side of actually giving too much to charity. Our trouble is, rather, that we think we ought to be giving more, but grudge actually doing so, and compromise by hating ourselves for our meanness or out of a mistaken idea of morality, and not enjoying the good things we lavish on our unloved selves.

8.17. MONEY

The fact that money obtains its value by conferring choice affects our understanding of its moral properties. In so far as it increases the individual's range of choice, it is a good thing, and equally it is good in extending our opportunities of concerting our actions in cases where the benefit would, in the absence of monetary transfers, accrue unevenly or to some partners not at all. But it also increases the burden of responsibility on the individual, who cannot disclaim many obligations on the score of not being able to discharge them. In the division of the co-operators' surplus each party is locked into an adversarial position, where his gain is somebody else's loss. And for many, many people money becomes an idol, not only for the good things it enables its possessors to enjoy, but also as a tangible token of success, a proof that one has won in the battle of life, and a means of demonstrating one's superiority over others. Although there are other idols—power, sex, prestige, even knowledge—the love of which engenders evil, the love of money is, of all the roots of evil, the most widely distributed.

Because money can take over, many feel that the only safe course is to abjure it altogether, as others are called to give up drink, or sex, or power, or to shun the limelight and look round for bushels to hide under. Such sacrifices, perfectly proper though they are for some, are not incumbent on us all. Total abstinence is not the only alternative to total surrender, and wise moderation is for most people what they ought to aim at.

Addictiveness apart, money presents two special problems in its responsible use: its adversarial aspect and its impersonality. The former can be dealt with by recognising that though business transactions are non-tuistic, they can, and should be, vosistic: we can have a general idea of the interests of the sort of people who want to purchase our wares or enjoy our services, and should ensure that they do not get a bad bargain. Although mediaeval ideas of the just price and just wage are too rigid to be applicable, the ideal of fair dealing is one we can apply to all sorts of situations in all sorts of circumstances, and will enable a responsible man to give an acceptable account of his business dealings.

The impersonality of money and the market is, as we have seen, a merit as well as a disadvantage. It liberates the individual from a suffocating web of personal obligations, and extends his freedom of choice. It transmits some relevant items of information very effectively, and enables us to make use of the efforts of remote operators. It is often taken to constrain our choices completely, so that we have no choice but to act as the market dictates, and no information other than that mediated through the price mechanism. But that, as we have seen, is a mistaken view. We have some room for manœuvre, and have other sources of information besides what is indicated by the market. We cannot, as individuals, do very much, and are not, as individuals, responsible for very much. But that is inevitably the nature of the case. It is a big beach.

Chapter 9
The Responsibilities of Office

9.1. DUTIES

If I take on an office—from the Latin *officium*, a duty—I render myself answerable for any failure on my part to do whatever needs to be done; and, conversely, if I have a negative responsibility, so that I am obliged to have an answer to the question "Why did you not . . .?", I must have some sort of duty. Else, I could brush off the question with a simple "Why should I?" Also I must have some power. 'Ought' implies 'can'. If I am to be held to account for things I have not done, they must be things I could have done, or again the question will not strike home. Responsibility and duty are correlative: if I am to have responsibility for something, I have to have the authority and power to act so as to discharge it. Responsibility thus implies, and is almost the equivalent of, 'power' or 'authority' in modern usage, or the Latin *provincia* in its original sense.[1]

We have some duties arising from the nature of the case. But such duties either are limited in scope or arise only occasionally, for the same reasons as were adduced against our being negatively responsible for everything.[2] For the most part, therefore, entirely general considerations will not determine our duties or negative responsibilities to see to it that certain bad things do not happen or that certain good states of affairs are maintained. Instead, our responsibilities are assigned. We take on obligations, and are commissioned to carry out various functions. Sometimes a person is specifically chosen for a job, and his duties are detailed when he is commissioned; in other cases he just comes to be in a position where he is expected to undertake a task, and is accorded the authority needed for carrying it out successfully. The very grant of a responsible commission either presupposes, or else confers, the requisite powers to carry out the task

[1] See §3.8.   [2] See §§3.4 to 3.6.

assigned. The power may not be very great, but at least it needs
to comprise some authority, and a right to adjure and cajole.
Often authorisation is important, although it is not obvious why
it should be needed. Against a general background assumption of
individual freedom, it might seem that each could do as he saw
fit, and answer for it in due course. But often we are acting in a
social context less individualistic than we suppose: people may
murmur "It is not his place to be doing that". Often, too, to act
involves trespassing on others' spheres of action: it is not that
what I do in the discharge of my official duties causes them
harm, but only that it does impinge, and could be construed as
infringing their liberty of action. We develop complicated co-
ordination norms, and these need to be modified if some new
common purpose is to be achieved, and a warrant is required for
my modifying them my way rather than someone else's doing so
some other way. However I come to hold it, an office confers a
complex bundle of authorities, duties, and responsibilities. I can
refer to my position to justify my taking decisions rather than
leaving it to someone else, to accord to those reasons that
weighed with me the weight that they ought to have in view of
what I was supposed to be doing, and to accept the legitimacy of
questions being directed to me rather than to anyone else.

9.2. RESPONSIBLE TO

Although I may be responsible for something, I may not be
responsible to some particular person. The question 'Why did
you do it?' or 'Why did you not do it?' may fail not because of
any internal defect, nor because it is wrongly addressed, but
because the questioner is not entitled to ask the question of me.
'Mind Your Own Business', I may say. Even though I may be
responsible, and may have to answer for my actions on the Day
of Judgement, I am not responsible to you. So far as you are
concerned, it was for me to make the decision, and you are not
to question it. In an army or a business we have a clear chain of
command and demarcation of responsibilities, and subordinates
are responsible only to their superiors, and need not, and often
must not, account for their actions to anyone else. In other cases,
I am responsible to you only in special cases or under some

special description. I have a duty of care towards you, *qua* neighbour, or purchaser, or client. If the goods I sell you subsequently turn out to be unsatisfactory, you can properly ask me to account for their poor performance, but Peter cannot, unless he can claim to be acting on your behalf, or as a representative of the public interest. I am not responsible to him, and need not, unless I choose to, answer correctly formulated questions correctly addressed to me, which are asked by him rather than by someone I am responsible to.

If I am responsible to someone, he is entitled to ask me why I did what I did, and I am obliged to answer him. This normally carries with it a further entitlement on his part to assess my reasons authoritatively, and reprimand me if they were bad, and instruct me for the future not to act on them again. This constitutes a chain of responsibility with subordinates responsible to those higher up being obliged not only to justify their actions to them but to accept guidance on how they should discharge their responsibilities in the future.

Where there is a chain of responsibility, responsibility is shared upwards. If I am responsible to you, you are responsible for what I do. The superior is responsible for what his subordinates do, because he can correct their reasoning. It is up to him to ensure that they are reasoning aright, and their decisions and actions can therefore be presumed to be in accordance with his intentions. At some stage the presumption fades into fiction, as in modern constitutional practice, where the minister is "responsible for" the actions of myriads of civil servants who are for the most part acting without either his consent or his knowledge. At the time of Crichel Down the Minister of Agriculture resigned after civil servants in the Department of Agriculture had been too zealous in promoting the public interest at the expense of private individuals, but common sense has since then eroded the doctrine, and ministers now do not regard themselves as responsible for what their departments do. This is right—but it requires a considerable rethinking of constitutional principle that has yet to take place.

It is often supposed that whenever I am responsible for something, I must be responsible to someone. After all, office-holders do not always decide aright. Often we cannot correct them, and have to bear with their mistakes as best we may, but sometimes we must review their decisions, particularly when they are in dispute with one another. We, and so also they, are only partly reasonable, only partly co-operative. There are many genuine disagreements about what ought to be done, and we often get on high horses and refuse to acknowledge the rightfulness of the other chap's opinion, just because it is his and not ours. We have to resolve disputes. This requires us to be apprised of the reasons behind the actions and proposed actions of the parties concerned, and to take a view of their strength. To that extent they must be not only responsible, but responsible to some authority.

The argument is a version of Hobbes' argument for there being an all-powerful sovereign, and fails for the same reason as his does.[3] Not all disputes are intractable, and in many cases we can live with a dispute being left undecided. Although the decisions taken by office-holders may be wrong, and the decisions given in justification bad, they are not all wrong, and there is some pressure towards adducing reasons which are, and are recognised by others as being, sound.

In practice the Crichel Down case illustrates the severe limitations to the extent to which *being responsible to* can actually control what an official does, and officials need to be responsible in a much wider sense than merely being responsible to some particular body. This follows from a theoretical limitation on the extent they can be called to account.

9.3. ACCOUNTABILITY

Although I need to attend to the questions of those who commissioned me to undertake some duty, I do not have to answer all their questions in minute detail: if I have some special duty, I thereby have an adequate answer to the question "Why did you do it?" I did it because it was my duty, my job, my commission. Every commission carries with it some discretion, some authority to decide as one thinks fit. Even if my commission is simply to go to the shop and buy a pound of sugar, I am thereby granted some right to choose, to decide which side of the road to walk along, which foot to step out with first. Unless there is some

[3] See §10.3, and J. R. Lucas, *The Principles of Politics*, Oxford, 1966 and 1985, §8.

reason for not doing what I did—for example, that that side of the road was dangerous—I cannot be faulted for carrying out my commission in the way that seemed good to me. For if my commission had been to walk on a particular side of the road, that could have been specified at the outset. Sometimes duties are specified minutely, and sometimes it is appropriate to do so, but there is a cost: the more closely a man is tied down by his instructions, the less he can be landed with the negative responsibility to see to it that things go well generally within his sphere of responsibility. If I specify exactly what route you are to take to get to the shop, and that route is blocked by roadworks, I cannot complain when you return empty-handed: you had not told me to go to the shop, but only to go to it a particular way, which task it proved impossible to perform. And so, *per contra*, if we ask someone to take on a negative responsibility, we *eo ipso* confer on him some authority to take decisions as seem best to him, and implicitly agree to accept his judgement in the absence of weighty reasons not to. So accountability is inherently limited: nobody can be required to answer for everything; in so far as people take on negative responsibilities, they acquire some right to have their judgement respected as regards the positive decisions they take.[4]

The underlying rationale for limiting accountability lies in the nature of reason. We find it difficult to articulate reasons; however much we specify reasons, we find occasions when it is reasonable to do something which outruns the reasons we have specified. Aristotle argues for ἐπιείκεια (*epieikeia*), usually translated 'equity', at the end of book v of the *Nicomachean Ethics*, and Gödel's theorem shows it an ineliminable feature of mathematical reasoning. We therefore cannot lay down somebody's duties completely and precisely, but must allow him some discretion. Moreover, it is inexpedient to tie him down too tightly, because, as we have seen,[5] we find it difficult to articulate reasons and often λόγον ἔχειν (*logon echein*), have reason, but cannot λόγον διδόναι (*logon didonai*), give it in verbal form: if we require people to act only on reasons they can subsequently give, we are preventing them acting on hunch or other intuitive reasons they believe are cogent but could not defend to a hostile questioner.

---

[4] See further §10.2, p. 208.   [5] See §4.2.

Instead of asking myself whether I am really doing my job properly, I concentrate on making sure that I can answer the questions other people may put to me when they are trying to haul
me over the coals. And other people's questions are easier to
parry than my own. Many people are severer judges of themselves than anyone else would dare to be, and have more intimate knowledge of failures and inadequacies, and can hold
themselves to account more exactingly than anybody else.

'Responsible to' is a partial, not complete, explication of
'responsible'. No superior can supervise all his subordinates' doings. They have, for the most part, to act on their own. They
need to be responsible, as well as responsible to, and not only do
what they are told, but identify with the values of their superior,
their firm, their minister, or their department.[6]

9.4. GIVING AN ACCOUNT

If I cannot brush off the question "Why did you not do it?" with
the counter-question "Why should I?", it is on account of there
being some retort "Because it is your business to do such and
such" which specifies the nature of my job, and hence also the
sort of answers I can give to the original question "Why did you
not do it?" and to further questions as to why I did whatever I
did do. The lollipop lady can justify her actions on the score of
children's safety, but not as a means towards inculcating Latin
grammar, or as an expression of her commitment to world peace.
A judge, a policeman, a civil servant, and a soldier all have public responsibilities, but very different ones, which require them to
be guided by different reasons in the discharge of their duties. So,
too, parents and children, friends and colleagues, have different
duties towards one another, and hence different types of acceptable reason that can be given in justification of actions, and are
allowed greater or less latitude in deciding how those duties are
best discharged. In general, the more senior an official is, the
wider the range of things a man is responsible for, and the more
momentous his success or failure, the greater the discretion
allowed him; when people complained to Abraham Lincoln that

---

[6] For a further argument, see §10.2 and §10.3, pp. 208–9 and 211.

General Grant drank, Lincoln is reported to have asked which brand of whisky he drank, so that he could send some to his other generals. It makes a difference, too, whether we are primarily concerned to minimise the damage wrong decisions can do, or to maximise the good that might be achieved if all goes well. Civil servants, trustees, and doctors could wreak havoc if they were negligent; so we tie them down closely, and are quick to mark if they do anything amiss. Poets, philosophers, scientists, and artists are in no position to do anyone great harm by a bad decision, and are not much good either if they merely keep their noses clean, and take care not to stray from the path of rectitude; a maximax, rather than a maximin, strategy is therefore appropriate, and a firm is content if the millions it has spent on research and development bring forth one winner amid a plentiful crop of blind alleys and failed inventions.

Nearly always some sorts of reasons are excluded. It is acceptable for me, as a private individual, to decide to buy a hat on whim, or to seek to please a girl by going in for a tournament, but I am not supposed to be guided by caprice, self-interest, fear, or favour when I am acting in an official capacity. Caprice is no reason at all, and the others, though intelligible, are not ones that would commend themselves to someone else.

Consequences are always relevant where negative responsibilities have been assumed. If I undertake responsibility, then not only is it my duty to see to it that bad things do not happen, but I carry the can if, despite my efforts, they do. Hence all my deliberations are suffused with a negative consequentialism. I cannot simply decide to do what seems the right thing to do, but must consider carefully the outcome of my decision, and take care not to do anything that might result in something untoward. Often the office-holder will justify his actions to the high-minded critic by saying, "It is all very well for you to say I ought to have been more understanding, and given him another chance. Indeed, it would have been kind, and he might have made it. But I would have had to carry the can if there had been an accident, and passengers had been hurt." An office-holder has to live with the consequences of his decisions, and the wider the responsibility he undertakes, the more he is constrained by the need to ensure that untoward events do not—and, more insistently, cannot—happen. He is constantly having to forgo the best in order to forestall the worst. Whereas the private individual, who is responsible for, and to, only himself, can afford to be high-minded and hope that others will be high-minded too, those who undertake office have to consider not only what ought to be the consequences in an ideal world, but what will be the consequences in this actual world, of what they do or do not do. The weight of responsibility not only bears on their time and their thoughts, but also burdens their consciences by making them regularly embark on courses which are far from being even a second-best, and which, even though the least of the available evils, seem disturbingly evil none the less.

The "lesser of two evils" is a dangerous doctrine. It can be invoked to legitimise some fairly evil courses. I may feel obliged to do on behalf of my country, my college, my family, all sorts of thing I should be ashamed to do for myself. My responsibilities may require me to act more prudently and less generously than I should naturally like, and the decisions I have taken may leave a nasty taste in the mouth. I am constrained to live in an imperfect world of cause and effect, where what I do cannot manifest the good intentions I should like to direct to those I have to deal with, but must be fettered by the need to take great thought for the morrow, what others shall eat and put on, who look to me to guard them against all manner of adverse changes and chances. Since things are what they are, and their consequences will be what they will be, we have good reason to be afraid of what might come to pass were we to act on the highest principles alone without exercising also a due measure of serpentine wisdom.

But consequences are not all-important. Inasmuch as negative responsibilities alter the answers that can be properly given, the questions too should be similarly amended. Inapposite questioning may make some office-holders feel uncomfortable, but lets others off the hook. Only if we are ready to acknowledge the relevance of consequences, can we pertinently question the man who has not weighed rightly the importance of principles also.

9.5. JUDICIAL AND POLYCENTRIC RESPONSIBILITIES

Judicial reasoning is in many respects untypical, but has often been taken as the paradigm way a responsible official should decide what to do in the carrying out of his commission, and thus has led to some misunderstanding of what he should actually be doing. We need to consider the judicial responsibilities of judges, not only to understand what they ought to do, but to realise how other judgements are properly reached by others whose responsibilities are different.

A judge adjudicates between two parties, each claiming to have right on his side. He must address himself to the individuals who are parties to the case; for that reason he must hear both sides of the case, and give full weight to the arguments adduced on either side. He concentrates his attention on the point at issue, and arguments adduced by either side for the decision being given in their favour. In deciding, he necessarily is deciding against one party, and in civil cases owes it to the disappointed party to explain why the decision had to go against him. Hence the need for giving reasons in public, but hence also the somewhat limited scope of the reasoning. Furthermore, because the reasons have to be very cogent if they are to persuade the disappointed party that he was reasonably decided against, they are implicitly omni-personal and universalisable, thus setting precedents for future decisions also.

Because judgements set precedents and need to be guided by them, the administration of justice tends to become complicated and cumbersome. The antithesis between justice and legality is widely felt, and re-emerges in each generation as a demand for some sort of equity to loosen the stranglehold of lawyers' law. Up to a point the demand is naïve. Justice is not completely determinate, and indeed there are conflicting canons of justice, so that there is no one naturally just solution, and the boundary between one man's right and another's must be, in part, a matter of legitimate expectation founded on convention. But although we cannot reckon on the just decision being always apparent to all men, intimations of justice are often widely shared, and too often are not encapsulated by the existing law. In the judicial oath "to do justice according to law" the legal qualifier has often become dominant, and the substantial commitment to justice eviscerated.

Often also the substantial commitment to justice is diluted by procedural requirements. Procedural requirements have their part to play: it is easy to reach a hasty or partial decision through not stopping to survey all the possibilities, or not adequately attending to one party's side of the case. Moreover, the law is a co-ordination norm, enabling individual citizens to conduct their affairs so as not to run foul of one another: it therefore needs to be publicly recognisable, and hence formal. But if procedural requirements are multiplied, the judicial frame of mind is lost. Instead of giving his mind to the substantial question at issue, the judge is concerned simply to go through the right hoops to ensure that his decision cannot later be faulted on procedural grounds. In all judicial processes there is a possibility that in the end a decision will be reached which is adverse to someone's central or chartered interest, and it is incumbent on anyone acting in a judicial capacity at some stage to give his mind to the question whether the decision should go against that person. It is proper to hold back from facing that question for a season, while all the relevant considerations are gathered in, but wrong not to focus on it while the issue is still fresh, before the mind has begun to harden towards some particular conclusion.

Other officers make decisions affecting people, but with other responsibilities. Unlike the judge, they are not concentrating on a single question at issue between two parties, and are not addressing their reasoning to the party that is losing the case. The bowler positions his men on the field so as to stop runs or get a catch, and may thereby give some fielder the opportunity to enhance his reputation, or deprive another of any such chance; he would be open to criticism if he did the latter out of spite, but is not otherwise required to give consideration to the hopes of each player. Winning the game is the point of the exercise, and it is right for only minimal consideration to be given to the interests of each individual. The same is true in the army, in business, and in many other organizations. The centre of concern is not concentrated on one or two particular individuals, but embraces many, or is not focused on individuals at all. Such "polycentric"[7] decision-making cannot give maximum consideration to each individual affected. Often it is concluded that it need not give any. But that does not follow. Sometimes, indeed, individuals waive all right to consideration, and want only to be used to

---

[7] I owe this term, and many insights, to Professor R. S. Summers of Cornell University.

further some great purpose; but often they are less than totally willing to submerge their whole identity in the common enterprise, and want, and deserve, some consideration by decision-makers. How much consideration should be shown to an individual depends partly on what interest will be affected, partly on the nature of the enterprise. The more important and central the interest, the greater the consideration: conversely, the more integral the action is to the enterprise, the more readily ensuring that it be done well should override the interests of some individual involved.

These truisms seem trite, but have often been obscured in political and legal philosophy, because we have supposed that if a question is justiciable at all, it must be completely dominated by canons of justice, so that if evidently other considerations must be taken into account, the decision cannot be a judicial one and considerations of justice should be excluded altogether. A citizen of the United States cannot be deprived of life, liberty, or property except by due process of law; but what about his reputation, possession of a passport, or licence to practise as a doctor? In conducting an examination I owe it to each candidate to give attention to his entry, and to be on the lookout for his merits as well as his faults, but I do not have to prove beyond all reasonable doubt that he should not be passed or given a good mark, and it would be perfectly proper, having considered the marks that other candidates have got, to draw the line with him below it rather than above. Public inquiries often result in orders which greatly damage the interests of some individuals. British law has sought to exclude all considerations of justice from their conduct on the grounds that they cannot be simply an adjudication of rights, and must therefore be an untrammelled exercise of the executive arm of government. But that is a fiction it has become increasingly difficult to sustain. The minister needs to be answerable not only to Parliament for the policies he promotes, but to the individuals who may be adversely affected, and show that in pursuing those policies he has also been sensitive to their interests, minimising the damage to them, and not attaining departmental goals at whatever cost to the citizens of the country he seeks to serve. In a wide variety of positions our decisions impinge on individuals, who ought to be the objects of our care and consideration. Canons of justice apply—not the elaborate procedures of the law courts with their artificial rules of evidence and burdens of proof that are often impossible to discharge, but a reasoned regard for each person who might be adversely affected as well as for other people and the general aims of the enterprise.

9.6. PROFESSIONAL RESPONSIBILITY

Professional people give themselves airs. They regard themselves as more responsible than other men, and like others to think so too. In other walks of life, people aspire to professional status, form professional associations, write letters after their names, and hope to hold their heads high too.

The responsibility of a professional man contrasts both with that of a businessman in his business relations and with that of the individual in his personal relations. Ordinary business relations are non-tuistic.[8] If I am doing business with you, it is not my job to make up thy mind as to what is really the best for thee, even though I ought to have regard for the customer's point of view, and give you what anyone in your position should regard as a fair deal. But beyond that I do not have to go. If there is a market for my wares, I do not need further justification: in the end it is up to the lady to decide whether she likes the hat.[9] A professional man, by contrast, has no customers whose value-judgements he can accept as conclusive. I go to a doctor because I do not know what is wrong with me, and cannot judge what would be the best treatment. If a double-glazing contractor offers to do my windows, it is for me to decide whether I really want them done, whether it will really be a saving in the long run: but if a doctor offers me a face-lift or a hysterectomy, I cannot reach a rational decision on my own. It would be highly unprofessional for him to talk me into an expensive operation which would line his pocket, but not improve my health.[10] A professional man ought to be guided in all that he says and does not by his own interests but by those of the people, or the God, or the ideals, he serves. The doctor puts himself in my position, considers my interests, does the best he can for

---

[8] See §8.3, p. 146.   [9] See §8.3, p. 147.   [10] See §5.5, p. 82.

me, and advises me what would be best from my point of view. In the same way a solicitor should try to keep his client out of court, even though some litigation would be greatly to the advantage of the solicitor. A schoolmaster should not stand in the way of a pupil transferring to another school, if that would be in his best interest. Similarly, too, the priest serves God, and seeks to advance His kingdom, rather than his own comfort or preferment, and the academic pursues truth, and should not lend his name to an intellectually dishonest piece of work, even though it is very much in line with contemporary fashion, and likely to be well received.

The assumed ignorance of the patient, the client, or the pupil is the correlative of the esoteric knowledge and values of the profession. Long training has given the professional an expertise and dedication which enable and entitle him to make up somebody else's mind for him and decide what is in his best interests. He defends his decisions by reference to the ideals and standards of his profession, not instructions from a superior or the pressures of the market. He is responsible, but not responsible to anyone.

9.7. FEES

The immediate objection to this picture of disinterested service is that professional men charge fees, and seek professional advancement. Occasionally a priest turns down the offer of a bishopric, or a schoolmaster the offer of a headship, but most professional men seek preferment, being susceptible not only to the last infirmity of a noble mind, but to the loaves and fishes which usually accompany greater responsibilities. Some are uneasy about it, and think it would be better if all professional services were rendered entirely altruistically, without thought of reward, but, recognising the impracticability of that, continue to pocket their fees while trying not to think about it.

It would be better if they did think about it. There are two reasons why the professional labourer should not be ashamed to receive his hire. If we suggest that he ought not to seek for any reward save that of knowing that he has done a good job, we restrict entry into the profession to those who have some other source of income or are prepared to live in great poverty. The Foreign Service at one time was open only to the rich, and the clergy in many countries are required to be celibate and cheap to maintain. But rich people are not always the best diplomats, and may have, and give, a distorted view of what is going on; and though there are other, much better, arguments for clerical celibacy and plenty of problems with married ones, some wifeless priests fall into sin or solitariness, and family life has not only supported many of the clergy of the Church of England, but enabled them and their wives to be more integrated with their parishioners, and fulfil their ministry far better.

A less obvious, but more telling, consideration arises from the nature of professional service itself. Although altruism is possible, it is for many people incredible. They cannot believe that someone else would put himself out for their benefit, and so are shy about asking. I hesitate to call the doctor out, because I fear my aches and pains will prove imaginary, and I shall have called him out needlessly. But if I am paying, I need not worry about trespassing on his good will. Eliza Doolittle offered Professor Higgins money to teach her how to speak proper. That entirely altered the aspect of the situation. He was not doing her a favour, but undertaking a professional obligation, which he had to discharge well if he was to retain his professional standing. The fee both confers on those outside the magic circle of the old-boy network the opportunity to avail themselves, simply because they are so minded, of professional services, and imposes on the professional a contractual obligation to do his best, which he cannot wriggle out of later, as he might if he had been giving purely voluntary help. In the years since the Second World War we have in Britain established a free National Health Service, and more or less free university education. Much of it has been very good, and many doctors and dons have maintained high professional standards. But a certain unsolicitude for the idiosyncratic interests of patients and undergraduates has manifested itself. Patients are having good done to them by doctors, and ought to be jolly grateful for the services they receive, and not complain if they are kept waiting for hours for an appointment or years for an operation; undergraduates are jolly lucky to be at university at all, and must not bother their tutors out of hours with their piffling problems. It would be better if patients and

undergraduates were encouraged to be somewhat more demanding, and to think that they were, though necessarily ignorant of
where their true interests lay, none the less entitled to some
extent to call the tune.

Fees, although they seem to weaken the claim that professional
services are rendered disinterestedly and not subject to distortion
by self-interested considerations, do serve to ensure that those
services are not rendered as a favour, but subject to stringent
standards of professional obligation, with some regard to the
rights of the individual concerned. But though they enlarge
choice, they also restrict the numbers of those able to exercise it.
It is good to allow anyone who wants to pay the fee to have
access to professional services, but not to make poverty a bar to
having them at all. And the receipt of money is not by itself
enough to ensure that in all other respects the professional acts
in a fiduciary way. Many insurance brokers both charge fees and
take commissions from insurance companies to guide business in
their direction irrespective of whether it is the best policy for the
client to buy. Other forms of remuneration are required besides
fees, and other safeguards of integrity than competition for business.

9.8. CONFLICT OF DUTIES

The traditional account, that the duty of the professional man is
to serve his client's interests, not his own, is too *simpliste*. For
one thing, not all professions have clients: the research scientist
and the journalist may be guided by professional values, but they
are not the interests of any assignable individual. Even where
there are definite individuals involved, it is sometimes not clear
whose interests are to be served, or whether those interests override other interests involved. If I am writing a reference for a
pupil, is my duty towards those to whom the letter is addressed,
or him about whom it is written? Traditional British understanding has it that I owe a duty of truthfulness towards those I am
addressing, and ought not to conceal factors which might tell
against the success of the candidate himself: modern transatlantic
practice holds that the duty is towards the candidate, and the
writer should do his best to get him the job. Apart from the con-

sequentialist objection, that the result of the new practice is an inflation of testimonials which renders them all useless, and forces institutions back on to the old-boy network in order to appoint suitable candidates, it is a sin against truth. Academics, and teachers generally, ought to value truth. Once we allow any force to that consideration, we can no longer seek to elucidate professional responsibility in terms of individual interests alone.

Even when there is someone to whom a prime duty is owed, there may also be duties to other, actual or potential, patients, pupils, or clients, and duties to the community at large. An infectious patient may infect others, a pupil given to bullying or stealing may make life intolerable for others. Up to a point we may resolve the apparent conflict by reckoning that the interests that are imputed to the individual as a basis for the professional's care of him are based on some concept of the reasonable man, and are circumscribed by the obligations that the reasonable man would acknowledge.[11] If you diagnose me as having typhoid, you can reasonably expect me not to want to spread the infection, and to be willing to take proper precautions, and if I say I am not interested in that, you are not then obliged to keep quiet about the danger I may be exposing others to. The duty to the individual is not absolute, though sometimes we may, for good reason, confer an absolute protection, as with the seal of the confessional or the privileged communications between solicitor and client.

Problems have arisen recently over AIDS, whether patients should be tested with, or without, their consent, whether the fact that a patient, or a medical employee, is infected should be disclosed. Our appreciation of the issues is distorted by the practice of insurance companies, the fears of the populace, and the vociferousness of the AIDS lobby. It is easier to think out how we should respond to other infections. In nearly every case we should attach paramount importance to not spreading a life-threatening condition. In time past a doctor who had contracted TB was required not to expose patients to the risk of catching it from him. If someone were dying from Green Monkey disease, all possible precautions should be taken to protect members of the medical staff from dying from it too. Nobody with cholera

---

[11] See §8.4, pp. 149–51 and §8.14, pp. 171–2.

should be allowed in a kitchen. But how far should doctors go in finding out and revealing unwelcome facts? General screening, like compulsory vaccination, is an invasion of privacy, not to be lightly insisted upon. Where it is relevant to the treatment that may be needed, or to the safety of the medical staff, it can be justified, though some assessment of the likelihood of infection, the stage at which it would be reasonable to look for it, and the actual hazard to others, should also be taken into account. "Is your test really necessary?" is a question that needs to be routinely raised in an era of over-elaboration.

Other medical dilemmas arise where there is a conflict between the interest of the patient and the rights of others: the interests of the mother against the rights of the unborn child; the interests of a young girl who wishes to be provided with contraceptives against the rights of the parents to know what is being done to their child and to bring her up in a non-promiscuous way of life. In other cases it is the true interests of the patient that are in dispute. Many doctors believe that they are entitled to lie to the patient if they think it would be bad for him to know the truth. But again, apart from the consequentialist disadvantages of this policy, it seems to be a sin against the truth and to derogate from the patient's status as a rational being. Although a patient is deemed to be unable to make informed decisions about his health, he is not necessarily a moral moron who must at all costs be shielded from the truth. Particularly at the limits of medical competence, when life is giving way to death, the interests of the patient are no longer simply to be kept alive and comfortable, but to be able to make his own decisions in the face of unpalatable facts: he may wish to make his will; he may wish to make his peace with his maker, his family, his friends. He may wish not to be resuscitated and artificially kept alive when there is no serious prospect of a real recovery. And if these are what in a calm hour he sets his mind on, then these are part of his interests which the doctor claims to serve. Although interests are what can be ascribed third-personally, they cannot be altogether divorced from first-personal actuality.[12]

Academics and journalists are in a different case from lawyers

---

[12] For a fuller discussion of these and other problems, see M. J. Lockwood, (ed.), *Moral Dilemmas in Modern Medicine*, Oxford, 1985.

and doctors in that they serve abstract ideas as much as people. Truth is difficult to empathize with, and her interests have to be discerned in other ways. We have a fair idea of what it is for an academic to fall down on the score of intellectual honesty: to plagiarize, to mislead, to write an untruthful testimonial, to give the wrong grade in an examination, to give promotion to the unworthy, or to block the promotion of the worthy. The failures are mostly failures of practice. With journalists there is considerable unclarity of principle. Sometimes they claim to be merely in business, concerned solely with circulation or ratings. But few would buy their wares except under the description of their being true. The sale for *Old Moore's Almanack* and the purely fictional newspapers in American supermarkets is small, and though falsehood is often purveyed by newspapers, it is falsehood that is parasitic upon truth. Truthfulness is thus a central value of the journalistic ethic, and carries with it many awkward implications, of not misquoting, not quoting out of context, not "improving" quotations, or putting a general characterization of someone's views into quotation marks. Many of these safeguards are difficult to abide by, especially within the tight time constraints under which journalists work; but their neglect leads to both a loss of public confidence, and also a reluctance to talk on the part of many. It may not matter to a journalist very much if he misrepresents the views of a doctor or a scientist, and leaves out some careful qualification, which to the journalist seems needless verbiage; but it matters very much to the doctor or scientist, who values his professional reputation far more than any amount of public exposure on the box, and would never live down the appearance of having said something silly or injudicious.

Issues of privacy and public acceptability and endorsement also arise. The right to know is not the only, or the most fundamental, of the rights of man: it is severely limited by the right to have one's confidences kept, and the right not to have one's private affairs made public. Academics, too, sometimes go to unreasonable lengths to decipher erasures, and piece together writings meant to be destroyed. Publication, furthermore, impinges on everyone, and carries with it some measure of endorsement. We are fairly well aware of the way in which communist regimes marginalised opponents by denying them publication; we are less sensitive to the argument the other way: that terrorists ought to be denied the oxygen of publicity, that to relay interviews with criminals is to confer on them an air of legitimacy, and that the media ought therefore not to do either, even though there might be a ready market for such material.

Journalism is a relatively new profession, and the responsibilities of journalists have not been properly thought out: the balance between the general obligation to tell the truth and make things known, and particular obligations to particular persons, or special exceptions to the general rule, is difficult to strike, and often depends largely on tone and context. Even in well-established professions there is much unclarity and confusion in the face of new situations giving rise to new questions. There has been a dearth of serious thinking during the past half century, largely due to subjectivist philosophies, which have led people to think that moral judgements are matters of arbitrary choice depending ultimately on feeling, emotion, or taste, not on sensitive discussion, careful argument, and hard thought. That era has happily passed, and now "practical ethics" is being seriously thought about again. But there is much to be done.

9.9. FALLIBILITY

Although most professional people try their best, they may make mistakes, and may be thought to even when they are not in fact mistaken. I may think that I am doing my best for you, but you might not be so sure. A doctor needs to accept the rationality of his patient's doubts on this score, and not only be ready to explain what he is prescribing and why, but to make it very easy for a patient to seek a second opinion. A schoolmaster is not really putting his pupil's interests first if he does not recognise that sometimes it may be in the pupil's interest to move to another school, and his duty to facilitate the transfer, even though it may seem an adverse comment on his school, and may result in pecuniary loss. A tutor should be at pains to make it clear that the tutor–pupil relationship is a highly personal one, and an undergraduate may well find him not *simpatico*, and, if so, smooth the way for alternative tuition. We try our best, but our best is not infallible, and may not seem good enough, and then our duty is to bow out gracefully, and not use our position of superior knowledge and authority to bolster our *amour propre*. Just as a gentleman does not require others to take him on trust, but volunteers security so that they shall not be embarrassed by having to ask for it, so a professional should not expect others to accept that his judgement is infallible, but should pave the way for them to check up on it as much as they wish.

And we do not all try our best. Besides the well-meaning incompetents, there are those whose commitment to professional ideals has entirely evaporated. The public needs to be protected from both. Competition is ineffective. If I do not trust the used-car salesman, I can bring a knowledgeable friend, or shop around; and if I do buy a pup, I shall know better next time. But I cannot check up on the doctor's advice, and if it is bad, I may not live to take myself elsewhere. Peer-group review is necessary, because only our colleagues can know what the standards are.

Many professions have professional associations, and in the Middle Ages guilds were widespread. Besides performing a useful function in helping members to define their professional responsibilities, we often look to them to see that their members live up to them. They are the appropriate institutions to articulate, inculcate, and maintain such standards, since only they have the knowledge to define what is needed, and to recognise when it has been lacking. Peer-group review can be more searching than the uninformed scrutiny of laymen. Trial by jury was originally trial by one's peers, who knew what were the canons of behaviour appropriate to one's walk in life, and could tell whether one's conduct was up to scratch. But peer-group review can become either too lax, or tyrannical. We are too ready to cover up colleagues' mistakes, instead of using our best endeavours to make sure that those who had put their trust in them should have reparation for their neglect, and others in the future should not suffer similarly. Doctors are notoriously unwilling to give evidence against other doctors in malpractice suits. Solicitors seem incapable of disciplining their members so as to provide prompt and competent service to members of the public. Journalists are reluctant to expose the misbehaviour of other journalists. Motorists, whether on the bench or in the jury box, are very lenient towards other motorists who kill or maim other citizens. It was the same with mediaeval guilds and with closed shops in other walks of life. The sense of solidarity with one's colleagues blunts the sense of responsibility towards members of the public generally. It is easy to say "There but for the grace of God go I" as one contemplates some professional lapse, but equally important to think of the patient or pedestrian who lost her life, the widow who lost her inheritance, or the parishioner not given the spiritual counsel she needed for her peace of mind.

It is easy for peer-group review to go soft. But often also it is used to damp down criticism of our ways of doing things, and to prevent innovation. We confuse two different senses of 'responsible to': in one sense the responsibility is to those that are served—it is their interests that the professional man undertakes to look after to the best of his ability; but since they, *ex hypothesi*, are not in a position to evaluate the answers that might be given, the responsibility has to be exercised in another sense to other professionals who alone can tell whether the reasons adduced stand up. One might say that one was responsible *to* one's peers *for* one's care of the person who had sought one's help, or one might say that one was responsible *to* him *before* one's peers. But neither prepositional nicety exactly expresses the underlying logic.

Professions have collective responsibilities not only to their clients and to the community at large, but to potential clients too. There is a standing temptation to restrict entry to the profession by raising the standard required, which provides a Rolls Royce service for those who get it, but means that many go without their Fords. With medical services in particular, one does indeed need to be careful, but medical auxiliaries who are actually available do more for health than highly qualified doctors who are not. A profession needs to take the wider view. So, too, in a different way, lawyers ought to take collective action about the dilatoriness of the law. It is easy for the individual solicitor or barrister to drag his heels when it is in the interests of his client to do so, and pass the buck when his client is suffering from the law's delays, and blame the other side, the courts, or the Inland Revenue. But society suffers. And the legal profession, if it is a profession at all, should take responsibility for identifying and remedying the causes of its failure to serve society properly.

The professions are under attack. In the United States of America they are squeezed between the law courts, which are ready to find malpractice whenever things do not turn out well, and a consumer culture which is intolerant of any suggestion that the professional man is more than a technician providing such services as the customer demands and is willing to pay for. In Britain, too, they are disliked by the egalitarians because of their élitism, by the centralizers because of their insistence on retaining an independence of judgement, and by the free-marketeers because of their refusal to accept the all-sufficiency of market values. And unfortunately they have done much to forfeit public esteem. But it would be a pity if they were to disappear. In their day-to-day practice they offer a third way of organizing affairs, which is neither ordered by the commands of superiors nor governed by market forces. They give to their members a meaning and significance in life not elsewhere to be found. And they embody ideals of great value.

Chapter 10

Responsible Government

Rulers often are responsible. It is a sobering experience to wear a crown, to hold a sceptre, to exercise power; and many tearaway Prince Harrys have become respected King Henry Vs. A supreme governor, a sovereign, a monarch, or a modern government cannot plead inability,[1] the way lesser mortals can, when taxed with having failed to keep things safe and sound, nor can he claim that it was none of his business. He has a general commission to oversee everything, and though not in fact omnipotent, he is normally granted a plenitude of power sufficient for the discharge of his manifold duties. The words which Harry Truman had inscribed on his desk, 'The Buck Stops Here', express the predicament of every government.

Many rulers have been responsible in a further sense. It is not just that they cannot evade the question, but that they have seen their being able to answer it well as constitutive of their role. They have seen themselves not merely as exercising power *de facto*, but as possessing a *de jure* authority deriving from their having been charged to undertake a great responsibility. Their power is not simply a naked *imperium*, a personal possession analogous to private property, for them to do with as they like, but a trust, which they have been called on to carry out for the benefit of the realm, and for which they will answer on the day of judgement.

The day of judgement is often anticipated in the minds of the rulers themselves, who, like most office-holders, seek success. They want not only to have done their job well, but to be recognised as having done it well. Politicians commonly crave not only

---

[1] Louis XV, however, pleaded "Fortunate Powerlessness"; see Bertrand de Jouvenel, *Sovereignty*, tr. J. F. Huntington, Cambridge, 1957, ch. 12, citing declaration to the *Parlement* of July 1717, in Isambert's *Recueil des anciennes lois françaises*, XXI, 146.

power but honour, and hope not only to have exercised power in their time, but in time to come to be held to have exercised it well. It is a natural propensity. Although at the time the holders of power may be able to ride roughshod over the opinions of others, and can say, if they wish, *oderint, dum metuant*—let them hate, so long as they fear, me—with the passage of time their capacity to inspire fear evaporates, and they would like to be loved, or at least well thought of. Augustus published a list of his achievements—his *Res Gestae*—in stone, and many modern statesmen write their memoirs in old age. Although primarily an exercise in vanity, often a defensive note creeps in, as the old man seeks to ward off criticisms and show how right he was to have done as he did, since even though it was misunderstood at the time, it was subsequently vindicated by events, or, alternatively, although with hindsight it would have been better to have done differently, on the information available at the time it was the rational decision to take. Politicians want people to appreciate what they did, and to think well of them. But they are likely to be disappointed. Historians record the follies of politicians and the consequent misfortunes of mankind, but take for granted their wise decisions: the glory of the Augustan age lies in the poets who wrote in it, not the Emperor who presided over it. This lack of recognition is not due just to perverseness on the part of historians, but to the logic of the responsibility of office, which tends for the most part to be a negative responsibility, while our concept of success is dominated by a means-and-ends analysis.

The dominance of means-and-ends analysis goes back at least as far as Aristotle. He most explicitly takes this as his paradigm in his account of βούλευσις (*bouleusis*) in book III of the *Nicomachean Ethics*[2] but his discussion of φρόνησις (*phronesis*) in book VI is clearly much influenced too. It is an approach in which, having adopted certain ends, we concentrate our thoughts on how best to achieve those ends. The intellectual activities of the man responsible for some sphere of concern are, by contrast, not all concentrated, but in part wide-ranging, sizing up the situation as a whole and keeping a weather eye open for potential snags. Although in some cases some *expertise* is necessary, it is

---

[2] *Nicomachean Ethics*, III. 3, 1112ᵃ18–1113ᵃ14; *Eudemian Ethics*, II. 10, 1227ᵃ7–13.

for the most part a generalist's competence that is looked for, the possession of common sense rather than any specialised ability. Specialists are all very well in their field, but all too often hopeless outside it, and practical problems are typically not confined wholly within one speciality but involve other factors which the specialist's narrow vision is unable to register properly. The all-in-all, holistic nature of the responsible man's reasoning stems, fundamentally, from the two points noted in Chapter 3: that all action, just because it is homeostatic, involves a sensitivity to changing circumstances which may require the agent to alter his behaviour to offset them, and that negative responsibility is concerned with possible states of affairs generally, to make sure that no untoward ones occur.[3] Means-and-ends analysis gives a very poor account of what we do in the discharge of responsibilities: we seldom seek to bring about an end *state*, much more often to maintain a certain *condition*, acting so as to restore equilibrium when it is disturbed by adventitious circumstances. Aristotle really knew this: his favourite example is of the doctor trying to restore the patient to health by curing the various illnesses that afflict him. But he was unable to articulate his understanding adequately because he kept trying to do so in terms of effective means towards definite ends. Modern thinkers make the same mistake. They like to construe purposeful action in terms of some end to be achieved, which gives the rationale of the action, and hold that we should always be setting ourselves goals, and working out how to achieve them. And then it is natural to construe success by reference to those ends, and the extent to which they have been realised. And then, it seems, there is nothing most office-holders can show as an achievement they can be proud of. The fact that during their tenure of office they saw to it that no disasters happened escapes notice. The doctor whose timely advice saved his patients from contracting heart disease or cancer, the schoolmaster whose swift intervention saved a child from being bullied on the way back home, the mother whose love and care saved her difficult children from growing up psychological wrecks, the diplomat whose soothing explanations prevented an unintended discourtesy causing a war, all have nothing to show for their pains, because their main concern was the avoidance of

---

[3] See §3.3, p. 38 and §3.7, p. 55.

indeterminate evil rather than the pursuit of some definite good. It is difficult to list things that did not happen, but the real *Res Gestae* of the statesman and all those who undertake wide responsibilities are, for the most part, non-events, the bad things which but for them would have happened, together with the unremarkable fact that thanks to their efforts to maintain the *status quo*, things were no worse when they finished their tenure of office than they had been when they began.[4]

10.2. Εὔθυνα

Although often disappointed, the desire to be well thought of can exercise a powerful influence. If I want people to appreciate what I have done, the reasons I give need to be ones that commend themselves not only to me and my immediate entourage, but to the ruled as well. If the story of my life is simply an account of how I got on in the world, a few people may admire or envy me, but those who were at some stage or other put out by the decisions I made in government will not be reconciled to me by my admission that I was feathering my own nest; whereas if I can maintain that it was for the public good that I crossed them, they may be brought to respect me and remember me for good.

Nevertheless, the desire of the ruler to be well thought of is often ineffective, and the day of judgement is a long way off, or so at least it has seemed to many suffering under the bad decisions of the powers-that-be. Although the distinction between tyrants, who have used power solely for their own benefit and aggrandisement, and benevolent rulers, who have sought the good of their peoples, is fundamental, it does not address the problem of the misguided decisions of well-intentioned governments who, against the considered judgement of those who have to live with them, sincerely believe that their policies are for the best. To remedy that, it is not enough that governments should be responsible to God on the last day, important though that is: it is also requisite that they be answerable to more immediate, if less searching, authorities within the term of this mortal life, indeed very often within their own term of office.

---

[4] I am indebted for the main argument of this section to Sir Geoffrey Vickers, *The Art of Judgement*, London, 1965, pp. 31–5.

The day of judgement can be anticipated by the day of demission, when the office-holder leaves office, and may give an account of his stewardship. Sometimes he makes a speech, sometimes invites questioning, sometimes is subject to formal scrutiny. The Greeks had a formal process, εὔθυνα (*euthuna*), to which magistrates were subjected on demitting office. In most cases it was simply a matter of auditing accounts, but other issues could be raised.[5] Detailed examination can probe deeply, and uncover particular pieces of misbehaviour, but cannot press home general criticisms without subverting the discretion of the office-holder altogether.[6] Pericles was able to brush off enquiry about one particular payment by saying that it was necessary, εἰς τὸ δέον (*eis to deon*);[7] in the Roman Republic retiring magistrates were examined by a panel of knights (*equites*), and it became a highly politicized part of a power struggle between the orders. In a very different context it was possible for judicial investigation to uncover specific misbehaviour on the part of President Nixon, but if impeachment were an easily invoked procedure in which the president's policy decisions could be reviewed and condemned, power would inevitably pass from the President to Congress. Office-holders can be required to account for their tenure of office, and it may be possible to press home very specific criticisms over incontestable lapses from the standards expected of those with public responsibilities, but for the most part we have to accept their reasons as given, and cannot, whatever our private opinion, formally fault them.[8]

In much modern writing it is assumed that some specific answerability to some definite authority is not only necessary, but a sufficient replacement of mediaeval ideas of a more generalised responsibility. That, as we saw in the previous chapter,[9] is a mistake. Quite generally, being responsible to someone is no substitute for being responsible *sans phrase*, because no human being knows all my doings or has time to question me about most of them. In particular, there has seemed to be a logical absurdity in holding the supreme authority responsible to anyone, for if it were, then it would not be supreme, and whoever it was responsible to would be supreme instead. So it was sometimes said in the

---

[5] Aristotle, *Athenaion Politeia*, §48.3–5; §54.2.   [6] See §9.3.
[7] Aristophanes, *Clouds*, 859; Suidas, s.v. δέον.
[8] See also §9.3, p. 186.   [9] In §§9.2 and 9.3.

eighteenth century that the English people, for all their vaunted constitution, were not really free except during general elections when Parliament was dissolved, and the people could really exercise an effective voice. That contention may not convince, but, besides raising the awkward question 'To whom are the people responsible?', it is enough to show that the concept of *being responsible to* is limited in scope, and cannot altogether replace in our political thinking the mediaeval insistence that all governments, whether monarchs, parliaments, or electorates, need, in addition to any institutions to secure effective answerability to specified bodies, a general sense of responsibility, acting only for reasons which will stand up if exposed to scrutiny.

10.3. APPOINTMENT AND CO-OPERATION

The most natural time at which to spell out the duties of office is at the time of appointment. We do not come into public office in the course of nature, as we find ourselves children and become parents. It is inherent in public office that it be publicly recognisable, and any rule of recognition needs some formal procedure for its application. The *lex curiata* that conferred authority on Roman magistrates indicated also what was expected of them, and the praetors in their edict bound themselves very closely in their adjudication of cases.[10] Even hereditary monarchs need to be crowned and to troop the colour so that people may recognise them as their sovereign. The coronation oaths, like the oaths taken by privy councillors, judges and Members of Parliament, indicate the general expectations we have of those who take them, and provide a basis for criticizing their conduct if they fail to live up to them.

The effectiveness of criticism is often underestimated. Political theorists commonly fail to distinguish constitutional criticism from other less cogent types, and mistakenly suppose that because it is not backed up by effective sanctions, it is necessarily ineffective. Any public figure is subject to criticism, much of it unfair, and must, in consequence, develop a thick skin. People do not like his ears, his taste in music, his favourite breed of dog.

[10] W. E. Heitland, *The Roman Republic*, Cambridge, 1909, §79, vol. i, p. 66; §1373, vol. iii, p. 423.

Such criticisms may be wounding, but are of no consequence. More serious are criticisms of decisions taken in the course of office. Some may be captious, but many are sincere and weighty, and these cannot be shrugged off if the bearer of office has explicitly undertaken to be responsible in his tenure of it. By so doing he has exposed himself to questions being asked, and though he may not be under a duty to answer a particular questioner to his satisfaction, he cannot, consonantly with being responsible at all, brush off all questions. Every time I undertake anything, I make myself vulnerable to remonstrance, should I fail to perform what I undertook to do.

But need a sovereign heed criticisms? Will he even hear them? The twentieth century, with its catalogue of lunatic dictators, has realised Plato's nightmare of the autistic tyrant, who will brook no opposition, no criticism even, and terrorises all into abject subservience. It can happen. But it should be seen as an aberration, not as the norm. The dictator who surrounds himself with terror-stricken *apparatchiks* deprives himself of his sources of information and counsel. He can kill the messengers who bring him bad news, but then will not learn of the enemy's advance until he is at the door. Hitler would not allow his generals to advise him, and paved the way for his own defeat. Stalin did not live to see the end result of his policies. He nearly destroyed Russia's ability to fight the Germans, and set in motion processes that have caused the collapse of communism and the Soviet system. No man is self-sufficient. Even the sovereign, who owns no superior, needs others, who will apprise him of facts and adduce arguments he cannot find out for himself. On this score the strict hierarchical argument of Hobbes' Leviathan fails, and though it needs must be that where there are disputes which cannot be otherwise resolved we must have a decision procedure that will give a definitive resolution of the dispute, the final say is not the sole say: whatever body has the final say must rely on a general willingness to co-operate on the part of subordinate bodies, and diverse responsibilities being exercised freely and relatively independently.

Government, then, is to be seen not as the exercise of untrammelled power by some self-sufficient despot, but as a function of society as a whole, involving the unfearful transmission of information and argument. People need to be able to tell the truth

and speak their minds without fear of reprisal, and non-patho-
logical regimes allow for at least some people being able to tell
rulers what they would rather not be told. Government by its
very nature has to be responsive, and since it is dealing with
autonomous human agents, it cannot be effectively responsive
unless they co-operate, and they will not co-operate unless it is
also responsible. The degree to which this *de facto* necessity is
translated into a *de jure* right is variable: it is the mark of a fully
responsible government that it accords very full provision for
public criticism of public policies. But always there is an inherent pressure in the nature of political society towards some freedom of speech, some ability to remonstrate with rulers if they
fail to keep their word. Hence the value of having them give
their word on admission to office to exercise their authority
responsibly and be guided by reasons that can be defended in
public.

A sovereign is limited in other ways too. Besides not being omniscient, and needing *glasnost* in order that he may be told the
truth, he does not have the time or the competence to take all
decisions himself, and must allow many decisions to be taken by
others. Even if they are nominally subordinate and responsible to
him, he cannot in practice oversee all their decision-making, and
even autocrats find themselves frustrated and controlled by their
apparatchiks. Even in a hierarchical organization *responsibility to*
needs to be supplemented by a more general *responsibility*, if the
organization is to be effective, and in most modern states there
are many different centres of decision-making which co-operate
without being effectively subject to any overall authority. Doctors
and schoolmasters and clergymen and local councillors are independent of one another, but work together. Throughout society
there is a separation of powers. There are many officials, each
with his own province of responsibility, and each needing to co-
operate with others. The diversity of their reasonings secures a
further point of entry for rationality. If no official is omni-com-
petent, each must communicate with others, using words, which
in itself requires him to formulate his reasons. The paper-pushing
of bureaucrats has its wasteful and tedious aspects, but it edges
each official towards giving, and hence having, his reasons, and
to that extent secures that public decisions are reasonable, if not
always right.

10.4. DISCUSSION AND DEBATE

The argument of the two previous sections shows how rulers, even supreme rulers, can be held responsible for their decisions by virtue of the account they will one day make and of the undertakings they entered into when they took up office. The same considerations apply in the intervening period, but there are further reasons then for discussing and debating decisions they may make. By opening their decision-making to scrutiny and criticism, rulers not only are bowing to the inevitable and seizing a chance of acquitting themselves well, but are sharing responsibility, and turning their decisions into ones collectively arrived at, and not theirs alone.

We have a strong tendency to identify. We have a natural *nisus* towards using the first-person plural 'we'. In modern times people have primarily seen themselves as members of some national group, France, Germany, or the United States. We are therefore predisposed to acknowledge the actions of our rulers as our own, but cannot easily do so without knowing what they are, and to know this, we need to know also the reasons for which they were undertaken. Rulers need to publicise their decisions, not only to have them obeyed, but even more to have them supported. Publicity is often enough, but it is difficult to publicise reasons, because reasoning is dialectical, and official reports are inevitably one-sided, and have a tendency to be monotonous. *Pravda* and *Izvestia* were not gripping reading. If the public is to be engaged, there must be some dialogue—not very much, perhaps, but some semblance—in which alternatives are canvassed and considered, and objections anticipated and met. In modern times much of this is carried out by the press, which not only informs the public of what is being done in its name, but, by canvassing arguments on either side, gives some understanding of why it is being done. It ceases to be what "they" do, and becomes what "we" do, worthy of our support, for which we take responsibility, and which we try to carry through to a successful conclusion.

As we saw in Chapter 5, responsibility can be shared.[11] We are responsible for what we assist in doing, and we can assist,

---

[11] In §§5.2 and 5.3.

French-wise, simply by being in on what was decided. But the sharing is not automatic, nor indefinitely extensible. One can dissociate oneself. And it is largely by reason of having been able to dissociate oneself but not having done so, that one can be presumed to acquiesce, and thus to have acquired responsibility.[12] We need dialogue not only for the effective communication of reasons, but for the spreading of responsibility. Although participation can be remarkably passive, it cannot be completely and necessarily passive, or it ceases to be participation. Public opinion must not only be able to form, but to carry some weight in arriving at decisions, if they are to be decisions the public are to feel collectively responsible for.

It is largely a matter of social psychology. Mediaeval monarchs were often better at securing public identification with their measures than modern bureaucrats, and it is a sad lesson of our times that the estimable liberals of the inter-war years were less able to engage the emotions of the populace than the fascist dictators. But although the bread and the circuses and the other pageants are important, there is a hard core of logic in the application of the concept of collective responsibility. If we are to be responsible for what the rulers decide, we must, sometimes, to some extent, somewhere down the line, be able to play some part in the making of those decisions. The king must take advice, not only because, as argued in the previous section, he is not omniscient nor infallible, but because, even though he may use the first-person plural, it will not be acknowledged as a genuine use of 'we' unless we have some real part in his deliberations.

Public discussion and debate not only plays its part in sharing the responsibility for what is ultimately decided, but engenders a responsible attitude in those who take part. Different people advocate different courses of action. If they do so in public, their arguments are on the record, not lightly to be disowned. It is easier to trim or be a time-server if one's support for different measures is hidden in private telephone calls and unrecorded votes in committees. Although in practice few people attend to what I say in public debate, I cannot be sure that some eager opponent will not dig up my words of yesteryear, and throw them in my face if I am grossly inconsistent. And even if others have forgotten what

[12] The argument goes even further: sometimes I am committed merely by having been heard, even though not agreed with. See further §10.5 below.

I said, I am disposed to remember, and attach importance to my stance in times past. I would be loath to have to disown it, and admit to myself that I had been mistaken in my advocacy then. Whereas in the secret confabulations of a court I can chop and change, in Parliament each time I speak I have committed myself and, remembering what I have said, cannot sit loose to the reasons I urged. I nail my colours to the mast, thereby imposing a certain degree of consistency and rationality on the courses I advocate.

10.5. REPRESENTATION

We cannot all take part in national debates. We cannot all assist silently in the French sense. If we are to be present at all, it must be vicariously, in the person of another. But that is often enough. Even when I am present at a debate, I am happy not to have to speak, and am thankful if another makes the points I want made, and lets me off the hook. What I want when public measures are being debated is that my arguments should be put forward, and often also my interests defended—that is, that someone should be looking at things from my point of view, and standing up for me if need be. Both functions can be performed by another, and often are better so carried out, as when I employ a barrister to represent me in a court of law. In many respects the government represents the people—notably in foreign affairs and the defence of the realm, but also in standing up for the public interest against purely sectional ones. In the Middle Ages the king often defended the common people against the nobles, and provided even-handed justice for all. But as affairs become more complex, debate becomes more divided, and the need for separate representatives to put different sides of the case becomes insistent.

Originally the House of Commons was a house in which communities were represented, and that function continues still, though much eroded by electoral reform to achieve equality of franchise. Communities cannot all be of the same size, and if we insist on constituencies having equal numbers of voters, we create artificial ones with no real community of interest. It often so happens that a particular MP takes up the concerns of some group of citizens, and speaks for the Jews, the Roman Catholics, fishermen, or the Police Federation, so that members of those communities have their arguments expressed and interests defended in the House, but this is now a grace note, not something secured by the Representation of the People Acts.

Representatives need not only to argue and defend, but to bargain on behalf of their clients and commit them to undertakings deemed to be in their best interests. This early became a prime function of Parliament—to agree on behalf of everyone to pay taxes. Somehow, in ways not clearly delineated, the function of representatives in representative government is to commit their constituents to abide by the laws and other decisions of Parliament, over and above the extent to which they actually agree with them. Even when there is no consensus, there is some sort of contract which binds me to obey the laws and acquiesce in the policies of the government, against my better judgement, and even in spite of my explicit and vehement opposition.

Representation is only one strand in the doctrine of the social contract. The people could enter into a compact with a sovereign who made no provision for representation, and so long as he kept his side of the bargain they would be bound to keep theirs. It is often argued that political obedience is the *quid pro quo* for the protection afforded by the laws and their enforcement by the civil power. More generally, we have already argued in Chapter 5 that we shoulder some burden of collective responsibility simply by entering into the benefits of belonging to a community. All these considerations carry some weight. But it is widely felt that the obligation to obey the government is greater in countries like Britain and the United States because there is some element of representation, consultation, and bargaining in the political process, so that people, even if the results are not all they would have liked, have nevertheless committed themselves to accept them.

10.6. VOICES AND VOTES

Once there are representative assemblies, there is a need to reduce the assemblage of different opinions being voiced to a definite view. In small committees it is often possible to reach agreement without a vote, and a good chairman can often devise a form of words that everyone will accept. Even in larger bodies it is sometimes possible to distil a sense of the meeting, and a monarch or minister can see how he should trim his sails in response to the currents of public opinion. But it is not always easy to discern the weight behind different opinions being expressed, and so it is correspondingly easy to ignore what is in fact a preponderant opinion under the mistaken apprehension that it is only one view among many.

Votes are standardised voices. Instead of each person saying what he thinks, raising his own questions and giving them his own answers, we ask him to give his answer to the same question as we are asking of everybody else. It is a single-question questionnaire, and the question is either whether we should do something (Yes or No) or who should be appointed (give name or names). Since the question is the same for everyone, the answers are in standard form, and can be counted and tabulated. And we can have some rule translating the individual answers of everyone into a collective answer of all.

There are many possible rules for converting voting results into decisions, and no single one of them is indubitably the right one. The advocates of proportional representation make valid points against the first-past-the-post system, the advocates of which in turn point out the disadvantages of each alternative proposed. The element of artifice needs to be acknowledged, especially in an age inclined to posit a divine right of democracies and to regard votes as sacrosanct. There is nothing sacrosanct about a 51 per cent majority, unless it is agreed that there is. If a majority vote is acknowledged as decisive, then it is: but equally if we were to decide matters of state by having the consuls look at the auspices, that, too, would be a legitimate decision procedure. Neither is constitutionally improper, neither is self-justifying. Either could be adopted, but always subject to further caveats, usually tacit, about the way it should be operated and results it may come up with.

The simple majority rule, though not sacrosanct, has the merit of yielding consistent results in the limit, of always yielding a decision, and, where Yes–No questions are at issue, of being symmetrical as regards the way the question is put. Those who are unanimous are always in the majority. Majority decisions can never be out of line with what we all want, whereas decisions taken in accordance with other rules can. Even the good chairman can sometimes mistake the mood of the meeting, and end up in a minority of one. Other majority rules are equally safe against being wholly out of line with what we all want, but may fail to give a decision at all. The Polish parliament had a unanimity rule, and Poland ceased to exist. In public affairs decisions have to be taken, and sometimes cannot be postponed. The simple majority rule, together with some provision for breaking a tie, for example by a casting vote, will always give a definite result. Also, that result does not depend on the way the question is put. If, put one way, the Ayes have it, then, put the other, the Noes will. There is less room for procedural manipulation and wrangling than where some greater majority is required, and there is much politicking to secure that the question is phrased in a particular way.

The advantages of the simple majority rule are real, but not overwhelming. Even if it does not matter whether the question is put in positive or negative form, there is still plenty of room for procedural wrangling over the order in which questions, especially amendments, are put, and substantial malpractice is possible. Although some decisions have to be taken without delay, they are very few, and often it is better not to be able to come to a quick, but wrong and possibly irreversible, decision. The Athenians voted in haste to execute the inhabitants of Mitylene, and, repenting overnight, were only saved by the heroic exertions of the rowers in the second trireme from a many times more monstrous Melian massacre.

Not only can a majority decision be wicked, but it can fail to conform to the internal requirements of a community's decision-procedure. Even near-unanimity is not enough to make the decisions of an Assembly valid. After the Battle of Arginusae the Athenians wanted to execute the generals who had failed to pick up the shipwrecked sailors after the fighting was over. Socrates happened to be chairman of the Assembly that day, and refused to put the question to the vote: it was unconstitutional to put anyone to death without a proper trial.[13] Even when there is no specific constitutional prohibition, proper discussion and debate are required. It is one thing to take a vote after a question has

---

[13] Xenophon, *Hellenica*, I. vii. 12–15; Xenophon, *Mem.* I. i. 18, IV. iv. 2; Plato, *Apology*, 32b; Plato, *Gorgias*, 473e.

been thoroughly canvassed and different points raised and attended to: it is quite another to take it purely mechanically, with no opportunity for opponents to argue their case or be given a fair hearing. A vote is a stylized voice, and makes sense only in the context of genuine voices being heard first. There is a requirement of due process, different from that in judicial proceedings, but a requirement none the less, if a vote is to have any validity.

There are also substantive restrictions on issues that may be properly decided by a vote of the public at large. The American prohibition on Bills of Attainder is sound. Where the central interests of an individual are in jeopardy, arguments in his defence deserve careful consideration, which a body of many people is too busy and too distracted to give. We cannot all attend to everything, and matters which demand a great deal of attention are ones we must leave to those who have the time and energy to go into them properly. Besides canons of justice, the general rationale of a society's existence and of its decision-procedures limits the decisions that may be taken: the South African Act of Parliament abolishing the franchise of the coloureds was unconstitutional; the subsequent Act to subvert the court that had pronounced it unconstitutional was *eo ipso* unconstitutional too, and all subsequent decisions, though often carried by majority votes, are tainted in consequence.

10.7. ELECTIONS

Elections are a prominent feature of modern government, and play an important part in rendering it responsible. Often, indeed, they are accorded an almost mystical significance, and it is supposed that there is a divinity about an elected representative that endows all his actions with authority. We need to be less misty-eyed, and recognise the demerits as well as the real merits of our electoral procedures.

In the British and American systems there are general elections every four or five years which determine the colour of the administration until the next election. In neither country is the issue decided by a simple majority vote, but instead an electoral college is chosen, according to rather unobvious rules, and the electoral college chooses the next prime minister or president by a simple majority. In America it does so for a fixed term with no right of recall, in Britain it is in continuous session, and could in theory at any time require the prime minister to resign or hold another election. Although formally the electorate votes for individual members of the electoral college, in practice they vote on party lines, choosing representatives who are pledged to vote for the party's candidate. In the United States it happened early on, in spite of Washington's earnest entreaties to his countrymen to eschew party politics, and in Britain, though as yet the process is not complete, it has been taking place as the franchise has been widened.

It is an inevitable result of a wide franchise and a democratic desire on the part of the people to decide something themselves. As with assemblies, so with countries as a whole, the more people who are in on a decision, the simpler the decision must be. If an election is to decide something nationwide, then every voter must address the same question: it does not signify my voting for Smith in Wandsworth and you for Brown in Bournemouth, but if we all vote for or against the government party, the nation's verdict will be clear. Moreover, this question is sufficiently simple for every voter to be able to answer without needing any special knowledge or investment of effort, and therefore puts all voters on an equal footing.[14]

Elections of this sort constitute a sort of εὔθυνα (*euthuna*). The verdict is on the government's stewardship during its previous term of office: if it is deemed to have done well, it is re-elected, and if not, not. It is a powerful dissuasive from visible irresponsibility, and an ultimately effective remedy if dissuasion fails. Western democracies are not immune from bad governments, but have an invaluable long-stop, in that sooner or later they are given the opportunity to exchange, without bloodshed, the worst for the less bad. Whatever the disadvantages of Western democratic regimes, they are "super-pessimal", not as bad as they might be—and this in our century is something to be thankful for.

Nevertheless, Western democracies fall short of being responsible governments both in theory and in practice. They are called

---

[14] Brian Barry, *Political Argument*, London, 1965, chs. 14 and 15.

to account by the electorate only seldom, and only one question is put, in which a multitude of separate points are blurred and smudged away. The individual, and even substantial minorities, may feel helpless, lacking the resources to mount an electoral campaign. Other, well-heeled minorities may be able to press their sectional interests to the detriment of the common weal. There is a strong tendency, especially in Britain, for governments to inflate the economy before a general election, and return to fiscal rectitude only after the votes are safely gathered in. Crude majoritarianism can likewise lead a member of an assembly away from a proper discharge of his duties, and to be responsive to electoral pressure rather than a responsible holder of office: he can see himself as dealing in votes, as other operators deal in oil—one elected American judge is reputed to have said in giving a decision, "Waal, I guess I canna let all that money go outa the State." Unless there is a reasonably frequent alternation of administrations, the opposition begins to lack experience, and consequently credibility, and no longer serves as a plausible alternative to the government in office. It is excessively difficult for new parties to break into the duopoly that the existing parties enjoy. The way in which votes are totted up in the United States is now simply an anachronism, and it is possible for an American president,[15] and common for a British prime minister, to gain office with only a minority of the votes—and the turnout in the United States, even for presidential elections, is remarkably low.

Many of these criticisms can be countered—but by appeal to other principles of politics than strict majoritarianism. Although MPs are too vulnerable to the prime minister's untrammelled power to dissolve Parliament to be able to press home criticisms of government policy as effectively as they should, they can make their voices heard, and the government often has its own reasons to heed what they say. The whips are too powerful, but not all-powerful. In the United States, though the electoral college has no continuous existence or power of recall, the Houses of Congress do sit, and have great powers which the president cannot ignore. In both systems the representatives see themselves as real representatives, not just cogs in a political machine, and not only devote much time to constituency work, but try to under-

[15] In 1876 and 1888.

stand and influence national policy. The traditions of both countries, though often inadequately articulated and understood, lead
Parliament and Congress to take a more responsible attitude to
their duties than crude majoritarianism would require. Even
crude calculations of electoral interest can argue for a responsible
attitude. The representative operates behind a veil of ignorance.
He does not know what his constituents individually think, and
his communications with them are public or liable to be publi-
cised. Any underhand deal is likely to be rumbled, and the only
reasons he can acknowledge in public are those that would weigh
with a responsible decision-maker. Constituencies are important.
They no longer are the communities that once returned burgesses
or knights of the shire to Parliament, whose representative enjoyed a large measure of support, and could use his judgement
on their behalf within wide limits of discretion. The modern MP
is returned in a contested election, often with an uncomfortably
small majority, comprising votes cast for different reasons by
different individuals with different priorities. There is therefore no
simple majority to be courted, but a shifting coalition of voters,
many of whom are likely to support their representative on some
issues but not on others. Under such conditions the best strategy
for the would-be re-elected representative is to be honest and
responsible in the decisions he takes: he will lose fewer votes than
he would by discovered dishonesty, and if he decides for good
reason he has a better chance of winning over floating voters
than if his reasons are bad.

These arguments do not add up to a complete rebuttal of criticisms. The traditions of Parliament and Congress have not
always prevented corruption and log-rolling. They often have
failed to curb the arrogance of governments. No satisfactory
safeguard against a sovereign body embarking on unconstitutional or wicked measures has yet been devised. Elections often
fail to provide adequate representation for particular communities and interests, and minorities often get short shrift under
majoritarian democracy. At present we too readily sing the
praises of democracy without being clear what we mean—often
in fact meaning something like 'responsible government': in fact
democracy, in the strict sense of the word, has defects not
sufficiently attended to, and special consideration is needed if
these are not to lead to dire results.

10.8. *VOX POPULI*

It is dangerous to deify the people, for then we are unprepared for their doing wrong, and find it difficult to defy them when they are minded to act irresponsibly. When Socrates refused to put to the vote the motion that the generals should be summarily executed without trial, there was an uproar, with people shouting that it was a terrible thing for anyone to prevent the people from doing what it wanted.[16] And it is not only the Athenian *demos* in the ancient world that ran away with itself: the Germans voted Hitler into power. However we arrange things, there is always some body not answerable to anybody else, and the possibility of power being exercised irresponsibly.

Some countries have taken the problem seriously, and sought to establish effective shackles on those entrusted with power, to ensure that they do not abuse their trust. The most notable is the United States of America, with its written constitution, separation of powers, and Supreme Court. Many thinkers in other countries have admired the American constitution, and thought that their own countries should follow suit. In the last half century, however, there have been second thoughts. Juvenal's question, *Quis custodiet ipsos custodes?*, has been raised afresh by the activities of the Supreme Court, which has taken unto itself wide-ranging legislative powers far beyond anything entrusted to it by the founding fathers. Not that all its rulings are bad; but many go beyond, and some clearly contravene, the plain meaning and original intention of those who drafted and agreed to the actual text of the constitution. It may or may not be a good thing to permit abortion and the sale of contraceptives, or to forbid the Lord's prayer being said at school assemblies: the one thing we can be reasonably sure of is that if any of these provisions had been thought to be implicit in the words put forward in the original constitution or the Bill of Rights, they would not have been accepted by the thirteen states. Historical and cultural explanations can be given for the encroachment of the judiciary on the other branches of American government. But clearly in any

---

[16] See above, §10.6, p. 217. For a similar occasion when Demosthenes was chairman, but was unable in the end to prevent a vote being taken, see Aeschines, II. 84.

country there is a danger, if the courts are charged with preserving the constitution, of their gradually aggrandising their role, and deciding that the constitution means what they think it ought to mean.

In Britain the House of Commons has gradually come to be almost, but not quite, supreme. It is still, formally, the Queen-in-Parliament that is the sovereign body, and the House of Lords and the Queen herself play minor, but not negligible, roles: in particular, the House of Commons cannot decide, without the consent of the House of Lords, to prolong its own life; and if this consent is not forthcoming, it cannot be dispensed with by means of the Parliament Act. But the safeguards provided by the limited veto of the House of Lords, and the conceivable refusal of the monarch to grant the royal assent, are inadequate, and there are suggestions to replace the House of Lords by an elected second chamber with greater powers. But there are difficulties. If the second chamber were elected on essentially the same basis as the House of Commons, it would be subject to the same surges of electoral folly; if it were elected on a different basis, like the Senate of the United States of America, it would perform a useful representational function, but engender endemic deadlock. Indeed, if the second chamber were elected at all, it would suffer from many of the disadvantages of the House of Commons: only dedicated politicians would run for it, and they would always be too much concerned with securing party endorsement for the next election to make the sort of contribution the Lords make now, or to be effective guardians of the constitution against the politicians.

It would be better to keep the House of Lords as it is now—it works; indeed, it works much better than most second chambers—but to merge the veto in a referendum. If the two Houses of Parliament could not agree on a bill, then at the end of a year both versions would be put before the electorate, and there would be a referendum on which was to become law. Such a provision would put pressure on each House to be reasonable, as it would have a better chance of its version being preferred if it went some way towards meeting the objections of the other side. And since it would be only a very occasional exercise, it would be less likely to encourage creeping aggrandisement than a constitutional court.

10.9. MINORITIES

The great weakness of majoritarian democracy is its treatment of minorities. Often in practice societies are considerate of minorities, but this stems from adherence to other political values, and the more explicitly the society adheres to modern democratic theory, the less reluctant it is simply to outvote those who disagree with the majority. Even where societies do not in practice ride roughshod over minorities, there is the fear that they might, fuelled by an unglossed reading of the democratic theory that is seemingly espoused. The prospects for a minority in a twentieth-century nation state have often been, and even more often seemed, grim. And where the minority looks like breeding itself into a majority, tension has risen to the point of open strife.

The trouble lies largely with democratic theory, which assumes that the people are fairly homogeneous, and in so far as they are divided by particular interests, these interests are shifting, so that they will be, by and large and in the long run, adequately represented by politicians who are anxious to be re-elected and hence sensitive to a wide range of concerns. These conditions do not hold when there is deep division that precludes the possibility of anyone being elected on lines that cross the divide. The Irish nationalists in Northern Ireland, the Basques and Catalans in Spain, the Flemings and Walloons in Belgium, the Hungarians, Slovaks, Germans, Serbs, and Croats in the Habsburg dominions, are places where modern democratic theory does not work.

A change of theory helps. If we view certain democratic procedures not as inherently and absolutely right, but as means towards securing responsible government, we can in principle accommodate the complaints and worries of minorities instead of ruling them out of court from the outset. We might also consider institutional safeguards. The electoral systems of the United Kingdom, the United States and other Western democracies are not sacrosanct. The House of Commons may be defended on the same grounds as the House of Lords: it works—not all that well, and certainly not as well as it might or should, but still better than most actual alternatives. Similar defences may be given of the arrangements adopted in the United States, France, Germany, Canada, Australia, New Zealand, and the rest: they have proved themselves relatively unbad, and nearly always worth holding on to for fear of getting something worse. But institutions which work in relatively homogeneous countries may well be unable to accommodate fearful, or assertive, or lunatic, minorities.

Minorities need to be effectively represented, and their representations need to be heard and heeded. Territorial constituencies exacerbate the problem, party divisions often alleviate it. It would remove many causes of friction if, at some levels of government, voters could choose what constituency to vote in, so that Hungarians living in Slovakia or Romania or Vojvodina could vote as Hungarians for a Magyar-speaking representative, and Germans in Galicia or Silesia as Germans for a German-speaking one. Although some questions are to be decided territorially—it would not do for Englishmen to drive on the left and French on the right—many are not: even the provision of schooling could be met by different groups having their own schools in the same area.

If minorities, despite being scattered geographically, can none the less elect their own representatives, they will be able to make themselves heard, and that will often be enough to secure reasonable treatment. They will be even more influential if the majority is not monolithic. In Israel the small number of Orthodox Jews have exerted great power because their support has often been essential for forming a coalition with a parliamentary majority. Members of minorities can often secure those things they care most passionately about at the cost of not having a say on wider issues: if my great concern is that the national airline shall not serve meat and milk in the same meal, I have a good chance of securing that, but cannot then choose a left-wing rather than a right-wing member of the Knesset. But often, once they no longer feared for their survival, members of minority groups would want to divide on the same issues as divided the rest of society. By providing for minority representation, we should in fact make it less self-consciously a representation of the minority *per se*, and more a vehicle for representing their views on wider issues.

Different tiers of government would be needed. Local government would be entirely geographical, and I should vote in local elections and pay local taxes in the area where I lived, irrespective of what nationality I espoused. But, in disputed areas at least, I could choose whether to vote, say, as a Romanian for a Romanian member of parliament in Bucharest, or as a Hungarian for a Hungarian member of parliament in Budapest, and I would pay national taxes, receive some social services, and live under family and other laws enacted by the national assembly of my choice. And again I would vote for a Romanian or Hungarian member of parliament in some European Assembly, and, irrespective of which constituency I had voted in, pay the taxes levied by that Assembly, and abide by the "federal" laws it had enacted.

It is not a new idea. The Ottoman Empire relied on the many minorities within its borders running their own affairs. The United States paved the way for a federal system whereby different communities could combine for some purposes while remaining separate for most. These, of course, were geographically defined states, whereas many nationalities in Europe are not geographically separate, but live intermingled in the same area; in any case, with the advent of modern communications, geographical contiguity is much less dominant a factor in the texture of our lives than it was. In Belgium different communities occupy overlapping areas, and the central government, the communities, and the regions exercise a wide variety of powers. "Person-related matters" such as family policy, youth welfare, health education, the delivery of medical care outside hospitals, and international cultural co-operation are the province of the communities. Although only the king, on the advice of the central government, can conclude treaties, the communities and regions can engage in international activities. In principle, though often not in practice, conflicts between the various levels of government are resolved by a "Concertation Committee", and can be decided by the jurisdictional subdivision of the Council of State, or ultimately by the Court of Arbitration.[17] Often, in fact, disputes between Walloons and Flemings have erupted into major, and often farcical, confrontations. But better a Belgian comedy than a Yugoslav tragedy.

There are many loose ends. Fire and, arguably, health services would need to be local: education, and perhaps other social ser-

---

[17] Yves Lejeune, "Belgium", ch. 6 in Hans J. Michelmann and Panayotis Soldatos (eds.), *Federalism and International Relations*, Oxford, 1990, pp. 142–75.

vices, would be for each nation to decide. There would be plenty of room for conflict as to exactly which sphere of government should be local, which national, which pan-European. But these conflicts would be diffuse, variegated issues of more or less, instead of the concentrated, fierce, all-or-nothing ones which territorial claims engender. I may feel angry if the electricity company will only do business with me under the commercial code of another nation, but I can still do business with my own circle according to the laws which we recognise and respect: I am not threatened with cultural extinction, as I am if the boundary is drawn so as to put me on the wrong side, and I have little incentive to join the guerrillas to fight for the lost lands of Greater Ruritania. Indeed, once we allow overlapping jurisdictions, every country can be its greatest self, and have maps showing its domain as including all the areas where its laws are, by some, acknowledged. The potent imagery of maps need no longer fire deep-seated instincts of territorial aggressiveness. Once overlapping national jurisdictions are allowed, each can survey the geographical scene with contentment, and national boundaries will cease to be bones of contention.

Much needs to be done. It cannot be done all at once, and probably cannot be done quickly. But we have already accepted the principle of expatriate voting, and are accustomed to paying taxes to different authorities at different levels. It would be possible to negotiate further under the Anglo-Irish Agreement to allow Nationalists in Ulster to vote for, pay taxes to, and receive social security from Dublin instead of Westminster: it might concentrate the minds of many to be faced with an actual choice, and to have to pay the economic price of their political preferences. Italy and Austria could work out rather different arrangements for South Tyrol. Austria and Hungary might find it very easy to formalise further their amicable arrangements for the minorities on either side of the frontier imposed by the Paris treaties after the First World War. And thus by trial, and occasionally by unhappy error, we could work out a *modus vivendi*, and ultimately devise political institutions under which deeply divided people could live together in peace, if not amity. But if we are to do this, and avoid the danger of further bloodshed, it will need much deeper thought than we have hitherto managed to give to the problem.

10.10. DEMOCRACY AND EQUALITY

The Athenian democrats were dubious about elections. They thought they were too élitist. Only those thought to be the best were likely to be elected, so that if the ordinary chap was to have a chance of holding office, he must be chosen in some non-selective way, such as by lot. Conversely the critics of democracy among the ancient Greeks complained that it was unreasonably egalitarian, both in theory—in supposing it was easy to govern, and anybody could do it as well as anyone else—and in practice—the majority of poor men would vote heavy taxes for the rich to pay.

Both sides of the argument have weight. They focus on different aspects of government. On the one hand to govern is by many thought to be a good thing. Ambitious men seek office, and even the unambitious like to be consulted and to feel that they have some say in what happens to them and their society. If I am to be part of We, what we decide must have some relation to what I think. I feel alienated if I have no part in the constitution,[18] and may well feel excluded if I sense that though I am free to stand for election, I never shall actually be elected. Many people are flattered to be summoned to serve on a jury: it shows that they are persons of consequence, and what they decide will have an effect on the course of events. Many offices do not demand more than average competence and reliability: Athens was right to make these available to the many who could not put themselves forward for election with any realistic hope of success, but who, given the chance, would show themselves on the job responsible citizens capable of doing their bit to keep society going.

But to govern is not only an ego-enhancing experience. It affects other people, and can be done well or badly. Sceptics have sometimes denied the latter, and argued, against Socrates, that since there are no agreed criteria of moral or political choice, political decision-making is in a class apart from that of the doctor, steersman, or shipwright: in the latter cases, admittedly, some practitioners are better than others, but where public affairs are concerned each decision is as good as any other.

---

[18] Aristotle, *Athenaion Politeia*, §2.3: οὐδενὸς γὰρ, ὡς εἰπεῖν, ἐτύγχανον μετέχοντες (*oudenos gar, hos eipein, etuchanon metechontes*), for they effectively had, so to speak, no share in the state.

The argument is invalid: the conclusion false. We do not need to have agreed on the criteria of assessment for assessments to be made. Often it is only in discussing and defending different assessments that criteria begin to emerge. More generally, disagreement is a sign that there is something to disagree about rather than that since we have not reached agreement yet it is pointless to go on arguing. And the conclusion is clearly false, for if there was nothing to choose between one decision and another, we should not take time deliberating what to do, but just toss a coin. The fact that we laugh at the Romans for seeking auguries and looking at the auspices is evidence enough that we do not really think that one decision is just as good as another. Some decisions we recognise as good, others as disastrous, and we reckon some decision-makers to be wise, others foolish or misguided. We do discriminate, and where matters of great moment are at issue, seek to have them decided by those who are most likely to decide them well. Government is, if not wholly, at least in part inherently meritocratic.

Both lines of argument are sound, and we need to accommodate both in the institutions of responsible government. It is an important merit of democracy that it underlines the importance of each voter in seeking his opinion on the future government of the country, and it would be good if minor offices were distributed so that ordinary citizens had a greater chance of holding them. But we need to be governed well. It is more important to us that we win the war than that the general's baton had its origin in a plebeian knapsack; it is more important to me, if I am on trial, that the jury can understand my defence, and not convict me merely because they reckon the police would not have charged me if they had not known I was guilty, than that some nincompoop should have a pleasant change of occupation. Egalitarian arguments are out of place in assessing people's competence for office. Only if the office is clearly within the competence of several candidates, would it be permissible to choose one rather than another on egalitarian grounds.

We should not be ashamed at being élitist in our choice of governors. We want to be governed well. But it is we who are being governed. We are at the receiving end, and are likely to know whether we are being governed well or not. The best shoes may be made by the best cobbler, but the wearer is the authoritative judge as to whether or not they fit. Feedback is essential if the job is to be done well, and elected representatives provide the feedback. These arguments, canvassed in antiquity,[19] are cogent still, but establish less than the full democratic case. They show that if the government is to be responsible, there need to be lines of communication from the governed to the governors, and only if they are responsive to electoral pressure can we be sure that the messages will be heeded. But the dangers of electoral manipulation and electoral bribery remain, in which the voters do not take the long-term view, listening to arguments and reaching their decision responsibly, but are passive pawns in an admass society, trading their votes for sectional advantage or according to which candidate plays on their prejudices to best effect.

10.11. RESPONSIBILITY IN PUBLIC LIFE

One of the attractions of communism was its double focus on the people and the party. It enabled adherents, especially the ambitious young, to gratify their élitist urges while placating their egalitarian pretensions. But the tension between the elect and the electorate is not peculiar to communism. Decision-taking requires time, and often effort and intellectual ability, and most people reckon they have better things to do with their time than to engage in detailed discussion of public affairs. Almost inevitably in a large society those who devote much time and thought to them are a largely self-selected minority. A democracy can function well only if there is such a minority, and only if that minority is imbued with a strong sense of public duty, and a recognition of the special responsibilities falling on those who seek to influence the course of events.

Always there is the duty of honesty, which in public life often involves speaking out, and not concealing unwelcome truths. Parliament provides feedback, but only if representatives speak their minds, rather than saying what will be to their own advantage. The minister needs to be told what are the snags in his pet project. In the Middle Ages loyal servants of the Crown would

---

[19] Aristotle, *Politics* III, 11, 1282^a. Aristotle has the proviso that the majority are not "too slavish" (1282^{a}15).

have to incur royal displeasure as they persisted in bringing to the king's attention unpalatable facts. A loyal public servant does not discharge his duty simply by doing what he is told, but must tell the truth, even to his own disadvantage.

In other ways, too, the responsibilities of those in public life are not limited to those particular responsibilities where they are responsible *to* a constituency, a minister, a departmental superior, or an editor. Although I may represent the electors of Bristol, or Kent, or Selly Oak, I should be concerned not with their interests alone, but with those of the whole country; although I take my instructions from the minister in charge of my department, my loyalty is to the Crown. I may be legitimately concerned to win the next election or to get the minister out of trouble, but I need also to consider how I shall answer for the plight of the country in ten years' time, or how my conduct will appear when the thirty-year rule reveals what I actually did. In the long run, maybe, we shall all be dead; but in the intervening period, when I but not everyone is dead, questions may be raised, which I should anticipate now, and make sure that what I do now will not be censured then.

The wider responsibilities of public life can lead to agonizing conflicts of duties—whether to vote against the party whip, whether to blow the whistle on illegal action on the part of the minister—but these are conflicts of a sort that occur elsewhere. Other responsibilities are more specific, and their discharge more counter to the natural motivation of public life. It goes against the grain to think well of opponents. But opponents are necessary if public debate is to be informed and effective, and will sometimes be successful in a bad cause. It is asking a lot of a politician to see their merits, and in the present party system it may be unwise for him to admit that he does. But still we demand a certain measure of honesty and tolerance in debate, for only so can rational discussion take place, and public questions be decided by reason and agreement rather than by force, chicanery and fraud.

Another virtue, equally needed and equally unnatural in those who enter public life, is modesty, both individual and corporate. Success, as we have seen,[20] is elusive, and it is tempting, espe-

---

[20] See §10.1 above.

cially in our age when political idealism is often a surrogate for religious aspiration, for a politician or a government to be dissatisfied with merely having kept things going, and to want to do something big to be remembered by. But big is seldom good. One can make one's mark on history, but most of the things that impinge on the collective consciousness are bad. Faced with the urge to Do Something, those in politics need to remember the first precept of medical practice, *primum non nocere*, Do no harm. Government is dangerous. Bad governments can do very great damage: good governments only a limited amount of good. Although there have been good governments, we need to be wary of government, and to forgo good things that it might be able to give if it were good, in order to forestall the evils which it will wreak if it is bad. Besides, governments are not very good at doing things. The cynical adage "If you want a thing done badly, get the Government to do it" is uncomfortably near the truth.

These arguments, though weighty, are exaggerated. Not all governments are bad, and some have been positively benign, and some government services have been competently run—for example, the Post Office in the Victorian age. We cannot have a minimal state, with strictly defined limits to government power.[21] Although the constitution of the United States of America tried to impose strict limits to the power of the federal government, the growth of national consciousness among Americans has led to the federal government taking more and more unto itself. Those in public life are maintaining and shaping the national identity, and need to accept the wide-ranging responsibilities that that role places on them. But they need to be cautious in what they do, and in particular in the exercise of coercive power; and generally to seek to minimise the damage they may do rather than aim at some maximum achievement.

10.12. CONCLUSION

Two strands of argument underlie our ideal of responsible government: the responsibility of office and the need for all to share responsibility for what their government does. Those who

---

[21] See §6.14.

govern undertake special responsibilities, and their performance can be judged on the basis of the task they have undertaken. It is a difficult task: decision-making takes time, and often calls for exceptional ability, and it needs to be done disinterestedly in circumstances where it would be very easy to allow considerations of self-interest to creep in. The main aim of this kind of argument is to ensure that government is good government: if all decisions are responsibly taken, then there will be reasons for them, which even if not the best of all possible reasons will be faceable reasons, and so the decisions are likely to be reasonably unbad.

We need good rulers. The old adage "Self-government is better than good government" was the reverse of the truth, and its acceptance by advanced circles in Britain after the Second World War consigned millions of human beings to misery and death. But good government is not easily had. Even if we choose ideal Platonic guardians on the best meritocratic principles, they may make mistakes. Rulers are fallible. Even if they do not suffer from ill will, they are not omniscient. Although we share some values, we do not share all, and even perfect Platonic guardians cannot know all my values unless I avow them. Some feedback, some input from the individual, is needed if the rulers are to be properly responsive to the needs of the case. A responsible ruler needs to be open to the opinions and preferences of the ruled. And not all rulers are responsible, and we need some remedy against bad rulers. Some measure of meritocracy may be necessary, but is not by itself enough to secure good government.

The second strand in our argument for responsible government stems from the need for all to share responsibility for what their government does. This is good for three reasons. First, it makes us feel good: instead of feeling outsiders, with "them" always doing things to "us", we can take pride in our society, identify with it, and feel at one with what is going on around us; corporate responsibility is ego-enhancing. Second, it gives us a good reason for obeying the law. If I feel that the law is our law, and that I am one of us, then I shall feel obliged to go along with it even when we have decided something against my own better judgement. Third, it encourages people to play an active part in their community, and to take initiatives and co-operate actively in carrying out public policy. Instead of the merely passive obedience that the previous consideration argues for, it engenders a strong readiness to take the initiative, and to help in all sorts of ways not foreseen by the government, and not laid down by any law.

These arguments are cogent. They do not lead to the simplistic democratic theory proclaimed by many, but they do show the need for some democratic element in our polity. They show also the limitations of democracy, sometimes the need for other than democratic elements, and above all the need for much wider constitutional principles, informing the whole of public debate, the way it should be carried on, and the considerations that ought to be given weight. They show also the importance of public life, the responsibilities of those in public life, and the importance of good people offering themselves for this particular form of service.

Chapter 11

Responsibility in Personal Relations

11.1. SOCIAL LIFE

Most of our life is constituted by relationships which are neither political and legal, nor financial. Most people spend only a small part of their time on politics, and only occasionally do something because it is required by law. And although money speaks, it does not speak very loud to many, who, within the constraints set by law and finance, are guided by quite other considerations. The happy man seldom sees his solicitor, and does not have to take much account of his accountant.

Some social institutions are fairly impersonal. The etiquette of the Bar is analogous to a legal code, though not backed by coercive sanctions. It would be difficult, however, to grade social institutions on the score of how impersonal they are: almost all generate, and depend on, a considerable degree of fellow feeling—graduates of the French *École Normale Supérieure* address one another in the second person singular, *tu*, even though they have never met. Most social relationships are coloured by some measure of intimacy, pretended or real, and are assessed—though outcomes are still important—much more by reference to what they mean than what they effect. Rather than try to treat them *seriatim*, as they become less and less like legal or economic relationships, it is more illuminating to consider them all as variants on personal relationships, but inevitably, in view of the fractured ideal of the *I–thou* relation, less than perfectly personal.

11.2. I–THOU

It seems incongruous to talk about responsibility in person relations. Responsibility is a cool virtue, giving reasons for what one has done, and taking care that what one is going to do is rationally defensible. Personal relations, on the other hand, are warm and emotional, and know nothing of the nicely calculated less and more. Again, personal relations are close and intimate, whereas responsibility, being concerned with reasons, deals with general features of the case, not the unique particularity of the individual person.

These are cogent considerations, to be elucidated more fully in the next chapter. But they do not license a general irresponsibility in my relations with other people—family, sweethearts, colleagues, and friends. Although often they will put up with me, far beyond anything I am entitled to expect, I ought not to presume on it, and owe it to them not to take their forbearance for granted, but to treat each of them as an ἄλλος αὐτός (*allos autos*), another self.[1]

But there are further difficulties. The very concept of an ἄλλος αὐτός (*allos autos*), *alter ego*, contains a contradiction. I alone am the ultimate arbiter of my actions, and determine what first-personal reasons to adopt. I am unique. There cannot be another me. You can never see the like of me again, because it would not be the centre of my consciousness, the initiator of my actions. Equally, there cannot be another thou, because thou hast a mind of thine own, and makest up thy mind for thyself what thou art going to do. If any other being were to count as a self, he would have to have a mind of his own, which he could make up differently from thee, and so be evidently differing from thee. Only if there could in no circumstances be any disagreement between the two of you, would we allow him not to be different from thee, and in that case we should say that there was only one person, though possessing two bodies.

The necessary uniqueness of each person precludes our ever being able to identify completely with anybody else. Yet we yearn for some such perfect union, and our personal relationships are always poised between two poles, trying on the one hand to merge our individual identities in the society of like-minded friends, and on the other seeking recognition of the essential differentness of personhood. I want to be at one with thee, and

---

[1] Aristotle, *Nicomachean Ethics*, IX. 4. 5, 1166ᵃ31-32; cf. 1170ᵇ6, where Aristotle uses ἕτερος αὐτός (*heteros autos*); ἕτερος suggests that there is only one significant other, whereas ἄλλος allows that one might have many friends.

feel that if we are to be truly we, we should have all things in common, but at the same time I want to be acknowledged as the unique person that I am, and not give up the special contribution that I alone can make.

11.3. PEERS AND PAIRS

The two poles are expressed by two paradigm social relationships, the peer group and the pair bond. They are paradigms only, and every actual relationship is not a perfect exemplar of either, but has features of both. The team needs its wicket-keeper, bowlers, and batsmen, making different contributions to their joint success: husbands and wives share many values, and have much in common. Nevertheless, the paradigms are illuminating. The peer group gathers together a number of people who are conscious of their being the same in important respects: the pair bond unites two people each of whom is the most significant person in the other's life. In the one I find my identity in that of the group. I, along with my compatriots, am an Englishman, along with my comrades a member of a school or a regiment, along with my fellow students a student, along with my colleagues a member of a profession, along with my partners a member of a firm; I congregate with other fans to watch football, or enjoy sport, and gather together with two or three to worship God. By myself my values seem insignificant and unrecognised, but in company with my brethren I discover what we stand for and find means of expressing it.

The relationship between members of the same peer group is symmetric and transitive, and hence inclusive. My comrade's comrade is *eo ipso* my comrade, and newcomers are readily absorbed into the group. But just as it is easy to join in, it is easy to drop out. None of us is indispensable. People will be sorry when I die, but as they march back from the funeral, the band will strike up a cheerful tune, and life will go on much the same without me. It is quite different in a family. I am irreplaceable, and my death will leave a gap that can never be filled. Above all in marriage each is indispensable to the other, and each enjoys an endlessly ego-enhancing sense of significance in being the other's significant other. To achieve this, the relationship must be exclusive, and without term or condition. I cannot be the significant other of someone who has other significant others. Only a one–one relation will secure to each the unique standing in the other's scheme of things that can underwrite the unique significance of the individual in the face of the anonymity of any one unit among the multitude of others. A temporary trust is similarly unsupportive. A deserted wife has little reason to think that her death will bring her ex-husband mourning to her grave-side, or leave an irreparable gap in his life. Nor is a conditional commitment a commitment to a person. I do not take thee, if I will keep to you only so long as you keep your looks, or cook me nice meals. Love can only be love if it is set to last, and loy-alty is to a person, not a bearer of desirable personal qualities.

11.4. PEERS

I must not let my mates down. We have a dim sense of the Prisoners' Dilemma, and a recognition that each of us will be tempted to shirk, and that everything would fall apart if that were countenanced. We shall not achieve anything unless we all pull together, and manifest our solidarity by ensuring that every-one shoulders his burden, and nobody lets the side down, either by not doing his bit, or by bringing our good name into disre-pute by some piece of misbehaviour.

Team spirit is a powerful corrective to individual selfishness, and much regarded by schoolmasters on that account. They are right in this: the herd instinct is one of the few available for countering the promptings of the old Adam inclining us to much more individual forms of sin. But corporate bodies too can be selfish, and a gang can easily degenerate into a mob. Beside the admirable loyalty to one's mates and willingness to make sacrifices for their sake, we need to set tendencies to hostility towards those outside the group and collective tyranny over those within.

As I identify with a group, and take responsibility for what the group does, I naturally also take its interests to heart, and see its successes as my successes. I am proud when my college wins the cricket cup, and downcast when my country is defeated on the field of battle. I am likely then to be partial to the interests of my college and its members, and my country and compatriots, and insensitive to those of the opposing side. And the very fact that I am being unselfish as an individual may blind me to our corporate failings in respect of those outside our magic circle.

My concern for the groups I identify with goes very deep, far beyond a crude calculation of interest. I value our good name, and am ashamed when any one of us besmirches it. We impose high standards on our members, and call to account those who fall below them. But it is easy to go too far. I not only want my lot to be honest, courteous, upright, and open, but demand that they always have the bottom button of the waistcoat undone, and never wear bow ties before 7 p.m. Such sartorial tyranny is venial, but when it is extended to all facets of life, it becomes insupportable. Brotherhood is admirable, but if I keep my brother on too short a leash, I destroy him. We may properly, as a condition of continued association, expect a high standard of behaviour from those we take responsibility for, but need to rein in our desire to exact complete conformity in everything.

Peer groups create very strong bonds, but not erotic ones. They are at a low emotional temperature, but long-lasting. No offence is taken if I forget your birthday or fail to visit you, but if we meet again after many years, we can take up the relationship again from where we left off. Usually they are single-sex, more often male than female. In our sex-obsessed age it is sometimes supposed that they must be somehow erotic, and much damage has been done to many by the insinuation that any close friendship must be homosexual. The reverse is the case. People value friendship because it is based on similarity of tastes rather than reciprocity of needs, and is correspondingly undemanding. Often there is some positive sense that an erotic note would undermine friendship. It may be for this reason that most peer groups are single-sex, and that homosexuality is strongly discountenanced in single-sex institutions, such as the army, for fear of the disruptive effect such intimate, intense, and exclusive bonds could have in a group based on an inclusive, low-temperature relationship.

11.5. PAIRS

Sex differentiates. A man and a woman are bound together because each needs the other, and no substitute will do. It is largely a matter of biology. The two of us together can do what neither could do unaided—mix our genes to create new people, who, being younger than ourselves, are likely to outlive us, and to some extent overcome our own individual mortality. Complementarity and creativity are built into the pair bond by our biological ancestry. Anatomically, socially, and emotionally, the sexes complement each other; and marriage is intimately related to the family, spanning the generations, and linking us with those who died before we were born and those who will be born after we are dead.

Because sex differentiates, it individuates. For most people the most personal part of their life is realised in their relations with the opposite sex and in their family life. We jealously guard our uniqueness: whereas my friend's friend is *eo ipso* my friend, my girlfriend's boyfriend is equally *eo ipso* not. Adultery, the turning of the loved one to anyone else, has always been seen as fundamentally disruptive of the marriage bond. It is by being the only person in the life of the only person in my life that I am assured of my own value. Family life concomitantly underwrites individuality. Fathers and mothers are as logically unique as husbands and wives, and though sons and daughters and brothers and sisters can be many, in almost every family each is given a sense of being loved individually and having an irreplaceable position in the family's affection. One important, and occasionally forgotten, aspect of family responsibility is never to undermine the sense of unique worth—the father asking a little girl at a children's party 'And whose little girl are you?' and being answered 'Yours, papa', or parents telling neighbours that if a sick child dies, they will have another one. Whereas in a peer group it is often right to stress the similarity of status by treating everyone the same, in a family fair shares are very often not equal shares, but differentiated according to individual needs, tastes, and situation: the youngest needs more care and protection, the eldest is entitled to stay up later and make more decisions on his own.

11.6. PLATO

Plato set out to abolish the family. It was part of his programme for abolishing the self. Believing as he did that the root of all evil was self-aggrandisement, πλεονεξία (*pleonexia*), he based his ideal society on a group of high-minded guardians who would merge their individual aspirations into a general concern for the good of the community and the discovery of truth. Plato recognised that sex and the family would disrupt the unity of the ruling class. Rivalries give rise to dissension, and even high-minded men favour their own progeny as they seek preferment and promotion. Plato could not adopt the solution of St Benedict and the monastic movement, that of denying sex altogether; nor that of Byzantium, of relying predominantly on eunuchs to exercise power immune from the temptations of jealousy and nepotism, for both these solutions, besides being dysgenic, were necessarily incomplete, and relied on outside, and potentially corrupt, sources for novice guardians. Instead, Plato sought to downgrade sex and cloak genetic relationships under a veil of ignorance. His actual prescriptions are messily distasteful, though, with the aid of modern techniques of contraception, artificial insemination, *in vitro* fertilisation, and surrogate motherhood, the same results could be achieved today without much upset to our sensibilities.[2] In fact, however, we have gone down a different path. Sex and the family are allowed, but downgraded. People may marry, but do not have to, and if they do, the marriage bond is easily broken. Sustained pressure from the Inland Revenue over many decades has led to the widespread acceptance of couples living together without benefit of clergy. Divorce has become easier and easier, and part of the normal expectation of contemporary life. Death duties have broken up family estates and family firms.

---

[2] For a fuller discussion of Plato's thought, see J. R. Lucas, "Plato's Philosophy of Sex", in *Owls for Athens: Essays on Classical Subjects for Sir Kenneth Dover*, ed. Elizabeth Craik, Oxford, 1990, pp. 223–31. In recent years the study of genetics has made clear the link between reproductive policy and social feeling. It is most clearly exemplified in the social insects, where the workers share the same genes, and are genetically very similar to their queen. The only mammals which are reasonably platonic in their reproductive arrangements are the naked mole-rats (*Heterocephalus glaber*), which live in the banks of rivers in Africa. See further P. W. Sherman, J. U. M. Jarvis, and R. D. Alexander (eds.), *The Biology of the Naked Mole-Rat*, Princeton, NJ, 1991.

Access, in the last century to the Civil Service, and in this to most positions of power and influence, has been by meritocratic examination. It ought not to matter, we have come increasingly to feel, who your father is in the course of your life: that adventitious circumstance is ruled out as irrelevant by the principle of equality of opportunity, which seeks to establish for all a career open to the talents. Although in private life sex looms large in our thoughts and fantasies, marriage and the family have been denuded of public significance by the canons of meritocracy. Plato would be pleased at the progress we have made.

But the family is likely to survive the meritocratic attack. Although meritocracy has much to commend it, the lengths to which Plato was driven should make us wary of adopting its principles without modification. His fundamental hostility to the self is mistaken, and coming into the world as we do, and having the instincts we have, and living under the shadow of mortality as we do, we need to accommodate our intimations of corporate identity as equal members of a group with our need to discover our own unique identity in marriage and family life.

Meritocracy is unstable. Equality of opportunity yields inequality of outcome, but every unequal outcome can be attributed to some antecedent inequality not sufficiently discounted or guarded against. If the proportions of those successful are out of line with those eligible, accusations of bias and discrimination will be levelled and largely believed. Every appointment is inherently discriminatory in that some are chosen and others rejected, and it is hard to prove that those rejected were rejected because they were less good and not because they were of the wrong race, wrong sex, or wrong social class. If equality of opportunity is offered, equality of outcome will be expected, freedom will be sacrificed, and the apparatus of totalitarianism installed. Plato's ideal state and the actualities of modern communism should be warnings enough.

Meritocracy is hard on failures. I can console myself for not being in the House of Lords by reckoning that it is because my father was not, and I would not have him have been anyone else. Under a meritocracy, however, the only reason for not getting on is one's own inadequacies, and since almost all people will not make it to the top, almost all are doomed to a low view of themselves.

Meritocracy is hard on women. They are unlikely to compete as effectively as men, because they have periods, and are likely to be off work having babies and looking after children. The family is their scene, and where the family is important, they are powerful. One of the root causes of contemporary feminism has been the diminution of women's role in society with the erosion of the family. When the home was central, they walked down the corridors of power, but secretaries in offices type only to dictation. Over the last hundred years women have won the vote, but lost their most influential say in the course of events. Plato's view that women were the same as men, only not so good in actual fact, is not one that should commend itself either to feminists or to thinking people generally.

11.7. THE FAMILY

The family is not perfect either, and can be suffocating, tyrannical, and incompetent. Children need to be liberated from the family, or they remain children for ever, unable to make decisions on their own, unable to recognise that they are not the only person that matters, and not realising that other people exist, on the same footing as themselves, who must be considered, and whose opinions must be accorded respect. Children are deeply conscious of their need for their peers, and are greatly influenced by them. They speak the language of their schoolmates, not their parents, and dress to impress their contemporaries rather than to please their mothers.

Although family relationships support the individual's sense of his own unique identity, they do not constitute it. To be merely a scion of my family, however distinguished, is not to be me. I need to do my own thing, to make my own way, to exercise my own freedom of choice. The son who is expected to follow closely in his father's footsteps, the daughter pressured to marry the man of her mother's choice, are being denied their personhood. We rightly frown on arranged marriages, even though our own arrangements do not work well. People need not only to be able to, but to be encouraged to, make their own decisions, free from the web of family relationships and expectations, for much the same reasons as it is good to be able to exercise freedom of choice by spending money unbeholden to anyone else.[3]

How best to wean children from emotional dependence on their parents is difficult to determine. The English upper-class habit of sending boys away to boarding school at a tender age has heavy costs, but by late adolescence some institutionalised separation has much to recommend it. In time past daughters were often sent to other families, more or less as *au pair* girls, in order to acquire domestic skills and discipline away from the tensions of their own home. The intense identification with the gang or the student body witnesses to an emotional need. Often young people also form a deep, but not erotic, friendship with someone of their own sex, a best friend with whom everything is shared, and who remains a friend for the rest of their lives. Once again, we do well, in the current climate of insinuation, to avoid any suggestion that any such relationship must have a homosexual basis. In general, however, it is difficult to be specific about other responsibilities of parents and children. Parents need to let go, but need also to stand up for their principles, and be firm about what is not acceptable behaviour. Children need to discover themselves, but also to realise that many forms of self-expression are objectionable on almost any grounds. To counsel parents not to expect too much conformity, and children not to insist on flouting their parents' values, is trite, but often, unfortunately, the best advice that can be given.

Families tend to be exclusive, and where the family is the dominant social institution, it easily engenders a caste system that is rigidly exclusive too. We naturally think that blood is thicker than water, that breeding counts, and that we have special responsibilities to our own kith and kin. All of this is true, but not the whole truth. We have not yet come to terms in our social thinking with what geneticists call "the regression to the mean". Children take after their parents, but over the generations become increasingly . average. Dynasties degenerate. Marcus Aurelius could exercise power well, but Commodus was a disaster. Many family firms have lasted two or three generations, but then foundered because the next in succession was a nincompoop; often, where they have survived longer, it is because there

---

[3] See §8.13, pp. 167–8.

was an only daughter who married the up-and-coming manager, thereby bringing new life into the family. From this it follows that we need to temper family affection and loyalty, so as not to make it exclusive, and not to rule out acceptance of the new man. It is not wrong, save in properly meritocratic contexts, to give the son of a friend a leg up, and often we have better reason to believe in him than in any other candidate buttressed with testimonials. But we should take care never to despise or overlook someone just because he does not sport a long pedigree, and to be scrupulous in keeping some avenues of advancement open to the *novus homo*, and making sure that those avenues are kept free of nepotistic influence.

We are inconsistent. Although we believe firmly that it should not matter who your father was, we want our children to do well, and do all in our power to help them. The French Revolution decapitated many hereditary aristocrats, only to install the bourgeois family at the centre of economic and social power. The Israeli *kibbutzim* sought Platonically to bring up their children communally, but have largely abandoned the attempt, as being bad for the children as well as repugnant to parental instincts. Although some pressure groups make out that "one-parent families" are quite all right, the evidence does not support that claim: we regard as irresponsible, and are likely increasingly to condemn, parents who divorce, and single women who make themselves pregnant, whether to get a council house or to fulfil maternal ambitions. Our children did not ask to be born, but can ask subsequently why they were, and there is much to answer for if they were brought into the world without the prospect of a proper home and the continuing intention to provide it.

11.8. DEVIANCE

It is easy to idealize the lifelong, exclusive union of two like-minded souls in mutual dependence on their complementary gifts and aptitudes. The reality often falls far short of that, and although many families are alike in being happy, the unhappiness of family life occupies a large part of contemporary consciousness. It is partly the tension between the two paradigms, each important, each always present to some extent, but each inclining us in opposite directions. More obvious is the biological underlay of our emotions. The sexual and parental instincts are powerful, as they have to be if the species is to survive, but often ungoverned and at odds with each other, or with other powerful drives. And, finally, the ultimate core of individual identity, the ability to make up one's own mind for oneself, means that people are always able to make their own assessment of their situation, and are often led to view it differently from the way we would.

Men have always been tempted to sleep around. At one level it looks like a good strategy for reproducing one's kind. But, for the same reason, once they take the responsibilities of fatherhood seriously, they are insistent that their women should not sleep with anyone else, for cuckolds leave no progeny to carry on their easy-going attitude to adultery. Men are, for simple Darwinian reasons, naturally polygamous and jealous, and find it hard to be faithful. Women are under no genetic pressure towards polyandry, and jealousy for them takes a different form. It is only at a fairly advanced level of civilisation, where it takes a great deal of effort on father's part to launch his children in life, that monogamy begins to receive biological support; the endemic fratricide among the sons of the Sublime Porte affords the best illustration of how polygamy does not in the long run pay.

It is not surprising, therefore, that in the modern world, with the advent of contraceptives, and until recently reliable cures for venereal disease, the adventitious arguments against sexual laxness have seemed much less compelling, and a general permissiveness practicable and attractive. If we regard *homo sapiens* only as a sophisticated animal, then since we have strong sexual drives, and obtain much pleasure from indulging them, there appears to be no good argument for not doing so. The case is altered, however, if we regard people as persons, and what they do as signifying the sort of persons they are, and carrying messages about what they intend, as well as being causes of change in the course of events. If any action is significant, then certainly sexual intercourse is. It commits. Just as the sharing of food and drink in a meal betokens fellowship and values held in common, so intercourse commits both partners to being together for time to come to share in the upbringing of the young and with a common concern for its well-being. These implications of sexual activity have evolved in an intelligible fashion, and remain part of our instinctive inheritance even when there is no prospect of progeny, just as having a meal or a drink together retains its emotional significance even when we are not actually thirsty or have no need of nourishment.

If sexual intercourse is a natural language of commitment, the questions we ask are quite different from those that arise if it is only a physiological process. The most insistent is "How will it end?" Will it end at the graveside, when one or the other departs this life, and all our hopes and plans are subsumed under our common mortality? Or will one party ditch the other, leaving a broken heart and a shattered life? Or will it end by mutual consent, both parties having got tired of the arrangement? The second is the most likely outcome in practice, but the least acceptable in prospect, and one which no responsible person could seriously contemplate. The first evidently points towards marriage. The third is often avowed by young people who shy away from the first, and are ashamed even to consider the second, but becomes increasingly unsatisfactory, the more it is thought about. Mutual consent is difficult to determine, difficult to time. What you want from me, as we settle down in some pad together, is not just that I shall continue to hang around, work the washing machine, and pay my share of the bills, but that I shall love you, and shall want to be with you. If I fall out of love with you, and start dreaming of another, it is not much joy if I do go on working the washing machine and writing a weekly cheque. Life together would be insupportable on those terms. We shall have to part "by mutual consent", but your consent was forced by my falling out of love.

But perhaps we could agree about this beforehand, and face the situation now, while we are still in command of our emotions. We could. We could agree now not to be committed, just as I could agree at a restaurant to share my table with another patron, without there being any common bond between us. The natural language of sex can be cancelled by explicit agreement, just as in a play I could kiss someone without it meaning anything real. But there would be a price. By cancelling the meaning of what we are doing we are depriving it of the significance it normally carries, and thereby making it harder for it ever to carry that sense again in future. It is not always absolute, but it is a corrosive tendency. Rakes and *roués* perfect their sexual techniques, but lose their ability to make personal contact. If you and I agree at the outset that we are not committed, we are agreeing to use each other as a means to physiological gratification, but not to signify any union of spirits. And that is the first step along a road that leads to utter loneliness.

The arguments against avowedly uncommitted sex are widely accepted, and though many people now, as in previous times, succumb to temptation, casual sex is seen as a lapse rather than an acceptable way of life. What people in this present age find difficult is to focus on the question of how their affair will end, and to accept the logic that any responsible answer entails. They are committed, but shy off the formal step of marriage until they have been together for some years, or until they have finished their degrees, got jobs, found a house, put down enough for a mortgage, or want to start a family.

It is easy to sympathize with such an approach. In modern Britain the process of getting married involves a formidable social hoohah which seems extraneous to the intimacies of love— the bridesmaids' dresses, the invitation to Great Aunt Agatha and her three undesirable offspring, the present list, the marquee, the choice of hymns and going-away dress. All these take their emotional toll, and can cause so much friction that the marriage itself is doomed from the moment the bride's mother enters the church. How much better a simple get-together with a few close friends, and break it to the parents later, when they will have to accept a *fait accompli*. And, indeed, that may be better. But the few friends are indicative of a need to make the commitment public. We need it to be known that thou and I are living together, so that an invitation to one of us should as a matter of course be accompanied by an invitation to the other, and each is known not to be available for other dates. A public commitment, moreover, is more committing than a purely private one. Thou knowest, if I have made public my commitment to thee that I shall be publicly ashamed if I ever let thee down, and that is a further security beyond the possibly fickle feelings of my heart.

Many modern couples avoid any formal commitment for some time, while they make absolutely sure that they are suited to each other. It is an understandable precaution against repenting at leisure, and can be seen as a sort of trial marriage, which will modulate into marriage proper in due course, all being well. Often all is well. But the course of true love does not always run smooth, and misunderstandings may be mistaken for evidence that the trial is not working out after all. Traditional marriage is buttressed by a determination to make it work, whereas the very fact that a trial marriage is on trial tends to weaken it. Although we may drift into a permanent relationship with each other, we have not made an explicit decision that we shall, and that lack may prove fatal.

But some trial must be made. We cannot have it that love will always be at first sight, and that the first hesitant invitation, or even the first stolen kiss, will be a commitment for life. There must be some opportunity for drawing back and breaking off an affair, even if it does mean heart-break on the part of the other. True; but once again the traditional guidelines, though not above criticism, are the least damaging to most people. We can trifle with someone's affections by paying a lot of flattering attention, raising expectations, and then fading out; we can make a verbal promise to marry, and then break it; but the distinction between the courtship which does not, and that which does, involve sexual activity, is supported by two independent considerations as providing the proper answer to the question "How far can you go?" In almost every culture the sexual organs are felt to be peculiarly private and intimate, the *pudenda*, and sexual intercourse to betoken an intimacy of union which is without reserve or qualification. Other deeds and words can express serious interest and tentative commitment, while leaving room for second thoughts and subsequent withdrawals, but sex has a completeness about it that is appropriate only to unconditional commitment. In the second place, the discovery of sex is for most people a major experience of their life, and therefore one best shared with one's partner for life. Even the *roué* James Boswell wanted to seek out the prostitute with whom he had first "celebrated the rites of love", that being a bond between them he would not willingly discard. Whatever subsequently happens, the memories of first togetherness remain. In retrospect, almost all would agree that it was best that these memories should be shared by husband and wife, and that, though forgiveness could wipe away previous fault, it would be a pity if either brought a shadow into their partnership in having had sexual memories the other could not share, and a sense therefore of there having been someone else with whom sexual experience had been initiated. And if this is what it would be rational to feel in retrospect, responsibility requires us so to act now that we shall not regret it then.

11.9. HOMOSEXUALITY

The most important thing to say about homosexuality is that we do not know the facts. Much is assumed, much is alleged, some conclusions are supported by some evidence, but we cannot be sure, and if the facts turn out to be different, may have to change our minds. If homosexual behaviour were, as was thought at one time, purely a matter of voluntary choice, it might well be stigmatized as perverse, on a level with bestiality or necrophilia. If it were entirely a matter of genetic inheritance, as is claimed by some homophile organizations now, it would be reasonable to regard it with sympathy or indifference, like colour-blindness. If it were engendered by environmental conditioning, and if, in particular, homosexual experience in adolescence could fix people in a homosexual orientation thereafter, as is still widely believed, then there would be weighty utilitarian arguments for discountenancing homosexual behaviour by means of the criminal law. It may well be that adolescents go through a homosexual phase in their development to maturity, and it may be that most will grow out of it naturally, whatever their experience; or it may be that homosexual experience does retard or inhibit further development. We do not know, but as often in practical matters have to make up our minds none the less, and must do the best we can, remembering always our own fallibility.

At the present time homophile advocates make two claims: that homosexual activity is on a par with heterosexual activity, and constitutes an alternative way of life; and that homosexuals cannot help having the orientation they have, and ought to be treated with toleration and sympathy. Either claim may be maintained, but not both. The former is putting forward a new morality, which may win acceptance, as being indeed the correct morality, which we all ought to pursue, but may, equally, be rejected as being, though sincerely advocated, mistaken and false. The plea for tolerance and sympathy, however, only makes sense

against a background of agreed principles. I can ask you to tolerate me, and sympathize with my plight, only if I concede that it
is a plight, and I am not calling your moral stance in question. If
I suggest that my position is not a plight but one that is on a par
with yours, I put you in the position of either conceding my
claim or else controverting it. And if you controvert it, I must
not complain, or say that I am being persecuted because you do
not acknowledge the rightfulness of my claim. Much confusion
and some aggravation has been caused in recent years by the
conjunction of pleas for tolerance with proselytizing campaigns
for homosexual equality. Clarity will be served, and perhaps
charity enhanced, if we keep the two contentions entirely separate.

Homosexuality has been a dominant feature of some cultures,
notably that of ancient Greece, and many homosexuals in other
cultures have made notable contributions to literature, learning,
and the arts. David and Jonathan loved each other with a love
surpassing that of women. Plato's affection for young members
of his own sex gave the Academy a firm foundation in natural
human emotions. And so, it is argued, we should accept homosexuality as a perfectly natural human relationship on a par with
the more usual heterosexual ones.

But the conclusion does not follow. There are two important
differences between homosexual and heterosexual relations which
greatly alter the view we should take of them. Homosexual
relationships are not based on a natural complementarity, and
are not naturally creative. Although homosexual partners may
possess or develop complementary skills or character traits, these
are not supported either by natural differentiation or by some
differing social expectation. The relationship is likely, therefore,
to be less binding and long-lasting than a heterosexual one. It is
difficult to argue this very strongly in the present age, when heterosexual partnerships too often lack permanence, but homosexual partnerships seem to be even more transient. In particular,
they lack the shared commitment of children. Again, homosexual
couples can, like childless married couples, develop other creative
concerns, intellectual, artistic, spiritual, or social, which give their
union a focus outside itself, and can carry them through to some
shared achievement. But it is difficult. Homosexual partnerships
lack the deep natural shared affection for children that most

married couples have, a shared affection which not only crowns a happy marriage, but often preserves others through unhappy patches. Homosexual relationships may be the best that homosexually oriented people can achieve, but they are not the same as heterosexual ones.

The relationship between David and Jonathan may, or may not, have been homosexual. There is no evidence either way. Young men at the threshold of adulthood often form intense friendships which are not at all erotic, and the language of yesteryear did not distinguish a union of souls from more fleshly encounters. David and Jonathan's friendship may have been like the many others that have been formed, and have enormously enriched the lives both of the two who are friends and of the many others they have affected. Certainly in later life David was far from being homosexually inclined. But his later heterosexual orientation may, perhaps, have been a natural development from an earlier homosexual phase. We do not know for sure, but some who have studied the subject maintain, with some evidence to support them, that men go through a homosexual phase in the course of their sexual maturation into normal heterosexual adulthood. It would be a natural way of accommodating the fact that they become sexually developed before they are able to shoulder the burden of looking after wife and children. That could be so. But it still would not establish the contention that homosexual unions are on a par with heterosexual ones. On the contrary, it would emphasize their transience. It might be natural for adolescents to go through a homosexual phase, but we should regard their attachments then as passing affections, which ought not to be made too much of, or allowed to stand in the way of some later, heterosexual and permanent, union.

To argue that homosexual relationships are not just like heterosexual ones, and that they do not constitute an alternative way of life on a par with them, is not to damn them utterly as immoral. Further argument would be needed to establish that conclusion, and the facts we know do not support any such argument. We cannot, on the basis of what we know, tell homosexuals simply to snap out of it, nor can they tell us that their situation is genetically controlled and unalterable. What we do know is that many homosexuals see themselves as unalterably fixed in that orientation, and that some who had thus viewed themselves have ceased to be in that case. It also appears that many, like Plato, have sublimated their urges, developing great sympathy with, and understanding of, young members of their own sex, without engaging in any sexual activity. Many of the contributions made by homosexuals have been through their heightened sensitivity to the feelings of others and the agonizing dilemmas that life forces them to face, and not through their having engaged in intercourse themselves. That seems the most responsible course to commend to present-day homosexuals, but if that advice is rejected, it is possible to respect their differing judgement of their situation, and to recognise the elements of fidelity, mutual support, and self-giving which can characterize their relationship as it can substandard heterosexual ones. There is a long tradition in literature and Christian teaching of the golden-hearted prostitute, who, though a sinner, shows much greater love than her respectably married sister, and is much nearer the kingdom of heaven. We do not commend prostitution—it does not normally lead to a golden heart, and most prostitutes are worse off, morally as well as materially, than most wives—but we can withhold condemnation, and see the good in the person and her way of life, even though something else would have been better. So too with the homosexual. The claim that it is as good a way of life must be rejected; but if that claim is not put forward, it need not be controverted. It has not been established that there are bad consequences that follow from tolerating homosexuality; and we can recognise the integrity and sincerity of those who want to live in lifelong exclusive unions with each other, even if such a union is not buttressed by a natural complementarity or the creation of new human beings.

11.10. FEMINISM

Feminist arguments have been much canvassed recently. They had attracted some support in the earlier part of the century, but faded away during the Second World War, and were revived in the aftermath of the student movement in the 1960s, when the gap between the egalitarian protestations of the leaders and their actual practice in their personal lives became too much for their female followers to overlook. The underlying causes were much deeper: the growth of meritocratic and egalitarian ideals and their application in industrial society. If all men are equal, should not that include women too? If the workplace rather than the home is the focus of social life, then women, no longer esteemed and revered as wives and mothers, but employed as secretaries, nurses, and receptionists, are evidently being treated as second-class citizens. A number of institutional injustices gave edge to indignation, which was formulated in the demand that women should be treated exactly the same as men, and that all discrimination on grounds of sex was immoral and should be made illegal.

But nature is hard to controvert. The irrelevance of sex may be proclaimed from the house-tops but is denied in the closet. None of us would be here unless all our ancestors had been sexists, evincing towards the opposite sex behaviour quite different from that evinced towards members of their own sex. Feminism taken to its logical conclusion yields the precepts put forward by the homophile lobby, and if we baulk at accepting the latter, we cannot go along with the former either.

Most feminists do not take feminism to its logical conclusion. They make an exception for sex. The sex of a person, they say, is irrelevant to everything save sex. Women are not to be debarred from dating men rather than other women, and—with considerable hesitation—it is allowed to choose girls as au pairs rather than boys. But once any exception is allowed, it is difficult to draw the line. Whether it is genetically controlled or due entirely to social conditioning, there are considerable differences in the aptitudes and attitudes of the sexes, and these are often highly relevant to the choices we make. To choose *is* to discriminate. Sometimes, under some conditions, for some purposes, we can require decision-makers to ignore some features they might otherwise regard as relevant, but a general requirement to ignore relevant factors is bound to be circumvented.

Feminist precepts are not only impracticable, but work against the interests of most women. Equality of opportunity does not guarantee success, though it is often taken to. It enters people for a competition, in which inevitably there are losers as well as winners. And women are likely to lose. Rather few women are likely to gain a place in the Oxford or Cambridge eight. Even where physical strength is not at issue, there may be sex-linked intellectual differences that have a bearing on the outcome of competitions. Although it is maintained by some that any imbalance between the sexes *must* be due to some bias on the part of the judges or unfairness in the procedures, such a conclusion is not the natural one, and is becoming increasingly implausible. It is more natural to suppose, though not conclusively established by scientific evidence, that women are less competitive in their attitudes and less well endowed with those abilities that win success in competitions than their male rivals, and so tend to lose out in the competitive arena of the workplace. If this is so, it is no benefit to women generally to force them to compete, when their instincts are to co-operate, and enter them for a race they will lose. For the sake of a few successful sisters, they are being made to feel failures, and, instead of fulfilled females, also-ran males.

The underlying logic of meritocracy plays down the importance of marriage, the family, and the home. But these are for most women the chief concern of their lives, and must be if the human race is to continue. The emphasis placed by feminists on women's rights in the workplace has the effect of devaluing the work that most women do. The message is that to be a housewife, a mother, and a home-maker is nothing much, whereas to be an advertising agent, an accountant, or a personal assistant to a managing director is something to be proud of. Bringing up children, making a home, loving and cherishing a husband—these are mediocre achievements, whereas deceiving the public, juggling figures, and pushing paper are important contributions to the welfare of mankind.

Most jobs are dull: that is why people are paid to do them. Although for some people—especially some of those who have been to university—a career is intrinsically satisfying, for very many others the chief reason why they work is to earn money, and a large part of the satisfaction derived from earning money is that it provides for the upkeep of a home and the maintenance of a family. Breadwinners do not want simply to eat bread themselves. They want to buy presents for their loved ones, give their children a good start in life, improve and beautify their homes; and their workaday labours are justified in their eyes as a means to that end. Feminist ideology implies a reversal of means and ends. In seeking to liberate women from the world of *kuche, kinder, und kirche*, it not only deprives them of the value of what they do, but also deprives men of the main purpose for which they work.

But some women want to have careers. Not every woman wants to devote herself to domesticity. Not every man wants to make founding a family the chief business of his life. In the Middle Ages vocations always involved celibacy, and there was no room for further conflict between family and professional obligations; but the modern world, rejecting that simple, though extreme, solution, has been confused and inconsiderate in its attitude to women who have felt the call to some career outside the home. We need to accommodate them; equally, they need to recognise that social institutions, such as marriage and the family, have to have simple and even crude outlines, if they are to be generally understood and accepted by people at large.

Many of the difficulties career women face are recent and of our own making: if we set our face against domestic service, then a doctor cannot both tend her sick children or go to their Christmas carol service at school, and be on call for sick patients. Egalitarian prejudice in the second half of the twentieth century has meant that all mothers are equally housebound, and has prevented many women from using their gifts, as they would have wished, for the benefit of their fellow citizens. But even where domestic service eases many problems, there is an underlying conflict of priorities: an eighteenth-century professor of chemistry at Bologna was criticized for neglecting her studies to play with her children, and a responsible mother cannot leave her children entirely to the care of nannies and au pair girls. Men, too, face a similar conflict, though usually less sharp: their careers may be advanced by accepting promotion to a different district, but their families may suffer from being uprooted. No simple rule can resolve this problem: sometimes it is right that family should take second place—as happens prospectively when anyone embarks on a profession rather than a better-paid job in business; but often also it is right to give up prospects of promotion for the sake of the children, and this applies to women no less than to men. If one wants above all things to get on and go far, one should travel light, and not take on encumbrances.

Professional people generally, and academics in particular, tend to despise those outside their magic circle, who merely earn their living in the workaday world. The arrogance implicit in the assumption that only professional work is really work, and that men employed elsehow, who merely provide for the needs of others and keep society going, are not really contributing anything worthwhile, is sometimes recognised for what it is, and condemned as intellectual snobbery: we need to be similarly sensitive to the snide disparagement implicit in the question "Yes, but what do you *do*?" addressed by professional women to their domestic sisters.

The professions tend to have a meritocratic career structure in which individuals, though co-operating with their colleagues, are also competing, and hope to rise by their own merits. Academics in particular think of life as a series of examinations, in which it would be unfair for anyone to be judged on anything but his own merits, and those of similar merits should be given similar rewards. They find it difficult to accommodate their thinking to the fact that many decisions are polycentric, with no one person who is the centre of concern, and all extraneous considerations excluded;[4] rather, there are a number of different people involved with different interests, so that in deciding about one, the side-effects on others have to be considered. In an examination it would be quite improper and grossly unfair to give a woman a different grade just because she was a woman, and hence it seems equally unfair to pay a woman less than a man for doing the same work. But the effect of equal-pay provisions on mothers and children has been altogether adverse. If men get no more than women, then fathers cannot afford not to send their wives out to work. In order to afford a mortgage for a house bought in competition with childless couples, a couple has to have two incomes, and children have to be postponed till the mortgage has been paid off, or parked out to baby-minders so that mother can go back to paid employment. It is difficult to believe that this is in the interests of the children, or always in accord with the wishes of the wives—but it is an inevitable effect of meritocratic principles being applied in the individual case without regard for the others who will be affected. Although it is tempting for a philosopher to fault feminism solely on the score of the logical errors and fallacies in the arguments put forward in its favour, the substantial objection is that, contrary to its protestations, it actually works out to the disadvantage of women generally.

[4] See §9.5.

Chapter 12
Beyond Responsibility

Responsibility is an important virtue, but not an amiable one. Its praises have seldom been sung. It is not one of the four cardinal virtues of pagan antiquity, nor one of the great Christian virtues singled out by St Paul. If we can regard it as the equivalent of φρόνησις (*phronesis*), we can count Aristotle as its great advocate, but must set against that Jesus' injunction "Take no thought for the morrow, what ye shall eat or what ye shall drink".

Responsibility by itself carries no connotation of spontaneity or warmth. I can be utterly responsible, but very boring and rather cold. You can rely on me: I shall not let you down, and you know where you are with me; but equally I shall not say anything new, and although I shall always treat you correctly, I would do the same for anybody else, and there is no indication that you mean anything special to me, that I like you, or want to share with you. If I am responsible, I am somebody you can work with, but it does not follow that I am someone you would want to live with.

Responsibility is like justice, very necessary in its way, but not by itself enough. If people are irresponsible, we find it very difficult to put up with them, and many friendships and marriages founder on unreliability and thoughtlessness. But essential though it is, we find, as we think about it, a pervasive sense of its inadequacy as a key concept in our understanding of mankind. It is all very well, but . . . It is difficult to articulate fully what is lacking. It is different in different cases. The economics of Chapter 8 are estimable but do not grip us. The political institutions of Chapter 10 are worthy, but lack glamour. Altogether responsibility lacks charm, lacks the human touch.

In part it is due to the logic of question and answer. If you ask me questions, I shall try to give answers you can accept. And so if you ask me why I did something, I shall tend to cite those omni-personal reasons which I can reasonably expect you to accept, rather than the first-personal reasons that peculiarly moved me, and are typical of the sort of person I am. I depersonalise myself in attempting to make my actions more acceptable to you. Instead of being me, the one and only unique character that I am, I portray myself as a standard-issue rational agent who acts just the same as anyone else in my position would. Responsibility makes Stoics of us all, and Stoics, though uniformly worthy, are uniformly dull, because they are not individuals but only instances of some impersonal rationality.

The Romantics reacted against the apparently Procrustean pressure of rationality by rejecting reason, and making emotion or feeling the most important guide in life. We have seen enough of unbridled emotionalism to be completely disenchanted with that: gut feelings are often nauseating. Although we recognise the critique of rationalism, and half agree with Pascal that the heart has its reasons of which the reason knows nothing, we begin to wonder what the reason is up to if there are reasons it does not know. In fact reason's ignorance of reasons is self-imposed: reason has been too narrowly defined, so that it is by definition unable to comprehend the reasons that the heart finds telling. If reason is defined as being purely deductive reason, the paradigm of the geometric method, then it is circumscribed indeed: even if we enlarge the boundaries of the concept to include inductive reasoning of various types, we have not enlarged it enough to include the reasons that move men to action. If we embrace all the reasons that different individuals find persuasive, we need to have reason infinitely complex in order to accommodate the infinite complexity of individuals. There are dangers here, which have made many philosophers draw back, for fear of extending the concept indefinitely, so that anything goes, and the concept of reason becomes empty. Those dangers can be avoided, and we have in Chapter 4 tried to develop a concept of reason which discriminates between good and bad reasons, but does not require good reasons to conform to set patterns. This makes it easier to see how people could act, even act spontaneously, and yet for reasons, and thus be responsible, but still be themselves.[1]

[1] See §4.6.

12.2. THE INADEQUACY OF DESERT

If we are responsible, and take thought about what we shall do in the light of the account we may one day have to make, we are likely to act for good reasons, and to be able subsequently to give a good account of what we have done. We shall have set ourselves worthwhile aims, and sometimes achieved them. We shall have deserved well.

It is not a bad thing to have deserved well. But it is not all that good either. Our achievements may earn us their due reward, whether in financial form or in the well-merited esteem of our peers, but these goods, though real, are not enough to satisfy the soul. We want more. We want to be liked, to be loved, to be valued for what we are and not only for what we have done. And love cannot be earned. I can make you—if you are reasonable—respect me, but I cannot make you like me. I can prove myself a worthy colleague, but not force myself on you as a friend. Friendship, liking, love—those are things outside my power to command or attain. They depend not only on my merits, but on your free choice. You may choose to like me, and if so, I am lucky: but you may find me uncongenial—I have the wrong chemistry for you—and then there is nothing I can do about it. If, therefore, I want to be liked, I make myself vulnerable to the unarguable-with choices of others, and aspire to something I cannot secure by my own unaided efforts. And I may express this by feeling that my actions and achievements are inadequate towards attaining what I most want, and hence entirely worthless. Lovers know they are unworthy of the love of the beloved, and so feel themselves to be worms, undeserving of the good thing they tremulously hope they may be granted. And in thinking that they are not worthy of love, they are right, for love is not the sort of thing one can be worthy of: but in concluding that they are altogether unworthy, they are wrong, for love is not the sort of thing one can be either worthy or unworthy of, and among those things of which such terms can properly be predicated there may well be many of which they are worthy.

The inadequacy of desert may also be argued for on other grounds. Under sceptical analysis both self and circumstance seem to dissolve to the point where they cease to be able to support a concept of the agent's being sufficiently much the author of his successes to be able to claim any ultimate credit for them. Rawls exploits this line of attack in advancing his claim that desert should not be a basis for allocation of benefits at all.[2] Williams, more moderately, observes that 'One's history as an agent is a web in which anything that is the product of the will is surrounded and held up and partly formed by things that are not . . .' and concludes that responsibility can be made coherent only at the cost of being rendered superficial.[3] Although we can counter, and argue that it is not all that superficial a concept, and certainly not one that can be easily dispensed with, we must concede that there is a considerable element of luck in life, both as regards circumstances that have afforded us opportunities, and in the more intimate encounters and experiences that have helped us become the people we are. We are knit together, and the picture that emerges from our discussion of responsibility, of self-sufficient men making up their minds for themselves, and answering for it to their peers or their creator, seems strangely atomistic and unreal. I am what I am partly through luck, and much more through the good offices of others with whom I have lived and from whom I have imbibed my ideals and developed my dispositions.

For these two reasons we begin to feel uneasy in our metaphysical moments at making much of responsibility and desert. Adequate though it is at an everyday level, it does not measure up to the great goods we sometimes aspire to, which cannot be earned or deserved, and if they are to be had at all must be had through the free choice of another. And though I ought to be ready to answer for my actions myself, a certain modesty overcomes me if I am honest, and prevents me arrogating to myself all the credit since I would not have had the personality to do them were it not for the example and encouragement, teaching and support, of many other people on whose shoulders I now stand.

12.3. ORIGINAL GUILT

As I acknowledge my fellowship with other men, I not only share credit for my good deeds, but responsibility for their bad ones. I

---

[2] See §7.4, p. 128.
[3] B. A. O. Williams, *Moral Luck*, Cambridge, 1981, p. 29.

am the beneficiary of ancient wrongs. My father got me on the vanquished maid,[4] and my fourth cousin twice removed made money exploiting African slaves in the West Indies. I am what I am not only through the good offices of others with whom I have lived and from whom I have imbibed my ideals and developed my dispositions, but thanks also to my having been nourished on the fruits of their extortions, and having been on the winning side in their unjust wars. Nor is this only a past inheritance that I have entered into late in time. Even now, wrongs are being done, sometimes wantonly, but more often inevitably and necessarily, as part of the system in which I participate and from which I gain my security and livelihood. Men are in prison that I may live in peace. It could not really be otherwise, but it is degrading none the less. I fail a candidate in an examination, I disappoint an applicant for a job, I shut up the village bore at a parish council, I do not give a petty thief another chance: in none of these cases am I acting wrongly, but in each I have rational grounds for some unease. There is a gap between what I had to do and what I would have wished to be able to do, and in that gap someone was wounded, and it was I who delivered the blow, not out of ill will, but as a member of society, a typical man representative of the human race. In some way still I feel that we, and I, have something to answer for.

We need to be cautious. It is easy to wallow in guilt without doing anything effective to put things right. It makes some people feel good to feel bad about things generally—it shows them to be moral without the inconvenience of actual action. Vicarious and collective guilt can be ascribed only under stringent conditions. I did not eat the apple; I did not commit genocide against Neanderthal man; I did not burn the temperate rain forests, dispossess the Indians, enslave the Africans. Nor have I really retrospectively endorsed those misdeeds. I may have entered into an inheritance founded on them, and may have thereby taken on some responsibility, but that would only amount to liability in tort with a duty of reparation, not criminal guilt with a call for punishment.[5] For that to be appropriate, some definite ill will on my part would be necessary. Only if I myself have flouted some

---

[4] A. E. Housman, *A Shropshire Lad*, XXVIII: "Couched upon her brother's grave, / The Saxon got me on the slave."

[5] See §5.2, p. 77, §6.9 and App. 1, pp. 278–9.

requirement, can I myself disown and unsay the intention to do wrong.

Some theologians—St Paul, St Augustine, and the Protestant Reformers—have discerned such ill will in themselves. It is not so much a catalogue of definite misdeeds—with a few juicy exceptions, the sins of the saints verge on the trivial—as a corruption of motive. The heart is deceitful above all things, they come to realise, and desperately sick: even in their most exemplary law-abiding moments, they are doing it out of concealed self-aggrandisement, a covert means of doing well by number one. Maybe: motives are mixed, and even when we are acting for disinterested reasons, we may also be aware of these actions being likely also to work to our advantage, redound to our good name, or improve our standing in the eyes of those we admire. In the ordinary way of thinking this is a fact of life—a fortunate fact, since it provides added encouragement to do good—which we may acknowledge, but need not bemoan. It is only against some duty of achieving perfect purity of heart that our mixed motives can be construed as a failure. St Paul believed, or half-believed, that he had such a duty. Was he right?

It is easy to see that at one level St Paul was wrong. He was setting himself an impossible task, and the harder he tried to achieve perfect purity of heart, the more aware he became of his self-awareness infecting his conscious pursuit of self-forgetfulness. It was only when he abandoned the struggle and accepted the fact that he was accepted by God that he could find peace and refreshment of soul. So too with Luther, so too with Wesley—we see them winding themselves up to ever more intense efforts of self-improvement, and release and relaxation come only when they turn their attention away from themselves, and meditate instead on God.

Thus far it is easy to psychologize about the evangelical experience, but it would be a mistake to leave it simply at that. The conceptual scheme which St Paul inherited from Judaism and passed on to the Christian Church was flawed, but there were truths he was trying to articulate which, though misformulated then and since, are truths none the less. The language of the law—duty, action, responsibility—is inappropriate to the private world of motives, feelings, aspirations, personal relations, and self-fulfilment; but, much more important, the self which has evolved, and which we have inherited, is not satisfactory, and is in need of a radical overhaul.

12.4. SICKNESS OF SOUL

Freud claimed that civilisation induced neurosis. It is not entirely true, and anyway living in uncivilised society can make one neurotic too; but it is true that the socialising process puts pressure on people, sometimes more than they can stand. Personalities need to be repressed if they are to be tolerable to live with; someone who is uninhibited is a menace to himself as well as to others. But we do not take to inhibition kindly, and often suffer severe traumas in being prevented from always getting our own way in everything. Many adolescents, in particular, try to break out before they are cut down to size by their pastors and masters, and fitted into a neat social slot. They want to make good, and be themselves, and sense that in conforming to society's requirements they are maiming themselves, and losing their virility and manhood. Although many in the end come to terms with themselves, settle down, and make a reasonable success of their lives, at least by conventional canons, some break out, and discover the hard way the emptiness of self-assertion. More drop out and, along with the more straightforward failures and misfits, become casualties of our over-demanding civilisation. Even those who do not actually break down may suffer still, sensing an emptiness in the heart of their own lives, the weariness of spirit eloquently expressed in the book of Ecclesiastes. However successful we may be, either individually or collectively, at one level, we have our moments of depression, when we are inclined to believe that the heart is, indeed, desperately sick.

The diagnosis is nearly always in terms of the self. "The fat relentless ego", in Iris Murdoch's words,[6] is the villain, and the suggestion is that if only I could get away from myself, all would be well. But myself is who I am, and I can no more get away from it than I can achieve the state of not being here. Plato, the Stoics, Kant, and many moral philosophers have equated morality with some form of selflessness, but this not only gives moral-

---

[6] Iris Murdoch, *The Sovereignty of Good*, London, 1970, p. 52.

ity an inhuman face, but fails in its effect: the old Adam finds highly original ways of coming back through the window, and making morality the new vehicle of his self-assertiveness. If we persuade ourselves that we are moral, we deceive ourselves, and become whited sepulchres, full of corruption within. A simple purge of self is impossible in principle, and ineffective in practice.

Freud and many other psychotherapists have maintained that it is none the less possible to cure our inevitable neuroses, and enable men to live with themselves. Christianity too claims to be able to heal the sickness of the soul, and free us from the disordered wills and affections of sinful men. In each case, instead of self-abnegation and self-hate, the therapy is based on self-knowledge, leading to some sort of self-acceptance. Not that we should be content with ourselves as we are. Some change of attitude, some new-mindedness is inculcated, but it is more the adoption of a new perspective than the self-sufficient striving to carry out a particular task. In the Christian case it is the recognition that one is loved of God that is called for, and the willingness to accept this and respond to it. Like the love of another human being, the love of God is ego-enhancing: however bad I am, I cannot be that bad if someone cares for me, and worthless though my own actions are in themselves, they are worth doing if they matter to someone else. Love is a solace to the soul stricken with a sense of its own worthlessness, and provides a motive for action untainted by egocentricity.

12.5. IDENTIFICATION

Love is not static. It is great to be loved, but few are content to bask in the admiration and affection of another. Love calls for love in return, and lovers seek further union, and ultimately a changed identity. I am no longer the miserable, insignificant me, but someone of consequence, whose values matter because they are not mine alone, but shared and endorsed by someone of consequence. My identity, by itself in jeopardy of evaporating altogether, is underwritten by my identification with a greater whole. Many greater wholes are, up to a point, sufficient to support my need for meaningful existence—the new social unit of the married couple, being a reliable member of a team, the school, or the firm, being a respected colleague, being a loyal citizen of the nation state—but each group identity is open to the same questioning as individual identity, and may be doubted too in the same despairing way. Only if we could ground our being in reality itself, could we be sure we had a firm foundation for significant existence.

But it is difficult to identify with reality. Reality might be of the wrong logical shape to identify with. It might be a collocation of material particles following predetermined paths according to iron laws entirely unmindful of us and our concerns. It might be a single integrated four-dimensional *deus sive natura* evolving from a point-like singularity some 15,000 million years ago, according to Einstein's field equations. It might be more mathematical still—some austere platonic form that necessitated its own instantiation. We might be awed by the starry heavens without, we might in our mathematical moods be moved to worship the world of the forms. But we could not identify with them.

Even if reality is personal, as the theists say, difficulties remain, as the ancient Jews found. The key concept in personal identity is the will, and it is in a union of wills that we chiefly manifest our identification with others. My identification with a greater whole has many emotional and conventional overtones, but the test of my identification is my implementing its values in what I do. The Jews saw themselves as God's people and sought to carry out His will, and to this day their shared obedience to the law is the core of their religious and cultural identity. But wholehearted obedience to the law is hard. I can conform my outward actions, but my inner motives have a recurrent tendency to egocentricity, and I do what I am required to do not because I want to do it, but because I want to stand well in the sight of my neighbours or reap some tangible reward at the hands of the Almighty. It is not really a union of wills but a two-person game, in which the other party is the public, or Nature, or God, but the person whose pay-off I am trying to maximise is once again the Great and Wonderful Me.

12.6. ATONEMENT

In orthodox Christian theology, the salvation of man is constituted by his reconciliation with God, which was accomplished by the death of Jesus Christ on the cross. Many theories have been put forward to explain how one man's dying a horrible death could enable all mankind to be at one with God. The most influential have explained the Atonement in terms of wrongdoing and punishment. We all are sinners, and were therefore estranged from God: punishment was called for if our wrongdoing was to be annulled and no longer stand between us and God. Jesus suffered the death penalty on our behalf. The penalty having been paid, albeit by him, vicariously, we were effectively ransomed, and free to be reconciled with God.

Penal theories, if taken literally, have always been difficult to make sense of, and all the more so if the account of punishment given in Chapter 6 is accepted. If punishments are unwelcome consequences adventitiously annexed to wrongdoing by an authority as an externally imposed penance, the necessity that was said to require man's sin to be purged by a punishment ceases to be an iron necessity that binds even God, and vicarious penance seems altogether inappropriate where man's relation to God is concerned. If I have committed mortal wrong, I may give myself up for execution to show how sincere is my repudiation of the misdeed, but it is difficult to see how someone else's execution can express my sincerity of repentance. If the Prodigal Son was not allowed to do penance, it is difficult to believe our Divine Father could not, or would not, remit punishment on our return to the fold. The metaphors of original sin, the wrath of God, the need for punishment, and Jesus Christ offering Himself instead of us, fall apart, and the explanations offered by penal theories raise more questions than they answer.

Penal theories are inadequate, but what they seek to explain has made sense to believers down the ages. The cross has been the pre-eminent symbol of Christianity, whose good news has been the reconciliation of man, in spite of his manifest failings, with God. If penal theories are inadequate to explain how this is possible, it is incumbent on us to show, in the light of our altered understanding of responsibility, identity, sin, wrongdoing, repentance, apology, penance, and punishment, how one person's death could overcome the corporate failure of mankind, and achieve some sort of at-one-ness with God.

12.7. CROSSLESS CHRISTIANITY

If people can be healed by coming to know that God loves them, it should be enough to apprise them of this fact, and let the good news do its work. But people will not be told. The Old Testament was full of messages to this effect, but the message did not get through. It was all very well for the prophets or the psalmist to say it, but were they telling the truth? How could God love us when He put Job so cruelly to the test, and many others likewise but without a happy ending?

The Incarnation offers a partial answer. Instead of a distant God, benevolently observing His creatures from afar, we are bidden believe in a God who is in with us, and involved in all our experience of life, bad as well as good. A Christmas God is one we can relate to, knowing that He shares in all our sadness as well as our times of gladness. But still we die, while He, presumably, does not. Something like the Resurrection is required to assure us that death has lost its sting and has no more dominion over us. But a Lazarus-type death and resuscitation would suffice for that, followed perhaps by an ascension like Elijah's. There were other religions in the ancient world, like that of Isis and Osiris, which offered communion with God and hope of immortality. A crossless Christianity could do the same.

The New Testament shows that Jesus courted death, though flinchingly. He set His face to go to Jerusalem, and was in no doubt about what the outcome of that confrontation would be. Why did He do it? He could perfectly well have lain low and avoided trouble, continuing to teach His disciples, and through them sharing with us more of His wonderful insights into the nature of man and God, until the times were more propitious for confronting the High Priest and Sanhedrin in Jerusalem. Others have courted death too. Socrates could have got off if he had agreed to a reasonable alternative, and had many opportunities of escape. Many brave souls in our own century have stood up and been counted for the gas chambers or the salt mines, when if they had kept their heads down they might have survived. But their necks were too stiff, and they held their heads high: they would not compromise their integrity in order to live. Jesus likewise had to stand up for what He stood for. A political leader, another David wise in this world's ways, could have made a tactical withdrawal until a more opportune moment for taking on the establishment, but Jesus was concerned with principles rather than power, and principles are less accommodating to the exigencies of expediency. Although Jesus did not have to go to Jerusalem precisely when He did, He had to go sooner or later and have it out with the powers that be. To have kept quiet would have been to back down, and to have backed down would have been to abandon His witness to the absolute supremacy of God. It was not just obedience to an external injunction from the Father that drove Him on, but an internal necessity to be true to Himself and His mission.

In the twentieth century governments have been very wicked, and have got rid of good men because they stood in their way. But neither the Jewish nor the Roman authorities were wicked, though later Christian writers made them out to be. The Sadducees and Pharisees were, in their different ways, zealous for the law and the prophets, and would in most ages be accounted as exceptionally good members of society. Pilate was evidently reluctant to allow Jesus to be crucified. He was done to death not by the Hitlers, Stalins, or Amins of the time, but by Britain or the United States. Moderately good men living under moderately unbad regimes find themselves none the less impelled to do bad things. It is customary to ascribe this to original sin—the way human beings are constituted and the way society is organized—and then it is true to say that Jesus died because of the sinfulness of man. Although individually neither you nor I had any part in what happened in 29 AD, we might well have done, had we been alive at the time, and collectively, inasmuch as we identify with humanity, we must acknowledge some responsibility—it is the sort of thing we humans do.

A crossless Christianity would have fudged the issue. It would not have made clear what the cost of integrity might come to, and it would have obscured the harsh realities of worldly ways. It would be a more comfortable religion, better for wiping away tears, and offering hope of an easier path through this world to the next. But it would involve an element of wishful shut-eye, and could not long commend itself as being the truth.

12.8. THE PLEDGE OF SINCERITY

We can explain why Jesus had to die in terms of integrity and the way that men in public positions choosing the lesser of two evils often are led to do bad things.[7] But it has meant much more than that. We are saved by the self-sacrifice of Jesus the Son of God. Much of the imagery is due to St Paul, arguing with Jews against a background of ritual sacrifice which does not admit of close analysis, but there is something that speaks to people far more intimately than the account of the previous section allows.

The previous section gives a sense to saying that Jesus died as a consequence of human wrongdoing, which was not just the particular wrong decisions of particular human agents a long time ago, but the sorts of things human beings generally, ourselves included, are always doing, and which are so much part of our way of life that we must, if we are honest, acknowledge some responsibility for their being done. In that sense we can say that Jesus paid the price of our sins.

It does not follow that our sins are forgiven. Forgiveness is two-sided, and requires both an owning up to the deed and a disowning of the intention on the part of the wrongdoer, and an acceptance of the apology and restoration to fellowship on the part of those whose values were flouted by the wrongdoing.[8] Where the values flouted are those of God, it is for Him to accept, and we find it difficult to believe that He really does. But if Jesus really was His son, it becomes difficult to doubt that God was in earnest in telling us that we are accepted and could be at one with Him. God so loved the world that He gave His only-begotten Son to the end that all might believe in Him and not perish but have eternal life. The Crucifixion was a token of God's sincerity.

12.9. THE PRICE OF PROOF

Dying is an expensive, if effective, way of proving one's love. I do not normally demand such proof of devotion from my

---

[7] See §9.4, pp. 188–9, and §8.14, pp. 169–71.   [8] See §6.4, pp. 95–6.

friends, and it would be most unfriendly to ask for it. Why should we have needed so much convincing? In one sense, as we have seen,[9] the necessity arises from God's side, not ours: having made the world, He is involved in it; he is not an impassive Buddha observing our antics from afar, but suffers with us. But there is a necessity on our side too: we are hard of heart, and unwilling to love the highest when we see it. We demand a sign, and to that extent are responsible for the priciness of the sign.

12.10. UNSAYING THE OLD MAN

St John the Baptist called on people to repent, and that has re-mained a central part of the Christian message too. It is a neces-sary condition for forgiveness. In the Christian understanding the new mind called for is more a reorientation towards God than an owning up to specific deeds and disowning the intentions they manifested, though there well may be specific misdeeds to be acknowledged and repudiated. In either case there is a problem of making our saying away sincere. Just as it is easy to say 'sorry' without really meaning it, it is easy to say that one is putting away the old man, but to continue as before. It regularly happens in church today. We need to offer tokens of sincerity too.

The difficulty is that there is nothing that will do. We cannot unsay ourselves, or perform some great task to show that we are no longer what we were, and still very largely are. For specific actions penance is conceptually possible, but for a whole state of mind it often does not make sense. Hence a further feeling of helplessness sinners have felt in disburdening themselves of their previous existence. I need to show in the value system I previ-ously upheld how inexpedient from that point of view was the action I then undertook; but from that point of view that point of view was the right one to adopt. I have no leverage on the whole system from within it. I cannot therefore show to myself, or to God, that I really am anxious to put off the old Adam, and thus do my bit to accept the acceptance freely offered, and over-come the estrangement from God, whose cause is, I recognise, within myself.

---

[9] In §12.7 above.

The necessity for tangible tokens of repentance seems to be twofold: I need to convince myself, and I need to convince God. But the latter necessity no longer obtains, once we abandon a penal theory: God does not require proof in order to be convinced, and we already have ample reason to believe that on His side no more is being asked for from us. It is only my internal difficulty that I have no leverage on the whole system to enable me to care about disowning it from within it. But it is possible to care about a man being killed unjustly. People care about Socrates and the modern martyrs in Germany, Russia, and the Third World. The cross speaks to us even in a fairly unregenerate state. The question 'Is it nothing to you, all ye who pass by . . .?'[10] does not elicit a universal 'Nothing'. Often we care a little, and sometimes we come to care a lot. Because we care, we are vulnerable, and as we come to care more we become more vulnerable, and to that extent are ourselves hurt. To some very limited degree we share in Christ's suffering. And the more we do so, the more clear it is that we are sincere in our repudiation of our old ways, and in our resolve to lead a new life.

12.11. IDENTIFICATION

Those who meditate on the cross, identify with Jesus; some so much so that they come to bear on their own bodies the marks of His passion. If I identify with Him, then it is natural to suppose that He identifies with me, and suffers not only for me, but in my place. And, as we have seen,[11] in an important sense He does, inasmuch as He identifies with the whole of humanity, and experiences the human condition from the inside, and undergoes the very worst that can befall us.

At the same time a second identification takes place. I identify with Pilate, with Caiaphas, with the Sanhedrin, with the soldiers, and with the passers-by, because I recognise in myself the propensities which led them to act as they did, and have entered into a human inheritance based on the sort of thing they and their like did and do. With this double identification it becomes possible to describe the Crucifixion as the evil consequence of my

---

[10] Lamentations 1: 12.   [11] In §12.7, p. 268, above.

(since I share responsibility for what we humans do) sin, which Jesus suffered on my (since He identifies with me) behalf. So He vicariously paid the penalty for the wrong which I, vicariously and collectively, had done.

It is a powerful metaphor. It has enabled sinners to feel properly purged of their wrongdoing, to be liberated from their past selves and to be accepted, in spite of their inadequate, creaturely status, by God, and to direct their gratitude for their liberation to Jesus and His self-sacrifice on the cross. But it has also been a metaphor that has misled many, portraying a wrathful Father quite unlike the *Abba* Jesus talked to and told us about, and construing the saving acts of God within a framework of penal legalism which it was the whole purpose of the New Covenant to put on one side.

12.12. UP TO A POINT

Responsibility comes out as an important but limited concept, and an important but limited virtue. It plays an important part in our interchanges with one another, especially our more distant ones. It underlies many of the concepts and institutions of social and political life, and we need to further greater responsibility in politics and business generally. Even as we move into the more intimate realms of personal relations and religion it remains important—there is no virtue in irresponsibility among friends or before God—but it is not all-important. In those realms what we do is not the prime manifestation of what we are, and what we are is more important than just what we succeed in doing. The fact that we are valued for what we are is—or should be—a perpetual surprise: it is certainly something we cannot earn or make happen; it depends entirely on the free choice of others, and is something for which we can—or should—only be grateful. There is a realm of responsible action in which I, along with others, am the means whereby rationality is made effective in the world. But I am not only a conduit for bringing rationality into effect in the world, but an individual person of my very own and am lucky to be appreciated as that.

APPENDIX 1
Aristotle

Aristotle was the first to discuss responsibility, and much of our understanding derives from him. It is appropriate to acknowledge and assess his thoughts from the standpoint of this book, but with some hesitation and caveats. Aristotle wrote from a very different standpoint, and was the heir of a very different tradition—Adkins says his *Merit and Responsibility* arose from his difficulty in understanding Plato and Aristotle's moral philosophy. In particular Aristotle's discussion is under the shadow of the Socratic paradox, οὐδείς ἑκών ἁμαρτάνει (*oudeis hekon hamartanei*), nobody errs voluntarily. Much of his argument is devoted to reinstating the common-sense view that people do in fact do wrong deliberately. Hence he is primarily concerned with the cases where something has gone wrong, and considering then to what extent the action was voluntary, and the agent culpable; in particular he discusses ἀκρασία (*akrasia*), weakness of will, and this discussion has attracted a lot of attention in recent years. To do justice to Aristotle, one needs to see what he was trying to do, and what alternatives were available to him, but here I am only concerned with a partial view, more to define the focus of this book in relation to Aristotle than to discuss him in his own terms and from his own point of view.[1]

Aristotle discusses responsibility in terms of the Greek words ἑκούσιον (*hekousion*) and ἀκούσιον (*akousion*). It is reasonable to translate ἀκούσιον (*akousion*) as 'involuntary', but, as J. L. Austin points out,[2] it is a mistake then to translate ἑκούσιον (*hekousion*) as 'voluntary'. The opposite of 'voluntary' is sometimes 'compulsory', sometimes 'required', sometimes 'paid', but never 'involuntary'. In so far as ἑκούσιον (*hekousion*) is the opposite of ἀκούσιον (*akousion*), we might translate it 'non-involuntary', though this is ugly. But no translation is really satisfactory, inasmuch as Aristotle himself sometimes uses the terms εκουσιον (*hekousion*) and ἀκούσιον (*akousion*) as contraries rather than contradictories.

[1] There are excellent scholarly discussions in Sarah Broadie (Waterlow), *Ethics with Aristotle*, Oxford, 1991, pp. 124–74; D. J. Furley, "Aristotle on the Voluntary", in Jonathan Barnes *et al.*, *Articles on Aristotle*, ii, London, 1977; T. H. Irwin, "Reason and Responsibility in Aristotle", in Amelie Rorty (ed.), *Essays on Aristotle*, Berkeley, Calif., 1980, pp. 117–55; Richard Sorabji, *Necessity, Cause and Blame,* London, 1980; and A. J. P. Kenny, *Aristotle's Theory of the Will,* London, 1979.

[2] J. L. Austin, "A Plea for Excuses"; repr. in his *Philosophical Papers*, Oxford, 1961, pp. 139–41.

Aristotle begins his discussion in *Nicomachean Ethics* III by locating ἐκούσιον (*hekousion*) on his moral map, as a necessary condition for praise and blame, which are clearly connected with ἀρετή (*arete*) (usually translated 'virtue' but better thought of as a desirable quality of character or mind). What is ἀκούσιον (*akousion*) is a matter for συγγνώμη (*suggnome*) (rendered 'pardon' by Ross, but better 'exculpation') or pity. He says that an action is ἑκούσιον (*hekousion*) when the agent himself is the spring of the action, ἀρχὴ τοῦ κινεῖν (*arche tou kinein*), and ἀκούσιον (*akousion*) when the initiating cause is external, ἀρχὴ ἔξωθεν (*arche exothen*).[3] Thus far he can be regarded as elucidating responsibility.

Aristotle reckons that the ascription of responsibility for an action can be defeated in two ways:

1. that what was done was done by compulsion, βίᾳ (*bia*), or
2. it was done through ignorance, δι' ἄγνοιαν (*di'agnoian*).

1. The paradigm example of something that happens by compulsion is being carried somewhere in a boat by the wind. In that case, it is clear that one is not responsible, because one did not *do* anything: 'I did not go—I was carried' is the proper disclaimer of responsibility. We make the point by using the passive voice. Aristotle, however, is concerned to identify the cause as being outside—ἔξωθεν (*exothen*)—the agent, the agent himself contributing nothing, and so talks of 'the wind carrying one somewhere', and then adds 'or men who are in control'. The added words have been taken in two ways: the natural reading is that they are just a further instance of being carried, for example in a ship after a mutiny, or simply being manhandled; but they have also been read as introducing the different case of actions under duress, which Aristotle then goes on to discuss in the following sections.[4] He takes a rather tough line. There is some doubt whether actions undertaken by someone at the behest of a tyrant who holds one's family hostage should be regarded as ἑκούσιον (*hekousion*) or ἀκούσιον (*akousion*), as also in the case of jettisoning cargo in a storm: one would not do it voluntarily (in the ordinary, English sense of the word, adumbrated by Austin above), but any sensible person would in the circumstances. Aristotle concludes that these are 'mixed'—μικταί (*miktai*)—actions, but more resembling those that are ἑκούσια (*hekousia*) since they were chosen at the moment of choice.

Aristotle's account of actions under duress is distorted by his emphasis on blame. He has confused two different ways of escaping blame: I may be not blameable because I am not responsible, but I may also be

[3] *Nicomachean Ethics* III. I. 3, 1110ᵃ1–3, and III. I. 6, 1110ᵃ15–18; cf. *Eudemian Ethics*, II. 6, 1223ᵃ9–18.
[4] Jonathan Glover, *Responsibility*, London, 1970, p. 6.

not blameable because although I am responsible, I have a perfectly good justification for what I did. The ship's captain escapes blame under the latter head: he was responsible; at the moment of choice he was able to make a choice, and did make a choice, a choice which in the circumstances was entirely reasonable, even though it would not have been reasonable in other, more normal circumstances. So too in most other cases of actions under duress. The agent did them because he had no acceptable alternative. This is often an adequate excuse, and we pity, rather than blame, the man who finds himself in such a predicament, though sometimes even death is better than the commission of a really wicked deed. In all these cases there is a choice, though a choice of evils, and we can properly ask why a man acted as he did, and detail the special circumstances of the case as exculpating him for doing what would in ordinary circumstances be reprehensible. Only in extreme case—torture or terror—would we reckon the man to be no longer himself, and not to be regarded as an agent at all. In almost all cases, however, he is an agent, responsible for his actions though not for the circumstances in which he has to act, and we can properly ask him about the former, though being ready to allow that it is in regard to the latter that blame, if there is any blame, is to be assigned, and about them we must address our questions elsewhere.

2. Aristotle reckons that for some actions the agent should be exculpated because they are done through ignorance, δι' ἄγνοιαν (*di'agnoian*). Again, the simple distinction between ἑκούσιον (*hekousion*) and ἀκούσιον (*akousion*) is inadequate, and he introduces a further distinction: everything done through ignorance is οὐχ ἑκούσιον (*oukh hekousion*), but it is ἀκούσιον (*akousion*) only if it is subsequently a matter of repine and regret.[5]

Intuitively we agree. If I throw a javelin in a tournament, and an unforeseeable gust of wind blows it so that it wounds a bystander, I cannot be said to have wounded him; but if the bystander was my greatest enemy, and I go on my way rejoicing at this lucky mischance, I make myself responsible for the consequences of my action. Responsibility is attributed to me on the strength of my subsequent lack of regret for the incident. The fact that I was causally involved—I threw the javelin— establishes a prima-facie case for asking me why I did it; the fact that I did not know that the javelin would be blown off course and hit a bystander defeats the ascription of responsibility; the fact that I did not feel sorry at this unforeseen outcome defeats the defeater, and renders me answerable again. I was causally involved, and though I did not in point of fact foresee the outcome, nevertheless it was one I should have been happy to bring about, so that if I had foreseen it, I would have

---

[5] *Nicomachean Ethics*, 1110^{b}19–24.

acted exactly as I did. Hence, if I had known I would have had the result to answer for, and I cannot plead ignorance to get me off the hook.

It is an important point. It is an example of "Cambridge Change", where a subsequent event alters the antecedent state of affairs: my not regretting now makes me to have been responsible then. It shows that responsibility is not just a physical concept subject to the standard physical constraints of locality and temporal antecedence, but is, rather, concerned with the significance of actions and their interpretation, where it is perfectly possible for the meaning to be altered *ex post facto*. Just as my not being subsequently sorry can make me responsible for the unintended consequences of my previous action, so I may become responsible for wrongs previously done by my society, and we, by punishing the wrongdoer after the event, may make us not to have been responsible for what he did.[6]

Aristotle has yet to draw a further distinction, between actions done through ignorance—δι' ἄγνοιαν (*di'agnoian*)—and those done where the agent is being ignorant—ἀγνοῶν (*agnoon*). He needs this distinction to block the defence of not knowing that the action was wrong. I can reasonably hope to exculpate myself if I can say that I did not know that the wind would blow the javelin out of its course and on to a bystander, but not, without thereby abdicating my role as a responsible agent altogether, if I say that I did not know that killing people was wrong. It is a demerit of Aristotle's approach that it is open to this defence, whereas if we see the issue as the correct description of the action, there is no opportunity to assimilate ignorance of morals to ignorance of facts.

In book v (the first of the common books), ch. 4, $1131^b25-1132^b$, Aristotle deals with punishment and reparation in the course of his discussion of "diorthotic", or rectificatory, justice. His account is dominated by his need to accommodate and neutralise its conceptual links with equality. So far as distributive, or social, justice is concerned, he takes over from Plato a distinction between geometric and arithmetic equality.[7] Equi-angular figures are "geometrically equal", or, as we should say, similar. Their angles are the same, but their sides are only proportional to each other, in contrast to congruent figures which are not only the same shape but the same size too. Their sides are "arithmetically equal". Plato and Aristotle hold that when benefits are to be distributed, they should be distributed in proportion to ἀξία (*axia*), merit. Perhaps partly to redress this, Aristotle finds a role for arithmetic equality in his account of "diorthotic" justice. He follows a distinction Plato draws in book ix of *The Laws* between voluntary and involuntary transactions, the former being the province of commutative, or eco-

[6] See §5.2, p. 77, and §6.4, p. 96, n. 9.   [7] *Laws* vi, 757.

nomic, justice, the latter of diorthotic justice. Aristotle's thought is that in an involuntary transaction one party gains an advantage at the expense of the other, who suffers a corresponding loss. What is needed then is to equalise the situation by taking away the illicit gain from the one, and restoring it to the other. The just outcome is thus a sort of equality, and also a mean between the one party being left with too much and the other with too little.

Aristotle's account is too schematic, and hence confused. He assumes simple theft as the paradigmatic involuntary transaction, where the thief's gain is the victim's loss, and taking away the stolen goods from the thief and giving them back to their rightful owner will restore the *status quo*. But such cases are rare. The typical involuntary transaction is not a zero-sum game, in which the gainer's gain is exactly equal to the loser's loss, but a negative-sum game, where the losses exceed the gains. Even when goods are restored to their rightful owner, he has been inconvenienced by not having them to hand in the interim. In general, therefore, we have to distinguish the loser's loss from the wrongdoer's gain, and address ourselves to entirely different questions, as we concern ourselves primarily with the one or the other.

If we address ourselves to the loser, our concern is with the loss he suffered, and how to make that good. Our aim is to compensate him, not to punish the wrongdoer. It is a case for the civil courts, not the criminal law: the wrongdoer has committed a tort, not a crime.[8] We do not need to make out that he flouted some precept or principle, only that he was careless, or even just unlucky, and that he failed to see to it that his actions did not have unfortunate consequences for the plaintiff. If that case is made out, then it is for him to compensate the plaintiff, and restore his position, so far as possible, to what it was before the involuntary transaction. It does not at all follow that the defendant only loses what he has illicitly gained. He may be much worse off: he may have gained nothing, but still have to pay considerable damages.

If we address ourselves to the wrongdoer rather than the person wronged, the case is very different. Our concern then is with the wrongdoer rather than the person wronged, and with the intention revealed in his wrongdoing rather than the consequences of his action; our purpose is, as we have seen,[9] to make sure that the wrongdoer does not get away with it, to see to it that crime does not pay. It is a different person's outcome we are seeking to alter—there may be no victim, or it may be impossible to repair the wrong—and we are not concerned with equality but with a *less than* relation: it would not serve our purpose if the wrongdoer were no better and no worse off than he had been before he

---

[8] See §5.2, p. 77, §6.9, pp. 111–12, and §12.3, pp. 262–3.
[9] See §6.4, pp. 97–9.

did the wrong; we need rather to make him worse off, so that from his, and other potential wrongdoers', point of view wrongdoing was a bad policy.

Once we recognise that most involuntary transactions are non-zero-sum games, with the losses outweighing the gains, the temptation to assimilate the wrongdoer's gain to the loser's loss disappears, and we see that we have to consider their positions separately, in the one case trying, so far as we can, to restore the person wronged to the same position as he occupied previously, in the other seeking to ensure that the wrongdoer is worse off than he would have been had he committed no wrong.

Some defence is needed for an account which is confessedly not fair to Aristotle, and is criticizing his account from my own standpoint, and pointing out what I think are confusions, and saying what I think he ought to have said. Plato gives one in his *Theaetetus*.[10] Philosophy is an activity, not just a set of doctrines, and in order to understand a philosopher, it is necessary to engage in argument with him, not just hear what he says. With those who are no longer living, we do not give them their due if we merely learn what they have said: we need also to engage them in dialogue, so far as we can, and do them the compliment of arguing with them as though they were still alive and able to answer back. Although on occasion an entirely scholarly approach is proper, and we ought always to take into account what a philosopher was trying to do, and what options were open to him at the time he was operating, he will not really speak to us unless we also speak to him, and say how his doctrines appear to us from our point of view. Reading philosophy is like reading poetry: the text by itself is dead. In order to come alive it needs to be lived by us, and the inevitable distortions of our subjective viewpoint have to be accepted as a necessary part of the process, though they should also be recognised and on occasion discounted for what they are.

---

[10] *Theaetetus*, 169e.

APPENDIX 2

The Which? *Guide to Theories of Punishment*

The account of punishment given in Chapter 6 is structured to fit the
general argument of the book. Many readers, however, are likely to have
to write an essay on the topic of punishment, and may want to start
from some other standpoint than that adopted in this book. The following notes list the different available theories of punishment, with their
merits and defects, advocates and critics, so that the reader can make his
own choice, and decide which for him would be the Best Buy.

1. Definition

Punishment is something unwelcome, deliberately imposed on somebody
by someone claiming to act on behalf of some society or community, on
account of some wrong he has allegedly done, and understood as such.
It would not be punishment if:

1. it was something pleasant;
2. it happened in the course of nature (unless it is seen as having been
   sent by God, who imposed it deliberately);
3. it was done for some other reason: for example, quarantine, conscription, sectioning, taxation.
4. it was done on account of previous misbehaviour, but not meant
   as a punishment: for example, passing over for promotion.
5. it was done by a private individual simply as a retaliation for an
   insult or injury done to him.

To be a punishment, the person being punished must know that he is
being punished, and the person imposing the punishment must claim
some *locus standi* entitling him to impose it.

2. Justification

There are two general types, utilitarian and retributive, based on two
general schemata of justification, consequentialist and deontological.

1. Consequentialist justifications are all utilitarian. They seek to justify
the infliction of something unpleasant by reference to the good that will
come of it. But these are blanket justifications: if they work at all, they
will justify inflicting unpleasantness on those who have done no wrong—

quarantine, conscription, taxation, vaccination, sectioning. They have great difficulty in accommodating the *concept* of punishment with its essentially backward-looking reference: "Why are you doing this to me?" "Because you *have done* wrong."

There are three brands: Preventive, Deterrent, Reformative.

2. Deontological justifications are retributive. They seek to justify the infliction of something unpleasant by reference to the bad that the wrongdoer has done. They have no difficulty with the 'have done' and the 'wrong', but, once having given this reason, they find it difficult to answer further questioning satisfactorily.

There are two brands: Vindictive, Vindicative.

Utilitarian arguments go a long way towards giving us an adequate justification for having the institution of punishment, but do not give a satisfactory account of the concept itself: retributivist theories give a better account of the concept, but an inadequate justification for using it.

We need to distinguish three retributivist theses, both as regards whether someone should be punished, and as regards how much he should be punished:

(a) Minimal retributivism: Wrongdoing is a necessary (but not sufficient) condition for punishment; only the guilty may be punished. The gravity of the wrong done sets a maximum (but not a minimum) limit to the amount of punishment that may be inflicted. Further justification is needed before it is right to punish the guilty, and consequences need to be taken into account in determining, up to the permitted limit, how much someone should be punished.

(b) Full-blooded retributivism: Wrongdoing is a necessary and sufficient condition for punishment; only the guilty may be punished, and all the guilty must be punished. The gravity of the wrong done sets not only a maximum but also a minimum limit to the amount of punishment that may be inflicted.

(c) Normal retributivism: Wrongdoing is a necessary and normally adequate, though not necessarily sufficient, condition for punishment; only the guilty may be punished, and in the normal course of events the guilty should be punished, though there are circumstances in which it would be right not to. No further justification is needed for punishing the guilty, but consequences may be taken into account in determining, within the permitted limits, how much someone should be punished.

(b) is the hard-line retributivist position taken by Kant and Hegel; (c) is the one adopted by most ordinary chaps; (a) is the position professed by Home Office officials, probation workers, penologists, and sociologists, who are utilitarians at heart, but cannot quite stomach the implications of thoroughgoing utilitarianism.

We need to distinguish two questions:

(a) Why are you administering this particular piece of beastliness to me?

(b) What is the general justifying aim of punishment?

Utilitarians can offer faceable answers to the latter question, but are in danger of justifying too much: punishing the innocent, having scape-goats to placate a lynching crowd, hauling potential criminals off to hospitals for treatment before they commit their crimes. Retributivists are quite safe on this score, and have a proper abhorrence of punishing the innocent, but in so far as they fail to address the question `Why punish at all?' seem to be relying on vindictive gut feelings rather than anything really rational.

Quinton[1] argues that it is analytically necessary that punishment should be for a wrong previously done—if that is not the reason given in the dialogue, then it is not *called* punishment, but conscription, quarantine, etc. We can then give a utilitarian justification for keeping the institution of punishment, but we still lack an account of its real rationale. The best compromise account is given by Hart[2] with a General Justifying Aim of Deterrence, but restricted to actual wrongdoers in order to reassure the innocent. This is further developed by Ten.[3]

3. Theories on Offer

Five brands: Preventive, Deterrent, Reformative, Vindictive, Vindicative.

(a) Preventive

Justification: Utilitarian.
Object of exercise: To prevent criminal from doing it (again).
Method: Incarceration; mutilation; confiscation; expulsion; execution; sacking; removal of licence.
Merits: Effective (very few drunken drivers mow down people while in prison); recognises importance of effectiveness.
Demerits: Inapplicable in many cases (fraud, seditious libel, Official Secrets Act, dropping litter); the logic of prevention is that it is better than cure, and so should be applied before, rather than after, the offence—most people could, with advantage, be prevented from doing most things; manipulative; no room for mercy.

[1] A. M. Quinton, "On Punishment", *Analysis*, 14, 1954; repr. in H. B. Acton (ed.), *The Philosophy of Punishment*, London, 1969, pp. 55–64.
[2] H. L. A. Hart, "Prolegomenon to the Principles of Punishment", *Proceedings of the Aristotelian Society*, 1959–60; repr. in his *Punishment and Responsibility*, Oxford, 1968.
[3] C. L. Ten, *Crime, Guilt and Punishment*, Oxford, 1981.

Advocates: Islamic fundamentalists, feminists, Conservative Selection Committees.

(b) Deterrent

Justification: Utilitarian.

Object of exercise: To deter criminal from doing it again, and others from doing it at all.

Method: Adventitiously annex unpleasant consequences to the commission of crime.

Merits: Widely regarded; may work (who knows how many potential criminals have been deterred from committing crimes that have not, as a result, been committed? Each of us can be reasonably sure that there are some things he might have done, were it not for the adverse consequences).

Demerits: Does not work with actual criminals, most of whom continue to commit crimes; manipulative?; no room for mercy.

Advocates: Bentham,[4] Smart.

Critics: Bradley,[5] Mabbott.[6]

(c) Reformative

Justification: Utilitarian.

Object of exercise: To reform the criminal so that he is no longer minded to be antisocial.

Method: Compulsory subjection to rehabilitatory procedures, such as boarding school or psychiatric hospital; teach useful trades; cure phobias; prefrontal leucotomy.

Merits: Well-intentioned; might work in some cases; not intended to do any harm.

Demerits: Manipulative; no limit to amount or range of treatment that may be deemed to be necessary; better to reform people before they offend than after, (and who can tell who might offend?); no room for mercy.

Advocates: Protagoras,[7] Plato,[8] Lady Wootton,[9] the former USSR.

Critics: Lewis[10]

---

[4] J. Bentham, *Principles of Penal Law*, in John Bowring (ed.), *Works of Jeremy Bentham*, Edinburgh, 1843, i. 365 ff.

[5] F. H. Bradley, *Ethical Studies*, Oxford, 1927, pp. 26–33.

[6] J. D. Mabbott, "Professor Flew on Punishment", *Philosophy*, 1955, pp. 3–33, repr. in H. B. Acton (ed.), *The Philosophy of Punishment*, London, 1969, pp. 117–18.

[7] As reported in Plato's *Protagoras*, 323d–325c.

[8] *Republic*, I, 335b–e.

[9] Barbara Wootton, *Crime and the Criminal Law*, London, 1963.

[10] C. S. Lewis, "The Humanitarian Theory of Punishment", repr. in his *First and Second Things*, Fontana paperback, Glasgow, 1985.

(d) Vindictive

Justification: Retributive.

Object of exercise: To pay people back for having done wrong.

Method: Adventitiously annex unpleasant consequences to the commission of crime so as to restore balance.

Merits: Widely regarded; no punishment of innocent; no excessive punishments.

Demerits: Ruat Caelum; often inexpedient (uneconomic); ultimate justification obscure; no room for mercy.

Advocates: Kant,[11] Bradley,[12] Armstrong,[13] Mabbott,[14] Lewis.

Critics: Most Modern-minded Members of the Chattering Classes.

(e) Vindicative

Justification: Retributive.

Object of exercise: To vindicate the law and the victim by making the wrongdoer visibly not get away with it.

Method: Adventitiously annex unpleasant consequences to the commission of crime.

Merits: No punishment of innocent; room for mercy.

Demerits: Excessive punishments not clearly ruled out.

Advocates: Feinberg[15] Cooper,[16] Ewing.[17]

Critics: Walker.[18]

Each of these accounts has its merits (presented in table form on pp. 92–3), though often its advocates concentrate on pointing out the demerits of its rivals. I have given only a few names, and even fewer references, knowing that the value of a reading list is inversely proportional to its length.[19]

[11] See quotation in §6.5, pp. 99–100, n. 10.

[12] F. H. Bradley, *Ethical Studies*, Oxford, 1927, pp. 26–33.

[13] K. G. Armstrong, "The Retributionist Hits Back", *Mind*, 70, 1961, pp. 471–90, repr. in H. B. Acton (ed.), *The Philosophy of Punishment*, London, 1969, pp. 138–58.

[14] J. D. Mabbott, "Professor Flew on Punishment", *Philosophy*, 1955, pp. 3–33, repr. in H. B. Acton (ed.), *The Philosophy of Punishment*, London, 1969, pp. 117–18.

[15] Joel Feinberg, "The Expressive Function of Punishment", *The Monist*, 1965; repr. in his *Doing and Deserving*, Princeton, NJ, 1970, pp. 95–118.

[16] David E. Cooper, "Hegel's Theory of Punishment", in Z. A. Pelzcynski (ed.), *Hegel's Political Philosophy*, Cambridge, 1971, pp. 151–67.

[17] A. C. Ewing, *The Morality of Punishment*, London, 1929; summarised by H. B. Acton (ed.), *The Philosophy of Punishment*, London, 1969, p. 14.

[18] Nigel Walker, *Why Punish?*, Oxford, 1991, pp. 21–33.

[19] This is not quite right. After I had enunciated this as my First Law of Bibliography in a lecture, an undergraduate wrote and pointed out that in that case a total absence of references would be infinitely valuable. The formula $V = 4x/(x + 1)^2$ will give the right result, so far as undergraduates' weekly essays are concerned.

Although punishment is not one of the fundamental problems of philosophy, it is one that confronts almost every thinking person. It is a good topic to think philosophically about. In attempting to clear one's mind, one is led to change it many times, as new difficulties obtrude themselves, and obstruct the latest clear and distinct ideas on the topic. Only by trying out different approaches and pondering their merits and demerits, can the reader think his way through to a solution which, while not the last word on the subject, is well considered and indubitably his own.

INDEX

The more important entries are indicated in bold type.